Durgnat on Film

by the same author

FILMS AND FEELINGS

THE CRAZY MIRROR

A MIRROR FOR ENGLAND

THE STRANGE CASE OF ALFRED HITCHCOCK

NOUVELLE VAGUE, THE FIRST DECADE
(Motion Publications)

GRETA GARBO
(with John Kobal)

LUIS BUNUEL

FRANJU

JEAN RENOIR
(University of California Press)

THE MARX BROTHERS
(Osterreichisches Filmmuseum)

EROS IN THE CINEMA
(Calder and Boyars)

SEXUAL ALIENATION IN THE CINEMA
(Cassell Collier Macmillan)

Durgnat on Film

RAYMOND DURGNAT

FABER AND FABER LIMITED
3 Queen Square London

First published in this edition 1976
by Faber and Faber Limited
3 Queen Square London WC1
Printed in Great Britain by
Whitstable Litho Ltd., Whitstable, Kent

ISBN 0 571 10656 0

Chapters 1, 2, 3, 4, 5, 6, 16, 17, 18, 19, 20, 21, 22
and 23 are taken from *Films and Feelings*, and
chapters 7, 8, 9, 10, 11, 12, 13, 14 and 15 from
The Crazy Mirror

Contents

Illustrations

Foreword

This book comprises a selection of chapters from two books, *Films and Feelings*, published in hardback in 1967, and *The Crazy Mirror*, published in hardback in 1969.

Apart from chapters on Chabrol's *Les Cousins* and Hitchcock's *Psycho* (reprinted in *The Strange Case of Alfred Hitchcock*), the principal omission from *Films and Feelings* is the bulk of a section entitled *The Harem Game*. Since traditional film aesthetics had tended to emphasise the specifically filmic nature of film content, or the transformation of the actor or star by context, or by the director as *auteur*, the section set out to redirect attention to screen personality as a usual centre of aesthetic focus, and the associated problem of emotional involvement as raised in, notably, Pauline Kael's bracingly astringent article *Fantasies of the Art House Audience*. The section also related actors' personality atmospheres (their personal style as content) with certain social issues and attitudes.

This was the second element of the book's overall structure, whose four parts discussed the contributions to a film's content of, respectively (a) aesthetic style, (b) personal style, (c) story structure, and (d) symbols, structures of symbols, and the transformation of symbols. Theory took second place to a review of examples chosen as constituting a crux for some widely prevalent assumptions, themselves existing without benefit of theory.

Far from deprecating theory, such an approach avoids certain dangers arising when theories are too brusquely or pedantically imported from other areas of study, or, still more seriously, from only *one* other area of study, particularly when this importation is compounded by the sometimes deliberate, sometimes involuntary, neglect of ground won by the more sophisticated aesthetic theories.

11

Although a group of left-wing critics concluded that the book's approach derived from that of F. R. Leavis, any similarities seem to me insignificant by contrast with a variety of radical differences, and the book plunges its roots into the area between and around the work of I. A. Richards and William Empson.

The final chapter, and appendix, included here, draws the threads together by considering *This Island Earth*, a film chosen as (a) anonymously school of Hollywood (no-one has ever proposed any of its creators as an *auteur*), (b) pulp-magazine science-fiction and (c) interesting without being a masterpiece. Though dismissible by the dominant critical schools, analysis of the interaction of its visual, personal,narrative and symbolic structures reveals just how wide the references within a run-of-the-mill movie may, consciously, but unself-consciously, be. It also suggests that the 'signs' in the 'text' on the screen need to be read in conjunction with ideo-emotional complexes which have no 'objective' reference on the screen. One may speak of *associative* as against *iconic* criticism, or rather as inclusive of it, since there's every reason why any functionalist structuralism whose aim is humanistic rather than pedantic should synthesise the two. No developing theory can dispense with observation and responsiveness, especially insofar as, in aesthetics, it is *their* systemisation which is the theory. Otherwise, every theory would derive its authority from that theory of theories which doesn't yet exist, and the premature lunge for objectivity concludes in metaphysics, predictably, given its intolerance of subjective variation, and its simplified view of interpretative processes, from which commonsense traditional aesthetics, or gestalt theory could have solved it.

The gap left in the structure by the omission of most of *The Harem Game* can, fortunately, be filled by certain chapters from *The Crazy Mirror*, subtitled *Hollywood Comedy and the American Image*. Indeed the sections relating the personal styles of slapstick comedians to machine-age speeds, ethnic groups and the immigrant plight, had originally been intended for the first book, and omitted owing to lack of space. Drawing attentions to gaps in film history which it couldn't itself fill, the book set out first and foremost to stress the tensions in, as against the innocence of, the spirit of screen comedy, and began by arguing a theory of comedy akin to that in Ralph Piddington's *Laughter*, a book first published in 1933, and recently reissued by Grove Press, New York, but regrettably ignored in subsequent discussions of humour, presumably because the prestige of Freud,

Bergson, Meredith and others pre-empted attention while obscuring the inadequacy of their theories. It seemed to me more important to figure forth certain principles, again by example rather than theory, than to attempt the massive task of rewriting the history of Hollywood comedy (and by implication of Hollywood). The omission of a longish section on Betty Hutton, a major comedienne of the '40's, was both involuntary and unnoticed, except by a private correspondent. If life were longer it would be interesting to research the gaps, and to consider such rediscoveries as Harry d'Abadie Arrast's *Laughter*, the rival views of Capra's political implications, and the subsequent evolution of American comedy. Five years later, the book would have gone on to trace the strange evolution of Jerry Lewis, the blossoming of Woody Allen and Peter Sellers as virtual *auteurs*, the nostalgic mode of Peter Bogdanovich, and the development, through such films as Jack Lemmon's *Kotch*, of a critical realism close to the book's heart.

Seven years later, its chapter on *Hellzapoppin'* would have taken on a new topicality by reference to the climax of Mel Brooks's *Blazing Saddles*. And a dramatic comedy of Harlem life, John Berry's *Claudine*, could have exemplified a mixture of TV situation comedy, kitchen-sink realism, and realistic comedies like Cukor's *The Marrying Kind*, and answered the pious hope expressed in the book's last sentence: "The time is ripe for Hollywood, five hundred years after Christopher Columbus, to discover America; to explore it, rather than descend briefly from daydream cloudbanks."

Acknowledgements

Several sections in this volume were based on a Postgraduate research thesis prepared under the auspices of the Department of Film at the Slade School of Fine Art, University College, London, during 1960–1. Others were revised from series first published in *Films and Filming* between October 1963 and January 1966. Part of *The Wedding of Poetry and Pulp* is translated back from a piece in *Midi-Minuit Fantastique*, February 1967. The chapter on the Marx Brothers formed part of a brochure written for the Austrian Film Museum's Marx Brothers retrospective in 1966.

My thanks are due to Professor Sir William Coldstream, to Professor Thorold Dickinson, and to Peter Baker and Robin Bean, successive editors of *Films and Filming*, for leaving me the reprint rights of material prepared in the first place for them; and furthermore to John Kobal for providing film stills from his collection. For rights to the stills used I must acknowledge the courtesy of Universal, Paramount, Columbia, 20th-Century-Fox, United Artists, M.G.M. and Barrie Pattison.

1 · The Mongrel Muse

The great difficulty in talking about cinema style is that the cinema is a *potpourri* of art forms, sharing elements in common with each, but weaving them into a pattern of its own.

In that it centres on actors, on the human form, it comes closest to the theatre. In its origin, too, it is associated with theatrical forms (the 'music hall' act). But it is 'deficient' theatre, for the show lacks the actor's presence. Instead of one person physically, constantly, present here and nowhere else in the world, we have only a Polyfoto presence, a pack of images, changing in shape and size—half-way to abstraction.

The cinema can compensate in other ways for its shortcomings in this. It can call on all the resources of photography. It can dispense with the human person altogether (the documentary) or merge him with the landscape (the Western). Its sense of place, in flexibility and realism far beyond theatrical possibility, confers on it something of the novel's narrative fluidity.

But compared with the novel its way with words, and therefore with ideas, is clumsy. The talkie's words take second place to the visual presentation of reality. Film visuals can show a 'lame old black cat sitting on a worn grey mat'. Or a 'playful tabby stretched out on a mat with a pattern of roses on it'. But they can't say, simply, 'the cat sat on the mat'. They can show a beautiful statue in sun, then in rain, then in snow, but they can't say simply, 'A thing of beauty is a joy for ever.' Their powers of abstraction are limited. They can't match the writer's swift, deft way with metaphors. Film is a reasonably good medium for persuading, but it's a very clumsy one for arguing. And by means of words, which present objective reality through ideas, the novelist can mix visual reality and ideas in a rich, intimate way. Here the cinema is infinitely poorer.

Yet its literary poverty is compensated by its visual richness. It is a visual art, like painting. In the words of Marcel Carné, 'One must compose images as the old masters did their canvases, with the same preoccupation with effect and expression. Cinema images have the same needs.' The film critic will often need to use the vocabulary of the visual arts rather than of literary criticism.

In sensitivity of line, tone, form and other plastic qualities the ciné-camera is, however, vastly inferior to the painter's brush. The very best cartoons, like Hector Hoppin's and Anthony Gross's *Joie de Vivre* (1934) may have something of the artist's freedom of line, but the cartoon isn't after all the mainstream of cinema.

The photographic cinema can compensate for its deficiencies here by its theatrical-narrative interest. And by the visual possibilities opened to it by its being a *succession* of images, in *movement*. Here it has its own possibilities of plastic, formal nuance and organization.

Indeed, it relates here to music and the visual arts at the same time. The visual art of architecture has been described as 'frozen music'—meaning that just as architecture is shapes and structures and tensions standing static in space, music is musical shapes and structures and tensions in time. It's true that there is a certain *time* element in architecture (you walk past a façade, or through an arch), just as there is a 'space' element moving in music (you are conscious of things happening 'simultaneously', in counterpoint). But these are secondary—'time' in architecture is reversible (few buildings are based, like symphonies, on a beginning, a middle and an end). And 'space' in music is a result, rather than a determinant, of form. Only the film is shapes and structures and tensions both in space (the image) *and* in time. Only the film synchronizes, interweaves, visual and musical shapes (picture and soundtrack). Norman MacLaren's *Begone Dull Care* (1949) represents the 'missing link' between painting and music. It shows us visual colours and patterns flashing, dancing, quivering in counterpoint to the Oscar Peterson Quartet.

Thus the cinema combines elements from the various arts into its own synthesis. It can also co-opt the various forms as a whole. The film adds words to pictures to music. As Resnais's camera roams over the surface of Picasso's *Guernica*, 1949 (breaking it down into a *sequence* of smaller images, that is, converting space into time), the commentator intones, first, statistics, then, a poem of Paul Eluard's

—thus making a new synthesis of two art forms. Of course, the film will not have the emotional impact of painting *added to* the poem—for so long as the spectator is attending to both, he cannot pay full attention, or respond with his full power, to either.

Elements from different media may be blended in many different ways. One of the most moving moments of Jean Renoir's *Partie de Campagne* (1936) has the camera tracking along a river stippled by raindrops, while a girl sings a wordless song. In Resnais's *Hiroshima Mon Amour* (1959) the camera tracks down streets and corridors while Riva's voice overlaid summarizes her thoughts—and Resnais experimented, matching different reading speeds to different tracking speeds, before finding the combination of speeds which was emotionally just 'right'.

The cinema is not the only 'art of mixed arts'. The opera is notoriously a *beau monstre*, a (sometimes rather absurd) blend of music and theatre. The theatre itself is a mixture of acting, lighting and text. 'Total theatre' is a blend of absolutely everything, taking even cinematic sequences under its wing. The cinema is another such synthesis of the arts.

Ever since the cinema began, aestheticians have sought to define 'pure' cinema, the 'essence' of cinema. In vain. The cinema's only 'purity' is the way in which it combines diverse elements into its own 'impure' whole. Its 'essence' is that it makes them interact, that it integrates other art forms, that it exists 'between' and 'across' their boundaries. It is cruder and inferior to every other art form on that art form's 'home ground'. But it repairs its deficiencies, and acquires its own dignity, by being a mixture.

The film medium depends on a blend of different media, and various films blend them in different proportions. A few films depend principally on criteria analogous to those one would bring to a short story or a novel. Thus for example Joseph L. Mankiewicz's *A Letter to Three Wives* (1948) is to a great extent a 'text' film. The films of Eisenstein require more 'painterly' critical descriptions than those of, say, Howard Hawks. Many films—Garbo's—can only be considered as 'star' performances, and one responds as one would to a 'star' performance in the theatre. The eloquence of Marcel Marceau, of Charles Chaplin, and less obviously Emil Jannings, lies in acting so stylized, so rhythmic, as to be nearer 'mime' than 'realistic' acting. Is Luis Bunuel's and Salvador Dali's *Un Chien Andalou* (1928) a Surrealist 'poem' (because of its 'symbolic meanings') or is it a Surrealist 'painting' (because it is a set of pictures?). An 'abstract' film like Norman MacLaren's *Begone Dull Care* accepts only those criteria that apply to abstract painting, linked with others that apply to music.

Yet each of these films is a mixture of the arts. Each of these films is 'pure' film.

Because there are so many varieties of film it is easy for the best-intentioned spectator to mistake a film's language. In *Strike* (1923) Eisenstein shows the Tsarist cavalry cutting down strikers with drawn sabres. To enhance the effect he intersperses the sequence with shots of a bull being slaughtered and hacked up in an abattoir. Some spectators find that the shots of the bull intensify the horror, while others, on the contrary, find that they distract from it. The difference seems to lie in the way the spectators' minds work. Some spectators get passionately concerned with the strikers and the cavalry. This action is completely distinct in their mind from the bull, which only interrupts, and so decreases, the tension. Others, presumably those who look at film *style* as such rather than identifying with the people *in* the film, are quicker to make the 'intellectual' connection: the bull=the crowd, the proletariat = cattle, people= lumps of meat. Many filmgoers today find that such metaphors in Russian silent films weaken rather than strengthen, especially when, unused to the thought and conventions of the time, we mistake a metaphor for a change of scene. Pudovkin means us to understand that 'the prisoner's joy is expressed by the breaking of the ice'. Instead we may assume a change of scene and get completely confused as to who's where. 'He was in his cell, now he seems to be standing by the riverside, has he been let out? or is this a dream? or are we with someone else altogether?' By the time we work it out, the film's gone as cold as a fish on the slab.

Similarly a spectator used to looking for detailed psychology, realistic acting, location settings, and so on, may be quite at sea with films whose subtleties are entirely visual ones. Most film critics (outside Italy) have a literary background, and the fact that films, like novels, tell stories, reinforces their tendency to consider the 'core' of film as being somehow 'literary'. Their indebtedness to a (waning) fashion *in* literary criticism usually leads to the further assumption that the 'core' of literature is 'psychological insights'—exact definition and motives, and so on. To these displaced persons a film's visual qualities are only 'style'. The documentarists' influence on film criticism completes the long-dominant emphasis on literary qualities, psychological realism, and social consciousness.

On the other hand, it was also apparent that the dominating creative 'charge' of many films was the director's, rather than the writer's or the actor's. So here was a paradox: the *quality* of a film depended less on the writers and actors, who one might have expected to contribute the literary-psychological interest, than on a man whose province was that of 'visuals' and 'style'. 'Visual' directors like Eisenstein, Murnau and Dreyer retained their prestige as 'geniuses' less, one feels, because these critics really understood or thrilled to their films, than before they were protected by an aura of 'prestige'. The critics of, for example, *Sight and Sound* whom, for all their individual differences, it is reasonable to consider as a team with a common attitude, typify a fading English critical orthodoxy, with all its confusions and contradictions—summarizable as: 'literary content' and 'style' are either indistinguishable or the same thing but the first is emphatically more important than the second.

This part attempts to offer some new ideas, to revive some very old ones which fell into disuse when the 'literary content' school acquired their stranglehold on film criticism, and to revitalize principles to which it consents in theory but obscures in practice. Space, unfortunately, forbids us from examining each point from as many angles as one would like to. It offers only a series of signposts, rather than a map.

Let us first look at the implications of the antithesis of 'content' and 'style'. Among film critics 'content' is equated with 'literary content', that is, anything in a film which a novelist could fairly easily put into words if he were writing 'the book of the film'. And 'style' becomes, virtually, anything which isn't 'content'.

In the other arts the uses of the word 'style' are rather different. In painting 'literary content' is obviously of minor importance, while much great music is absolutely devoid of all 'literary content' whatsoever. By this definition abstract paintings and symphonies would be 'pure' style, altogether devoid of meaning—and importance? Clearly then there must be a sense in which 'style=content'.

The opening definition of 'style' in *The Concise O.E.D.* is: 'Manner of writing, speaking or doing . . . as opposed to the matter to be expressed or thing done.' In other words, an artist's 'style' is his answer to the problems with which he is faced in the course of creating his work of art. On the one hand, he has a certain intention, a certain 'vision' or 'drive', an experience to communicate (even if he isn't himself too sure in his conscious mind of exactly what it is). Similarly, the film director has a scene in a script, or a certain plot point to make. This scene is built around this point, so he thinks of it, for a while, as what the scene 'contains', his 'content'. But his sense of craftsmanship, certain practical exigencies, the need for a slick, easy flow of ideas across the screen, etc., confront him with various practical problems. Should he make the actor walk into shot? or should he pan the camera to pick up the actor? There may be no particular reason for his choice, except, in the case of a dull director, habit or convention, or, in the case of an original director, some intuitive, inexplicable preference. It just feels right to him— more smooth, more elegant, more lively than other possibilities. That choice is his 'personal' style. The writer, the actor, the cameraman, the director, will each have such a personal style of his own— favourite, intuitive, unexamined ways of doing things. Often he will be quite unaware that other solutions would have been possible. The director, as *integrator* of everybody's work, has more 'stylistic' problems than anyone else; hence his 'style' usually flavours the film.

Now let us look at 'style' in a medium other than the cinema. Two actors will declaim Shakespeare's words ('content') in altogether different ways ('style'). One makes Hamlet a warrior-hero who can't make up his mind. The other makes him a neurotic intellectual who can't steel himself to action. The 'literary content' is exactly the same but the 'theatrical content' (gesture, voice) is altogether different. So different that it transforms the meaning of the text. Here, the style is just as much a part of the content as the 'content'. In fact much of what film critics call 'literary content' is in fact 'theatrical content', depending less on the text than on acting and staging, and, to this extent, the ordinary fiction film is nearer the theatre than literature.

Of course, not all features of 'style' make much difference to the 'content'. It may make no difference whatsoever whether an actor lifts his left eyebrow before or after he waggles his right finger-tip. This is a change of 'content' too, but only a minor one.

From this definition, the question whether style is more important than content is a misleading one. Style is simply those pieces of content which arise out of the way the artist makes his basic points. These may (as often in painting and poetry) be only a pretext, a wire on which to 'thread the beads'. If style is 'manner of doing', then we can say that the way a thing is done is often a way of doing a different thing. To say 'sorry' *superciliously* is doing a different thing from saying 'sorry' courteously or servilely, etc. Certain tones of voice make 'sorry' mean: 'Look where you're going, you clumsy imbecile.' 'It ain't what you do it's the way that you do it.' 'Le style, c'est l'homme.'

Let us look at one or two screen examples. Here are two frame-stills from Dreyer's *La Passion de Jeanne d'Arc*, 1928 (Plates 1 and 2). In a sense, they both have the same 'content'—Joan (our identification-figure) is being bullied. In general composition, both shots have marked similarities. But they also have many differences. In each case her tormentors have different faces and characters, so that the kind of threat is very different. The spatial relationships are an important part of the human relationships. Thus, in the second shot the perpendicular inquisitor towers gaunt, cold, dry as a cliff. The other shot conveys a sense of boiling wrath, of directed attack. Joan's different postures (the turn and tension of her neck) express different feelings. The content is in the style.

Suppose a director has filmed four takes of the same scene which shows an argument between two equally sympathetic characters. Take (1) shows the scene as a series of 'reverse angles' (alternating full-face close-ups). Take (2) is a continuous two-shot of two profiles. Take (3) shows B's full face, but the back of A's head prominent on the screen. Take (4) is an 'over-shoulder' of A, with B's head not very obtrusively present over to one side of the screen. In (1) we will feel each person's responses intensely during *his* close-up, and the other's responses will be temporarily soft-pedalled, even forgotten; until we return to him with a little 'shock'. Our identifications alternate. In (2) we see and feel both responses simultaneously. Our reaction to A's words is continuously modified by B's reaction, which may be sceptical or pitying. We feel a smoother, softer, mixture of feelings. In (3) with the back of A's head, almost in the middle of the frame, we will be very conscious of his constant 'obstruction'; he is a real force, but an enigmatic one. In (4) we may almost be unaware of him and be aware mainly of A's feelings—although the vague presence of B makes for a more complicated composition and 'feel' than a mere close-up.

Are these differences of style, or of content? Both. And the differences are not a matter of *information provided* about the characters so much as of *the spectator's participation* in their feelings.

The distinction between '*literary* content' and 'visual style' is particularly misguided because even in the work of literature much of the 'content' comes from the 'style'. Suppose we call someone 'slow but thorough' we feel this is, on the whole, a compliment. His slowness is a trifling disadvantage, the last word acts as a summing-up, an assertion of his value. But if we call him 'thorough but slow' there is an implication of criticism. The ideas and the words are exactly the same—but to change their order is like inserting some invisible words. One order says: 'We can rely on him.' The other: 'He should pull his socks up.' More often, literary 'style' is a matter of choosing different words—different ideas, different content. My friends are 'unfaltering', my enemies are 'obstinate'. I show 'intensity of purpose', you are a 'fanatic'. Our friends are 'original', our rivals 'eccentric'. Writers show such concern over points of 'style' (e.g. *le mot juste*) because of their concern over points of 'content'.

Such nuances of order, sound (especially in poetry), vocabulary, and so on, don't just *colour* the 'content' of a passage. They *constitute* its content. The passage may be badly written, but of interest as a description of an interesting event—traffic accident, a battle or a riot. But this event is not its 'literary content'. It's only the *subject*. Another passage may describe an apparently boring event, but bring to it a wealth of ideas and insights. And in this case we may speak of the author's 'style' as enlivening a banal 'content'. But this wealth of ideas and insights isn't 'mere' style—it is 'content'. And, here, to ask whether style or content is more important is like asking whether water is more important than H_2O. The words are different, the things's the same, which phrase one uses depends on one's context and emphasis. It is not the importance of their subjects, but the richness of their 'content-style' which distinguishes good artists from mediocre ones.

Another quite common and useful sense of the word 'style' is to refer to the whole mass of details which go into a film, but which happen to be confusing and difficult to describe in words. Thus a *specific* reaction—horror, joy, etc.—tends to be called 'content' because it is easy to define, it offers a nice, solid idea to lean on. On the other hand, an actor's postures, gestures, smiles, the quality of his glance, the tension of his facial muscles, the director's spatial relationships, the tones of grey caught by the cameraman, all these may be very eloquent and forceful in communicating experience (and so are 'content'). But because it is difficult to analyse or explain their exact meaning in words they tend to be referred to, vaguely, as 'style'. But here again 'content' and 'style' are indissoluble. In fact, here, the 'content'—horror, joy—is a spectator's deduction from what the screen actually contains. This is why spectators so often disagree on what a film's content is. The screen contains the style, but not the *content*, which is the spectator's deduction, and not contained on the *screen* at all!

If we speak of an artist's 'style' as being as individual as his face or his finger-prints, it is because he tends to bring similar insights and details to every subject which he treats. Dreyer's style is the visual expression of certain attitudes, interests and feelings which arise in him whether his subject is *La Passion de Jeanne d'Arc*, *Vampyr* (1932) or the naughty carry-ons of *The Parson's Widow* (1921). In this sense, 'content- style' is the quintessence of an artist—although often his choice of subject also is determined by his personality. Thus personal 'style' is a matter, not of mere visual mannerisms, but of plot, characterization, and so on. For example, King Vidor's heroines are tomboys expertly wielding shotguns in *Duel in the Sun* (1946), *Beyond the Forest* (1949) and *Ruby Gentry* (1952), and there are reminiscent traits of forceful independence in the heroines of *The Big Parade* (1925), *The Fountainhead* (1947), *Man Without a Star* (1955) and *Solomon and Sheba* (1959). His heroines' *style* is an important part of King Vidor's vision of the world. (Always when we speak of an artist's 'personal style' we might as well speak of his 'recurrent content'.)

In a sense, the total content of a film is made up of a vast array of details. But the meaning of each detail is heavily influenced by the context. For example, Karel Reisz writes '. . . the discreet distance which Ophuls' camera keeps from his players reflects a lack of identification', and Andrew Sarris '. . . Bunuel's . . . camera has always viewed his characters from a middle distance, too close for cosmic groupings and too far away for self-identification. Normally, this would make his films cold and his point of view detached. . . .'

These are fair enough as critical approximations, but it would certainly be wrong to conclude that identification is weak without a high proportion of close-ups. Silent films used far fewer close-ups than films of the 40's, and cinemascope Westerns use fewer again, but this has little effect on identification, compared with the main determinant, which is the spectator's affinities of emotion, experience and moral sympathy with the screen characters (their 'resonance' with him). Further, artists who don't know where the spectators' sympathies lie, how to make them chop and change from one character to another, how to create the anxious tensions and suspense of 'split sympathy', won't stay out of the bankruptcy court very long.

Where a film has a very popular star, the spectators so keep their eyes glued on him that even when he's in long-shot *physically*, he's in close-up *psychologically*. This is not to say that camera distance has no importance; only that it is only one of many elements of style-and-content working simultaneously. I'd suggest that the only partial identification made by most spectators when seeing a Bunuel film for the first time is mainly due to the fact that his characters are very complex individuals, and presented with a certain mystery. Seeing *El* (1953) for the first time, my principal emotion was one of fascination, of passionate curiosity; but at a second viewing, when the film's main pattern had been understood, a much stronger identification with the characters was possible. In Ophuls (and here space forces one to schematize) a purpose of the long-shots is to show the characters in their décor (close-ups tend to 'abolish' décor). His characters are 'glimpsed' amid their richly period setting, there is a quality of *nostalgia*. But the significance of 'style' can never be defined exactly, any more than the meaning of a line of poetry can be defined exactly, not only because any work of art worth having arouses a complex chord of emotions, but because different spectators' minds work in different ways (as we saw in the case of *Strike*).

One or two further examples may make our point clearer. When the camera tracks forward swiftly (as in, say, a musical number) the spectator often feels a mild exhilaration, as if he in his seat were gliding effortlessly through the action. There is a general sense of well-being, of dynamic excitement. But in Truffaut's *Jules et Jim* (1961) the helicopter skims swiftly over a hilly landscape—and a hill rearing up before us suddenly reveals a sheer drop on the other side. Here any 'exhilaration' is modified by the turbulence of the landscape, and killed by the 'sudden drop'. In the same way, the film is about the turbulence and unsteadiness of human relationships (Jeanne Moreau's song: 'chaqu'un pour soi et hop parti—c'est le tourbillon de la vie'). In the same film, there is a sense of chaos, of confusion, when, seen from the helicopter, the train carrying one of the *ménage-à-trois* steams out of the country station. The last scenes of Joshua Logan's *Picnic* (1954) have a similar theme—a train seen from a helicopter, carrying William Holden away from Kim Novak. But the whole tone is different. Not only is the landscape different (level), but the dramatic context is different—this time the lovers are determined not to be separated for long. There is no sense of chaos—our helicopter shot is, so to speak, a 'fate's eye view', a map revealing that their paths will cross. It is the exact opposite of the 'similar' effect in *Jules et Jim*.

Within the general framework of a two-shot many different 'spatial relationships' are possible. In *The Magnificent Ambersons* (1942) Welles expertly puts his characters in tough, angular, separated compositions, creating an effect of loneliness-by-antagonistic-wills. In Renoir's *La Règle du Jeu* (1939), more fluent and informal arrangements leave plenty of space for the characters to move around, to change their minds, to remain individuals while being members of free and easy groupings.

Suppose a film ends with the camera tracking back from the lovers embracing alone on the beach. This may mean 'how tiny and unprotected they are' or 'how frail and futile their love' or 'the whole wide world is theirs' or 'this is the moment of destiny' (for plan views can suggest a 'God's-eye-view') or 'Good-bye, good-bye', depending on which emotions are floating about in the spectator's mind as a result of the rest of the film. Hence style is essentially a matter of intuition. There is no possibility whatsoever of an 'objective', 'scientific' analysis of film style—or of 'film' content. It is worse than useless to attempt to watch a film with one's intellect alone, trying to explain its effect in terms of one or two points of style. Few films yield any worthwhile meaning unless watched with a genuine interest in the range of feelings and meanings it suggests. To any work of art one must bring one's own experience if one is to take from it its experience. Indeed, professional film makers have a point when they accuse film 'highbrows' of an almost fetishistic attention to whichever aspect of style happens to be in intellectual fashion. In the 20's it was *Caligari* décor, from *Potemkin* (1925) on it was montage and it was dubious whether cinema art could survive the hideous barbarism of the spoken word, in the 40's it was camera angles and location photography, and today it's camera movements.

The reputation (rather than direct influence) of *Cahiers du Cinéma* and of its late doyen, André Bazin, has recently been goading British critics to a new interest in style and theory. Yet a certain 'fetishism' often cramps Bazin's intelligence. For example, writing about William Wyler's *The Little Foxes* (1941) and *The Best Years of Our Lives* (1947) Bazin calls their deep focus more 'democratic' than shallow-focus because it enables the director to have more important characters on the screen simultaneously, thus permitting the spectator to choose whichever character he will look at and identify with. Yet in these films Wyler had effectively determined which characters the spectators would be interested in, by the moral and emotional traits with which he endowed them, and which he balances one against the other with just as much care and control as do such shallow-focus films as *Johnny Guitar* or *This Island Earth*, as we shall show later. Within the limits of their tendencies to moral schematism, tendencies from which Wyler is not exempt, American directors can calculate audience sympathies to the nth decimal place, with a finesse which, given the cultural diversity of their audience, is a far from inconsiderable 'classicism'. The spectator is no freer, no more 'democratic', in Wyler's film than in the others.

Conversely, Welles uses deep focus in his *Citizen Kane* to present an extremely 'egocentric' universe, Kane's. There's no reason why Leni Reifenstahl, Hitler's cinéaste-laureate, shouldn't have used the 'hierarchical' possibilities implicit in deep focus to Fascist effect (the Leader in big close-up with 'the people' reduced to little faces peering hopefully up from far away, and so on. In practice of course the points made by the visuals would counterpoint rather than repeat those made by narrative or dialogue or audience assumption—e.g. one would enhance the Führer's real grandeur by showing him far away and small).

Often the best way for a director to sensitively nuance every aspect of his medium is to forget about 'style' altogether and immerse his conscious mind in his feelings and ideas; just as the thoughtful spectator will often arrive at the most sensitive understanding of a film by giving the artists the benefit of any reasonable doubt, and, within the spirit of the word 'reasonable', assuming that every aspect of the film is the way it is as the result, not of mere 'mechanics', but of an 'intuitive intention'. (This generous responsiveness also exposes the 'twee', bad, 'stylist' more surely than bluff indifference to nuance.)

'Style'—or rather, *nuance*—is conventionally associated with the creation of a personal, a subjective, a 'non-objective' world—a world that is *this* artist's (or *this* character's, or both). And in the next chapter we shall try and consider, in view of this, the cinema's reputation as a particularly 'realistic', 'objective' medium.

2 · Ying Realism, Yang Fantasy

Cecil M. Hepworth tells a delightful story about early days. He was giving a film show to a church literary society, and half-way through the reel realized he'd forgotten to remove a striptease sequence from his last show. At the last minute he had an inspiration, and introduced the item as 'Salome Dancing Before Herod'. The vicar was delighted and in his closing remarks said he had no idea the 'cheeney-martograph' had been invented so long.

This story neatly enshrines a point regularly overlooked by the theoreticians for whom the cinema's 'essence' is realism. Just because the moving photograph satisfies our sense of reality, it is an ideal medium for making fantasy seem real. And cinemagoing is notoriously as near dreaming (images rising up in darkness . . .) as looking at everyday life.

Even the completely realistic film includes impossibilities of many kinds. The camera's quick changes of viewpoint within the scene, the cut, the flashback and cross-cutting all outrage simple 'literalism'. So does the tilted screen for which Carol Reed's *The Third Man* (1949) is famed (although this 'expressionistic' device had been used more selectively in Duvivier's *Un Carnet de Bal* in 1938 and James Whale's *Bride of Frankenstein* in 1935). Background music is an outrage against realism, but, when creatively used, can have an effect as powerful as the visual images. In *The Third Man* and François Truffaut's *Tirez sur le Pianiste* (1960) zither and piano add their own colour to the atmosphere created by the visuals—expressing life's, fate's, bitter, mocking indifference to the characters. And Sir William Alwyn testifies to the contribution made by the most conventional background music, 'I can't tell you what *Henry V* was like until the music was put to it. Though I say it, I wouldn't have believed it possible that the music could make so much difference. I used to go and see run-throughs of the bits I had to put music to, and really I could hardly keep awake for five minutes.'[1]

Quite unliteral is the use of overlaid commentary (in any newsreel), and of *today's* voice over *yesterday's* actions (as in many flashback sequences). Splitscreen is common enough in musicals (Donen's) but doesn't break the spell in serious dramas. Thus in Robert Wise's *Two For the Seesaw* (1962) Robert Mitchum and Shirley MacLaine, telephoning from different apartments, are shown side by side on the screen. Alf Sjoberg's 1951 version of Strindberg's play shows Miss Julie as a young woman in the foreground remembering, while Miss Julie as a child enters from the background. Thus time, space and personal identity are all outraged, with no flaw in 'real' emotion!

When we are confronted with films like Josef Von Sternberg's *The Blue Angel* (1930) and Eisenstein's *Ivan the Terrible* (1945) the term 'realism' scarcely serves to describe our feelings. We know we are in a 'hallucinated', a dreamlike, universe, that the clothes, the décor, are not just 'realistic', they embody emotions just as emphatically as the characters do. Everything on the screen is as rhetorical as the verbal poetry of Olivier's *Henry V* (1945).

So while the old-fashioned film criticism is still permeated with the assumption that the cinema is at its 'best' when it records 'real life', the cinema in fact accommodates fantasies and fairytales of every kind and style—cartoons like Disney's *Bambi* (1942) satirical allegories like *Two Men and a Wardrobe* (1958), elaborate nowheres as in Welles' *The Trial* (1962) and in *L'Année Dernière à Marienbad* (1961), crazy comedies like *Million Dollar Legs* (1932), expressionist films like *Waxworks* (1924), metaphysical struggles as in Murnau's *Faust* (1926) and Cocteau's *Orphée* (1950), fairytales like the Powell-Berger-Whelan *The Thief of Baghdad* (1940), science-fiction like *This Island Earth* (1955), surrealistic serials like Feuillade's *Les Vampires* (1915) and Franju's *Judex* (1964), and fantasies of libidinous emotion like the endless variations on *Dracula* and *Frankenstein*.

---

[1] The theoreticians' dislike of background music is a leftover from their campaign against sound films (as well as a reaction against Hollywood cliché). In fact, silent films were never shown in silence, and the lone pianist was found only in the tinier fleapits. Every self-respecting suburban hall had its own orchestra, often of substantial size; and some cinemas even had special sound-effects machines. The crudest Hollywood soundtrack is simply this orchestra on the film instead of in the pit. But the film society habit of reverently watching silent films in reverent silence is an artistic barbarism.

G. W. Pabst, celebrated for his 'realism', reacted vehemently when questioned. 'Realistic? me? . . . From my very first films, I chose realistic themes with the intention of being resolutely a stylist. . . .' And on neo-realism, '*Sotto di Sole di Roma* is a great film, but because Castellani has *style*. Renoir and Carné are great directors for the same reason. Realism must be a trampoline from which one bounces higher, and it can have no value in itself. It is a matter of going beyond reality. Realism is a means, not an end. . . .'

An end to what? To showing, surely, something deeper than the surface of life, whether it be the subjective experiences of the characters in the story, or a clarification of social processes, or the artist's feelings about these things. All these things are invisible to the camera-eye; which can't see the inside of a man's mind, or a historical process, or a sociological generalization, or a theological or philosophical belief, or the artist's own responses. These 'invisible' realities can, must, be reached through diverse methods, or by different methods in various combinations: the 'sample moment' of *cinéma-vérité*, expressionism, or studio trickwork, or dialogue, or music. . . .

Even if we consider the visual surface of life, we find different approaches and styles equally valid. This is reflected in *literary* style (and content!). Thomas Hardy describes landscapes, rooms, faces with an almost pedantic visual exactness (often surpassing Robbe-Grillet). His novels are conceived in visual 'scenes', and he shows the most developed visual and filmic eye in English literature. Whole chapters of his novels are shooting-scripts, complete with establishing long-shot, tracking-shots, etc. He writes, 'A passer-by might have seen . . .' and goes on to put himself in the place of the camera. Colette also has an acute visual eye, but, whatever the scene, selects a category of detail quite different from Hardy's: furnishings, make-up, *feminine* detail. At the other extreme, a writer like Dr. Johnson has no visual eye whatsoever; he is almost 'blind'; he describes everything in sonorous, abstract phrases, which have their own (very great) beauty.

Suppose all three writers were describing the same person in the same room. Each would select his own types of detail. One might not even realize that Colette and Dr. Johnson were working from the same model. Which of these three is the 'realist'? All of them.

Much of the confusion has arisen from the 'abduction' of the word 'realism' by left-wing critics, to mean 'a realistic picture of the individual in society—i.e. 'social realism'. Similarly, in painting, the anti-thesis 'realism-or-artificiality' has little or no meaning in relation to, say, Titian or Turner. They are both 'realistic', or unrealistic, but each displays his own rich, rewarding subjectivity. In a real sense, Rembrandt's 'mythological' subjects are just as 'realistic' as his 'realistic' ones.

Some aestheticians still deny that the cinema can still be an art, because the camera *mechanically* reproduces whatever is put in front of it. Pudovkin summarizes the certainly true, but incomplete, de-fence with which film theoreticians have been content ever since. 'There exists between real events and their reproduction on the screen a fundamental difference, and it is this difference which makes film an art.' This difference is that of *selectivity*. The cameraman does not merely reproduce, he interprets reality, by his selection of certain details, angles, and so on. Then there are creative possibilities of choice of lens and lighting, and all sorts of manipulations on the cutting-bench.

In fact, except in the case of a minor genre, documentary, much of the creative effort takes place *in front of* the camera. It's the face and the performance of the actor, the sets and lighting which between them carry most of a film's meaning. The camera doesn't record 'reality' at all. It records a fictional 'construction' which is already a work of art, or rather, designed to become so on film. To the 'pri-mary' elements (what the camera sees) there are added the 'secondary' elements (derived from the possibilities of photography) and 'ter-tiary' elements (from manipulating the strip of film). These three elements can't be separated, but at least the distinction reminds us that the film is a work of art even before it's in the camera. The director and art director can *build a painting* and photograph that— the décor of *The Cabinet of Dr. Caligari* (1919) is a work of art which (like architecture) was built to accommodate movement in three dimensions, but (like a painting) appears in the flat on the screen. With its painted décor and daubed-on faces, Weine's *The Cabinet of Dr. Caligari* is half-way to being a cartoon.

In one scene, the somnambulist Cesare (Conrad Veidt) carries the heroine (Lil Dagover) away along a painted path. The perspective of the path is subtly foreshortened, so that Cesare scuttles from fore-ground to horizon in three strides flat, giving an effect of nightmare speed. Here the effect is gained by the 'primary' elements. On the other hand, Orson Welles often uses low-angle close-ups with wide-angle lens, so that his characters tower over the camera gigantically. When they step away from the camera, they diminish in size so rapidly that in two steps they seem to have covered about twenty yards. Here the same effect of 'giant stride' is obtained by 'secondary' elements (camera lens). German silent films often isolate the central character by a spotlight (primary effect) where Griffiths would use a mask or iris-in (secondary effect) and where a modern film would cut from three-shot to close-up (tertiary effect).

Traditionally, film criticism has overstressed tertiary and secondary elements and forgotten that the director does the bulk of his creative work in setting up what the camera sees, in his *staging*. It's a matter of the *pictorial* and the *theatrical* element of the cinema.

Let us take another example. A rule of thumb in film appreciation is that scenes of fast and exciting movement, like railway trains rushing along or gay dances, need plenty of fast cutting. Certainly, they can be handled in this style (as in Jean Mitry's *Pacific 231*, 1949), but they can also be presented just as effectively by deliberately slow cutting. In *La Bête Humaine* (1938), Jean Renoir builds a train journey into a sequence of great visual tension by using a few long takes of countryside seen from the train. Hedgerows, bridges, viaducts, stations, tunnels, horizons, flash past the camera in a flowing series of contrasts. And in the climactic dance of *French Can-Can* (1955), Renoir's cutting is not particularly fast. The dazzle and frenzy is created by the way in which the dancers' clothes and movements are played off against one another 'inside' the shot. It's a matter of *staging*; fast cutting would ruin the effects. The movement is located *within* the image and virtually demands a fixed, consistent camera-viewpoint.

In an essay typical of the *Sight and Sound* line, Tony Richardson tried to draw a distinction between those directors who were *artists* and those who were merely *metteurs-en-scène* (as artists he excluded German expressionists, Dreyer, Ophuls, Visconti and Kazan). But we propose here to use the term *mise-en-scène* in a different way; to refer to the creative arrangements of things *within* the screen. Some directors manage to get a particularly intense performance from their actors. Others direct for cutting. We wish to draw attention here to the *mise-en-scène*—strong, eloquent arrangements within the image (or series of images).

This *mise-en-scène* has two aspects, often allied. There is the 'theatrical' element—the dramatic scenes are staged (for the camera), the characters arranged in space, with their exits, entrances, movements, gestures and so on. (Matters of casting and acting, equally important, are 'theatrical' without being *mise-en-scène*, which we may define as 'staging for the camera'.) And there is the 'pictorial' element (pictorial composition, 'painterly' qualities, and so on).

It is obvious that the 'theatrical' and the 'pictorial' must often overlap, and often provide two different names for the same effect. In fact during the First World War Max Reinhardt's stage productions paid as much attention to the *pictorial* organization of the stage as did the silent German films of the 'golden age' (many of which were influenced by his work). Similarly it's reasonable to attach some little importance to the 'theatrical' element of certain paintings —say, Géricault's *The Raft of the Medusa*. Indeed Tintoretto and Gainsborough used to work out their paintings with the aid of a model theatre, testing the effects of light and shade with models, cutouts and candles.

The traditional prejudice against the 'pictorial' element of films is typified by two remarks in Paul Rotha's *The Film Till Now*. Of Dreyer, 'The damning fault of *La Passion de Jeanne d'Arc* was ... the beauty of the visuals, which were so pleasing in themselves that they were detrimental to the expression of the theme. . . .' And, 'Sternberg seems lodged in this gully of pictorial values . . .' to which Rotha's disciple, Richard Griffith, adds, 'Sternberg's . . . strange, compulsive preoccupation with pictorial composition . . . action and even continuity were progressively drained away in favour of an ordered flow of a pattern of images, often lovely in themselves, sometimes floridly vulgar, but always empty of real dramatic meaning.'

Our viewpoint here is that this 'gully of pictorial values' is actually one of the principal elements of film art, and that unless the critic accepts, and keys his sensibility to, pictorial values, he will be unable to pay more than lip-service to the real richness of such directors as Eisenstein, Sternberg, Dreyer, Pabst, Murnau, Ophuls and many others. It is no accident that Eisenstein evolved away from his 'cutting' style to the slow, elaborate pictoriality of *Ivan the Terrible* which, stylistically, is very near Dreyer and Sternberg.

A sensitive response to *mise-en-scène* means paying just as much attention to make-up, lighting, décor, costumes, gesture, and other 'technical', 'stylistic' details of a film as to dialogue and plot—noticing them not for their own sakes, but for their emotional meaning, their psychological impact. The mask which Jack Pierce created for Boris Karloff in James Whale's *Frankenstein* (1931) is no more 'childish' an effect than the make-up daubed on Werner Krauss in *The Cabinet of Dr. Caligari*, it is just as much a *vision* of the personage. And Christopher Lee's sensitive mime as the Monster in Terence Fisher's films is an aesthetic effect of the same idiom as Conrad Veidt's lean, spidery Cesare.

The Pierce-Karloff vision of the Frankenstein Monster is prefigured in the weird being dreamed up by Goya for *The Chinchillas* (Plate 3). Many horror films, like Goya's etchings, offer a *demential* insight into the disorders of human nature and society. And, for all their implausible situations and comic-strip dialogue, they may have a visual flair which makes them, creatively, the equal of well-written dramas with only mediocre visuals.

The costumier's art mingles with the art director's. Any criticism of *Ivan the Terrible* must pay as much attention to costume as to dialogue. Dress may establish character in ways about which the script remains silent. In Richard Fleischer's *The Big Gamble* (1960) Irish adventurer Stephen Boyd brings his new French bride (Juliette Greco) back to his puritanical family. She wears a black leather coat, a tightly moulded red dress, and a white flower in her buttonhole. The coat suggests she's knocked toughly around the world. The tight red dress suggests promiscuity (as when in Victor Fleming's *Gone With the Wind* (1939) Rhett, thinking Scarlett has slept with Ashley, makes her go to Melanie's party wearing a red dress). And the white flower says she is pure at heart. The dramatic modulations of atmosphere possible through wardrobe are neatly described by Cecilia Ager, describing Garbo's in Cukor's *Camille* (1937):

'. . . the colours of her costume change from white, in the carefree beginning, to grey when the forces of tragedy gather momentum, until, at last, sable black, with all its dark meaning, appears. First, in an all-black velvet dress and large black hat that she wears for her journey to the country. Then, when it seems that she is to be happy, white again, in cannily picturesque lawn dresses with only a black cloak to remind you her fate is sealed; black again after her renunciation—shimmering black net with sequins, but black. For her death, so that you are not too miserable, and may find solace in something, a white gown ecclesiastical in feeling with its monk's cowl, sending you to religion, there to take courage to bear it. Adrian has never been more touching, not, fortuitously, more decorative.

35

Garbo's *coiffure* also acts; the frivolous curled bangs that cover her forehead in the beginning are gradually lifted until at the end the whole serenity of her brow is revealed; there is something spiritual about this process too.'

Thus there exists a whole sensuous 'layer' of film meaning with which film criticism has scarcely begun to deal. Michael Caen underlines the importance of colour and clothes in Terence Fisher's *Dracula* (1958) and its sequel. 'What more can be said of Jack Asher's forests in *Brides of Dracula* except that they are more Gothic than ever Bram Stoker dreamed them? or of the glasses and decanters in which liquors shimmer in all colours from crimson to *crème-de-menthe*, except that they contribute to the sheerly decorative richness a note of that baroque which is precisely the key to the Victorian era? Fisher as no other knows how to use soft blues to lyricize the sepulchral atmosphere of these haunted crypts. . . . As part of a spectrum so hypersensitized, black takes on a new, its full, power. It ceases to be that meaningless tonal value rendered by panchromatic stock . . . it takes on life, substance (the shiny black of satin is played off against matt velvet), it acquires the value of an ethical symbol . . . it inserts itself like a wedge into a colour world where the mauve gowns and turquoise *déshabillés* stress the vulnerability of the women selected as victims. . . .'

A black-and-white analogy occurs in Franju's *Les Yeux Sans Visages* (1960) about a megalomaniac surgeon who cuts off girls' faces. In its pattern of surfaces, it is an *epidermal* film. There are elaborate contrasts of clothing—satin, leather, rubber and towelling. The camera dwells on the rainy 'surface' of the sky (Franju notoriously keeps his whole unit, expensively, waiting for the weather to be dramatically exact), on black branches dancing in car headlights, or reflected black-on-black, in the sleek 'skin' of a Citroen Déesse. The furnishings form part of the same visual complex—blacked-over mirrors, carpets, portraits, the patterned leading of windows. Franju's film evokes the Surrealist remark that, 'Fear, the incongruous, and the fascinations of luxury are emotional factors to which we never appeal in vain', and Baudelaire's, 'The furnishings seem to be dreaming, endowed with some somnambulistic consciousness, like that of plants. . . .' Franju's, like Minnelli's films, like *L'Année Dernière à Marienbad*, are *décor* films.

Connected with film 'pictoriality' is a sense of bodily physique and sensations. King Vidor's films are frequently eloquent in their physical movement and tension: Bette Davis's dying crawl at the climax of *Beyond the Forest*, echoing her earlier greedy writhing on the fur-coat she covets; the jagged, fierce, forked-lightning-fast movements of Kirk Douglas in the extraordinary dance-banjo-and-gunplay sequence of *Man Without a Star*; the rhythms of digging in *Our Daily Bread*, the death-crawls and dying embraces of *Duel in the Sun* and *Ruby Gentry*. Against the slow narrative rhythms of Arthur Penn's *The Left-Handed Gun* the fiercely *choreographed* gunduels have a quite explosive impact. *The Olympiad* (1936) is one of the great 'physical' films of all time. In Leni Reifenstahl, even Nazism, alas, can claim its genius.

Films abound in sensuous, even sensual, experience. Von Stroheim's are particularly rich in such moments, whether of luxury or revulsion—close-ups of black blobs of caviare, of fur slippers, of corpses dragged through wet mud, of violets held near a glinting cavalry boot, verbal references to the smell of new-mown hay, or Von Stroheim as the seducer in *Foolish Wives* (1921) dabbing perfume behind his ears and on his eyebrows. Throughout *The L-Shaped Room* (1962) Bryan Forbes' camera dwells on such little nastiness as a cake of soap studded with bedbugs, flat beer jigging in a glass on a piano-top, and (nauseous in close-up) a mess of cat-food. This is the world 'sensed' through the physical responses of a depressed and pregnant woman.

Dreyer described the film as related more nearly to architecture than to any other art. It may seem astonishing that he should compare so *static* and so *fluid* an art. But the film entails, like architecture, the creation of a visual world through which people move. Sometimes the two coincide, as in the opening sequence of *L'Année Dernière à Marienbad*.

We have come a long way from the 'literary' conception of a film as 'explaining' or 'analysing' people's psychology. The film's job is not so much to provide 'information' about the characters' minds as to communicate their 'experience', whether intellectual, emotional, physical, or a blend of all three: The *temps-mort* in which Renoir's films are so rich, which Becker schematized, and which Antonioni's camp-followers abused, is, more quietly, a constituent part of many purely commercial films. The pleasures and miseries of 'getting up in the morning' are evoked, vividly, at length, and quite independently of the plot, in such films as Jerry Lewis's *The Ladies' Man* and Daniel Mann's *Butterfield 8* (luxuriously), and (drably) in de Sica's *Umberto*

D, Gilles Grangier's *Gas-Oil* and Sidney Gilliatt's *Only Two Can Play*.

Quite apart from 'literary' values, the average audience is interested in 'how things are done'—and many feature films take in their stride little moments of documentary interest. Rossellini's *The White Ship* shows how wounded men are transferred from a ship at sea to an ambulance aeroplane, and not simply as a symbol of the pure Christian charity with which the Fascist forces cared for their injured crusaders: the procedure is in itself matter for art. Wyler's *Ben Hur* shows how sea-battles were fought in Roman times. King Vidor's *Hallelujah* celebrates among other things, the simple efficiency with which cotton is baled in the deep South. A tragedy of Flaherty's career was its steady decline from the eloquent *practicality* of *Nanook of the North* (1922) to the middlebrow *schmalz* of *Louisiana Story* (1948).

This emphasis on styling and staging enables us to refute those aestheticians who deny that the film is an art because the director can't do everything himself and is at the mercy of collaborators and of accident. Even Peter Ustinov falls for this nonsense, when he says, 'The script is no blueprint. And in the practical world of the cinema, if a director decides to use a certain cameraman and that man is not available, then he will already get a slightly different result from the cameraman he actually uses. He is not entirely in control. The man who is most in control is the man who is looking through the camera and who sees the shot at it is being made . . . and you as a director have to rely on him . . . it is really remote control . . . films are full of accidents. . . .'

But this argument also proves that music, ballet and the theatre are not art forms. Composers like Bach and Beethoven now have no control over what conductors and performers do to their music; and it is because the player's interpretation really does alter the meaning of the piece that we give him the status of a 'creative artist'. Who is 'in control'? The composer? or the conductor? or the soloist, who actually plays the music? None. Equally, a ballet may be a compromise between different creative interpretations: the choreographer's, the conductor's, the dancer's (and two 'stars' may have very different ideas). And who is 'the' creator of a play? The author? The producer? The star actor? In the practical world of the theatre, isn't the casting just as much at the mercy of 'accident' as choice of a cameraman?

Peter Ustinov's argument leads him to the peculiar position that a play is a work of art when it's read by the author, but not when it's being performed on the stage by a company!

The fact is that the film is only one of many media in which art takes in its stride the effects of collaboration and of accident, which in any case may help as well as hinder. Such novelists as Dickens and Hardy didn't write in a vacuum; they wrote *for* their readers, and in a very real sense they 'collaborated' with them. The desire to *communicate* is itself an acceptance of *collaboration*. Even self-expression requires compromise with accident—composers have to settle for what's playable on what musical instruments exist. The whole development of thought in a poem is constantly being affected by the need for rhyme or rhythmic patterns.

But let us return to film practicalities. Gérard Gozlan described how André Bazin once rhapsodized over Wyler's very personal handling of a scene in *The Little Foxes*. Wyler, who was present, embarrassedly explained that he filmed the scene the way he did, not for Bazin's deep philosophical reason, but to hide the fact that Herbert Marshall had a wooden leg. Similarly a director may have to choose a particular camera-angle because his glamorous leading lady turned up this morning with a pimple on her left cheek.

But André Bazin's remark isn't so foolish. Given a 'pimple' or a 'wooden leg', different stylists will find different solutions. One changes the camera-angle; another introduces a last-minute panning shot; another will retain the original set-up, but throw heavy shadows to conceal the offending detail; another will interpose a pot of flowers or a table-cloth to conceal the trouble spot from the camera. The director has ample opportunity to maintain his style in the face of 'accident'. And it's no exaggeration to say that such stylists as Dreyer and Bresson would imperturbably maintain their characteristic style even if the entire cast suddenly turned up with pimples *and* wooden legs.

Of elaborate critical interpretations, Fritz Lang made a very fair comment. 'I always laughed when people came to see me and explained what it was that I was trying to do in my pictures. And then I happened to think in the following way. My profession makes me like a psychoanalyst. Unconsciously, when you write a story you have to psychoanalyse the characters. Then I have to make myself clear why the characters act the way they do so that I can explain it to the actors. Maybe the critic is a psychoanalyst too. Perhaps he finds I do certain things of which I am not conscious.'

We return to one of our definitions of the word 'style'. Personal style is the content which the artist contributes, intuitively, to every subject with which he deals. Inevitably, it is frequently the deepest, the determinant part of the content.

3 · Sensation, Shape and Shade

Although there is no clear line of demarcation between the 'theatrical' and the 'pictorial' elements of the cinema, we have described *mise-en-scène* as the way the action is *staged* and the way the images are *composed*. If we go on now to make a few comparisons between cinema and theatre on one hand, and cinema and painting on the other, it is simply a way of exploring, or emphasizing, particular 'wavelengths' of the cinema's spectrum. We don't intend to press the analogies too far, nor to set up any profound philosophical similarities.

Among the many ways in which British film critics can be grouped and regrouped, there is a distinct chasm between those who *contrast* 'literary content' and 'style' and those who respond to the 'theatre' elements—notably, of course, the personality of the actor, which finds its extreme in the star system.

The second group of critics are of course far nearer the habits of the general public than the first. All critics are aware of the unique quality of a few 'grand' stars—Garbo, Bette Davis, and so on. But outside this little group, 'intellectual' criticism currently pays relatively little attention to the central importance, in the film's content, of the actor's personality, and the way in which, by lighting, and all the features of his own style, the director can modify that personality. This neglect is a comparatively recent development—the English magazine *Close-Up* (1927–31), and its French contemporary *La Revue Du Cinéma* are very responsive to personality.

Unlike the 'legitimate' stage, the cinema can accommodate complete amateurs (to whose authenticity or spontaneity the director can contribute the necessary artistic control) and it can accommodate actors who can't act in any real sense but have an emotional vibrancy

41

of some sort (like Alan Ladd, Joan Crawford or Clara Bow). But if the popular cinema can manage without actors, it couldn't manage without personalities; 'documentary' is condemned to be an ancillary genre. Many of the screen's favourite personalities graduated from the 'illegitimate' stage—music-hall, revue and cabaret. The appeal of many film stars compares with that of music-hall personalities who, like Harry Lauder, or Vesta Tilley, display, not 'acting talent', but a warm and resonant personality-role. As Jean Renoir remarked, 'As for actors, the best training-ground for them used to be the café-concert. Which doesn't exist any longer, but it's in the cabaret, in night-club numbers, that you can find your future stars.'

The general public is very quick to recognize these qualities, once, at least, they have found their 'role'. As early as 1915, a brief glimpse of an extra looking with sad adoration at Lillian Gish in *The Birth of a Nation* (1915) brought torrents of enthusiastic letters from all over the States. Alas, the extra had been paid off, and Griffith never managed to trace him. George Raft recounts how 'Mae West was in one of my early pictures . . . and she had one line in the picture which knocked me right in the box . . . she comes on and checks her rag, saying, "Check it!" Just that. . . . From then on, she became a definite personality and the public wanted to see more of her. . . .'

The 'acting' required is qualities as simple and subtle as those which made music-hall stars of Jack Warner, Gracie Fields or Will Hay. The light, crisp, exhilarating dancing of Fred Astaire isn't just a *tour de force* to be admired for its cleverness; it creates a *physical* well-being amongst the audience. Even when he's not dancing, his very walk is so light and sweet and easy it's a pleasure to see him walk across a room. And when this slender figure begins to dance it's as if mild Kent Clark had turned into a pint-size Superman with anti-gravity. . . . A brief pen-portrait by Michel Mourlet nicely registers the kind of quasi-physical nuance which registers so powerfully with screen audiences, 'Charlton Heston is an axiom. By himself alone he constitutes a tragedy, and his presence in any film whatsoever suffices to create beauty. The contained violence expressed by the sombre phosphoresence of his eyes, his eagle's profile, the haughty arch of his eyebrows, his prominent cheekbones, the bitter and hard curve of his mouth, the fabulous power of his torso; this is what he possesses and what not even the worst director can degrade.' Richard Roud seemed to feel the idea of the relevance of physique rather unpleasant ('nutty and crypto-Fascist'), but it's not a new idea.

In the words of Sarah Bernhardt, 'There is a fitness of things intellectual and a fitness of things physical, and the latter should receive as much attention as the former.' And Ellen Terry was accustomed to say, 'It is no use an actress using her nervous energy battling with her physical attributes. She had much better find a way of applying them as allies.' Indeed, one of the most eloquent aspects of Welles' *Touch of Evil* (1957) is the contrast of personalities between Welles' fat, gross, crooked cop, who has run both physically and morally to seed, and Charlton Heston's incorruptible Mexican. The latter character is built on the internal tensions between his 'liberal' part and the actor's 'Bronze Age' personality.

In the same way, many of a film's meanings lie in physical gestures and parallels. Whenever the Belmondo character in Godard's *A Bout de Souffle* (1960) is uncertain of himself, he rubs his lips with his thumb; and as she watches him lie dying, through her treachery, Jean Seberg 'catches' his gesture. Riccardo Freda's staging of *The Spectre* (1963) is influenced by Barbara Steele's lean, expressive hands—as she and her lover caress, her hands rove round his face and neck, restless, aggressive. Freda proceeds to invent, or to stress, actions which make us watch her hands—screwing up paper, opening a snuffbox (which then oozes blood), wrestling with a heavy coffin-lid, tugging her lover's corpse upstairs, shaving her paralysed husband (with murder in her heart), then 'flagellating' her lover's face, with the same razor, in an action which is itself a variation on 'shaving'. In E. A. Dupont's *Variété* (1925) henpecked husband Emil Jannings powders, pats and dries the baby; later he rubs down his youthful mistress (Lya da Putti) after her trapeze performance. Here the meaning lies less in the nuances of movement than in the action itself—a kind of doting fatherliness, shading into a weak motherliness.

Altogether the cinema is freer of literature than even the theatre. The camera's darting, analytical eye is made to stress such gestures and can dispense with speech altogether. In Visconti's words, 'The cinema which interests me is an anthropomorphic cinema. Of all the different aspects of a director's work, that which excites me most is what I do with the players. Experience has taught me that the weight, the presence of a man is the only thing that really counts on the screen. . . . I could make a film in front of a blank wall if I was sure of finding the real human elements of the character placed in front of this bare décor. . . .'

The fact that the cinema *can* use the amateur, the man-in-the-street, and an almost-deadpan acting style, is sometimes used to suggest that it *ought* to use these styles in preference to others. But, in fact, it accommodates artificial styles equally well, whether the expressionistic style of Emil Jannings, the stylized mime of Charlie Chaplin, or the 'Lyceum' performance of Bette Davis.

One can distinguish the following principal styles of film acting.

(1) The 'semaphore' style—the stylized gestures and signals used in early silent films.

(2) The 'pantomime' style of Mack Sennett. Chaplin refined and sensitized this and brought it near the 'poetic mime' of Marcel Marceau.

(3) The 'expressionism' of Emil Jannings and the German silent cinema's 'Golden Age' (1919–25). Later German films compromised between this and a more 'realistic' style.

(4) The 'Kulyeshov' style of early Eisenstein and Pudovkin. Brief shots of 'fixed' expressions. (Kulyeshov made the experiment of intercutting the same shot of Mosjoukine, absolutely expressionless, with a soup-plate, a woman and a corpse, and spectators complimented him on Mosjoukine's lyrical expression of hunger, love and grief.)

(5) The 'later silent' style—including pretty well anything which audiences of that time accepted as 'realistic'. Some actors have dated more than others: Louise Brooks in Hawks' *A Girl in Every Port* (1927) is quite as 'modern' as Kim Novak; of Hawks and Kim, more later. Mosjoukine in L'Herbier's *Le Feu Mathias Pascal* (1923) ranges from heavy 'expressionist' poses to Chaplin slapstick.

(6) The mainstream sound style is a modification of this silent style. Again, there is great variety within the range. The 40's and 50's specialized in glum, deadpan faces (Ladd and Lake, Audie Murphy, Kim Novak), succeeded by another kind of realism, the 'Method', a conscious, perhaps, somewhat cerebral, reaction against this lack of feeling, towards a deeper, more revealing and spontaneous, kind of self-awareness.

(7) The heavy 'monumental' style in highly pictorial films, like Eisenstein's *Ivan the Terrible* or Dreyer's *La Passion de Jeanne d'Arc*.

(8) In contrast, the swift, fluid, responsiveness of Renoir's 30's films. Visconti's *Ossessione* (1942) is a Renoir-ian film, and, as such, the first 'manifesto' of the great wave of Italian neo-realism.

(9) Visconti's *La Terra Trema* (1948) is a brilliant blend of the last

two styles. Antonioni's first feature, *Cronaca di un Amore* (1950), also has an extraordinary deliberate sense of bodily posture.

(10) The English 'documentary' style of 'understatement', so fashionable during the war. Its, not falsity, but artificiality, is revealed by the comparison with:

(11) *Cinéma-vérité*—which isn't a style at all.

Different styles can be combined in the same film. Thus Marlene's Lola-Lola in *The Blue Angel* hasn't dated at all; here is a laconic, 'underplayed' performance; Jannings' is more expressionist and dated, especially at the climax, when it is liable to seem ludicrous unless one makes the effort to adapt to it. And Mosjoukine switches style very smoothly from one scene to another in *Le Feu Mathias Pascal*.

With Eisenstein and Dreyer, we feel, not that the actor dominates the image, but that the actor is part of a visual composition—that he has practically been hammered and planed into shape. The 'theatrical' is subordinated to the pictorial. These directors often work on their actors by liberal use of make-up, or, by scrubbing their faces clear of make-up and etching every wrinkle, *carving* every feature, with a sculptural sense of light and shadow. They work on their actors in another way too. To play Joan of Arc, Dreyer took a young woman, Falconetti, whose smile was dazzling and modern enough for the toothpaste advertisements on which she featured, and talked to her, worked on her, in his stuttering French, until her mind transformed her features from within. He wasn't above a little physical—not torture, exactly, but lack of consideration, keeping her kneeling lengthily on stone floors—but his whole effort was devoted to locking on to her features, sculpting them into, feelings which hitherto had been dormant within her, or merely passing moods. He superimposed his portrait of her *on* her face.

Dreyer's visual flair is very strong, very simple, very strange. The 'low angle' in Welles makes the character seem proud, as he looks down at others. The 'low angle' in Dreyer makes Falconetti humble (often because from this angle even her *level gaze* seems to be looking imploringly upwards). He photographs Falconetti from a low angle, so as to increase the slight downward curve of her very vigorous mouth, giving her an air of tragic dejection—he uses perspective to change the shape and 'meaning' of her features. He lets on to the faces a white light which seems to grind them down, to scrape them clean, to impart to them the permanence of stone. He photographs a face as if he were photographing a piece of sculpture. Maybe he can't chip and chisel away at his actors' bodies to get the shape and pose he wants, so he arranges their clothes—flowing monks' robes, which he can 'compose' quite freely, some into sharp, mean crooks and cranks, others into billowing explosions of their wrath.

One group of directors, like Eisenstein and Dreyer, tend to think of each screen 'picture' as a little composition of its own, so deliberate and strong that one becomes aware of each image, organized as a whole, following and replacing its predecessor, with a little impact. The pictures are *joined* by their 'collision', which sets a kind of solid, hard-edged mood, much as brushstrokes set mood in painting. And these directors often strengthen the 'impact'—one shot will be, for example, a strong diagonal, the next a scatter of round forms, the third a bold horizontal-vertical, and so on. These directors, as if by temperament, incline to ask from their actors strong, deliberate movements. Others, again, like Renoir and Rossellini, are pretty nonchalant, even sloppy, about compositions, leaving them 'loose' so as not to cramp the actors' spontaneity and quasi-improvisation. They ask the spectator to concentrate on the flow of postures, gestures, movements, streaming steadily through the shots. Each image as a whole becomes 'invisible', for the movement flows smoothly through the images. And these directors tend to prefer lighter, more fluid styles of acting. Renoir's sensitivity to his actors' bodies and gestures is as fine, in its very different way, as Dreyer's.

Renoir's exceptional awareness of posture and gesture reveals a visual concentration of a deliberate, disciplined kind. In Renoir's words, 'I began to realize that the gesture of a laundress, of a woman combing her hair before a mirror, of a streethawker near a car, had an incomparable plastic eloquence. I made a sort of study of French gestures through the paintings of my father, and those of his generation.'

No better example could be set for any aspiring film director—to learn to *see*, through paintings, through life. Far from being a 'dissipated' talent, Renoir in his greatest films has contrived to 'load every rift with ore'.

Between the extremes of Dreyer and Renoir come men like Pabst, Antonioni, attentive both to compositions and postures, finding some sort of compromise between the two.

For Dreyer, the face is a *landscape*. (Plate 4.) Following Pierre Bargellini's brilliant study of the 'cinematic' aspects of Giotto, we can compare such a Dreyer close-up with a 'close-up' from Giotto, where the modelling of flesh and physique is similar. Posture is controlled as carefully as in any painting. At the other extreme, Renoir is nearer Degas. Renoir's being an art of movement, most stills betray it, though some (Plate 7) suggest the wealth of 'behaviour' that can crowd the screen.

If Renoir leaves visual space so that his actors are free, it is because, for him, human nature is flowing and free. Whereas Dreyerian space, so carefully patterned and sculpted, expresses his *protestant* sense of human nature as tight, tense, *locked*.

Of course, the fact that a director or cameraman has a consciously 'visual' style does not mean that his style is of interest. There are bad (banal) visual styles, just as there are bad scripts, bad dialogue. Laurence Olivier tried desperately hard to give *Hamlet* (1948) a worthy visual style, but, as Renoir remarked of its barn-sized sets and deep focus compositions, 'You feel dizzy when you look down from a great height? So what? What has that to do with Shakespeare?' The style *confuses* the issue. Similarly, Alexander Korda's *Rembrandt* (1936), conscientiously uses Rembrandt-era furnishings and sets and reminiscent faces, but the only lively thing in the film, apart from Laughton's stylish performance as Charles Laughton (never as Rembrandt!) is the highly individual face and style of his wife, Elsa Lanchester, who is almost the Barbara Steele of the early 30's. There is only the crudest resemblance between the massive visuals of Eisenstein's *Time in the Sun* (1932) and all those peasant-faces-against-the-clouds-shots in Emilio Fernandez's *The Pearl* (1946). Only schizophrenics go through the day feeling 'noble and pure' all the time, and visuals which keep insisting on this are just as fake.

Among the visual academicians we must include Aleksander Ford (cf. *Young Chopin* (1952)), Blassetti, despite one or two nice shots in *1860* (1933) and *Fabiola* (1948), and Arne Sucksdorff, especially the pseudo-*cinéma-vérité* of *Rhythm of a City* (1947). Nor can visual analysis settle for primitive rules of thumb like 'diagonals for urgency, visuals for repose, low-key shadows for drama, high-key shine for comedy'. After all, Autant-Lara, Wilder, and Kubrick all use very gloomy lighting for their comedies—witness *La Traversée de Paris*, *The Apartment* and *Dr. Strangelove*.

Here we can only make a few *ad hoc* points. Far from aiming at being even an introduction to a 'theory' of film visuals, they are meant only as examples, to illustrate the wealth and subtlety possible when directors, instead of merely 'illustrating' a script, *think* in graphic terms.

There is no need for each image to be a 'careful' composition or to be a lyrical expression of one particular feeling. The muscle of art is subtle contrast, so subtle that the spectator doesn't notice it as such. For example, one of the best ways of making the spectator conscious of fast or vigorous movement is by discreetly juxtaposing the movement with something very solid and static. In Pabst's *Kameradschaft* (1931) the miners' lorries, as they move off to the rescue of their French comrades, contrast with the heavy, immobile buildings and gates of the mine, or the lines of women and children silent along the roadside. Throughout the climax of Pabst's *Der Dreigroschenoper* (1931), when London's starving proletariat ruin the Coronation by mobbing the Queen, the crowds stream and bustle along past such 'static' features as a bend in the road. Similarly, in Eisenstein's *October* (1927), the scattering of a crowd under machine-gun fire is underlined by a very static visual feature—the immobile space of the square as they thin out.

A second point is that there can be no 'grand style' without emotional intimacy. The academicians like Fernandez always try for a 'grand', 'heroic', 'cosmic' style, all beautiful clouds, crags and skylines. But such effects are meaningless when there isn't also a sense of human joy and pain, of the ordinary, everyday scale. Dreyer's style is highly organized, formal, monumental, anything you like. But his characters are not really 'on a pedestal'. His eye is very sharp, piercing, in a sense, informal. The sense of 'face as landscape' is a kind of intimacy. This frame still is as 'intimatist' as anything in Humphrey Jennings' admirable documentary of World War Two *Fires Were Started* (1943) (Plate 8).

Analysts of composition in paintings love to cover the canvas with what looks like an underground map of lines and circles, and this is very sensible, for the canvas is a static design over which the eye moves to and fro, analysing and reanalysing the picture into its various patterns of colour, chiaroscuro, perspective, mass, balance, symbolism, etc. Screen visuals are usually rather simpler (for the equivalent to the canvas is the sequence, a series of 'details'). Further, the composition of a screen image depends on the narrative interest. The spectator usually has a definite centre of focus—the hero's face, the central event—and any compositional effect must be noticeable in relation to his 'centre of focus' rather than to the image as a whole.

Screen visuals usually make their point by one or two contrasts rather than by an intricate organization. A favourite device is to set off a strong architectural feature—a colonnade, a jetty, a bridge—at a diagonal to the line between the faces of two dramatically important characters. Or characters' bodies, arms, glances and positions in space may comprise a clutter of sharp, tense diagonals. The angles between two walls, or between walls and ceilings, may be brought into play. This still from *La Passion de Jeanne d'Arc* (Plate 12) contains a set of tense, painful angles—the pike, Joan's head (against her body) the two men who carry her, the 'heavy', 'unsettled' diagonal of the roof. The pyramidal form of the men carrying Joan creates a sense of weight, of struggle.

Similar 'lines' may be set up by the play of spotlights through darkness, by colour, by shift of dramatic centre, and so on.

Or a composition may derive its beauty from a simplicity of outline on a flat plane. (Plate 10.) Or from *hints* of depth (Plate 9)—how beautifully the visual suggestion reinforces the psychological uneasiness.

Pabst and Ophuls are specialists in multi-plane compositions. The central action is glimpsed through a foreground 'screen' of hats, flowers, bottles on a shelf, minor characters or furnishings, and beyond the main action we become aware of a 'background' plane—dancers, lookers-on, a door into another room, or perhaps a mirror reflecting the main action from another angle. Contrasts of spotlight and shadow can be used to direct the eye and prevent the picture being a clutter; while the abundance of environment gives a very powerful sense of atmosphere. Pabst's *Der Dreigroschenoper* and Ophuls' *Madame De* are particularly rich in such effects. Both directors specialize in using light and smoke to make one aware of the air around the characters.

A beautiful recessive pattern of movements is shown in this frame-still from the riot sequence in *La Passion de Jeanne d'Arc* (Plate 11).

The first still from Eisenstein's *Alexander Nevski* (Plate 13) is a masterly combination of bold outlines, simple form and complex detail. Its near-symmetry would be stodgy were it not for the projecting beam which gives it such life, leaping out from the tower like a cry. Yet every visual feature echoes the same basic shape—the cowls, the crosses, the tower, the helmets, are all variations on the one theme of virile upthrust, which is in grim contrast to the hanging man. A simpler, but equally subtle, 'theme and variation' is offered by the shot of the three Teutonic helmets. (Plate 14.) Each helmet is a brutal face. First our attention is drawn by the watchful eyes in the largest helmet on the right. Then we see the more closed helmet, second in size, on the left. And finally, ramming the message home, we see the even more metallic face between them, like reinforcements lying in 'ambush'. The degrees of 'closedness' form a climax.

In a very different key, Renoir's *French Can-Can* offers another form of theme and variations. One after the other, three young friends of Nina (Françoise Arnoul) present themselves for an audition as can-can dancers. The first, a laundress, shows a brave spirit, but can't dance very well. The second, a frail, pale, long-faced girl, with lanky limbs and a thin lock of bouncing hair, is apparently a gymnastic expert, for she does high kicks in an almost laughable mechanical style—we feel like laughing until, as she gathers confidence, she relaxes and shows an exuberance which really is impressive. After her comes our third candidate, a haughty, physically opulent milady who cannot raise a leg without wobbling violently. And this succession of 'twists' is further diversified-and-unified as Nina, a trim redhead, dances expertly beside her friends to encourage them. All this is taken by Renoir at a cracking pace, as if to stress the contrasts. Quite apart from the *characterological* interest of each different girl, there is a magnificent variety of emotion—nervousness, disappointment, and so on. Though this little sequence exists in time, and as a narrative, it is constructed on the same principle of 'theme and variations' as the shots from *Alexander Nevski*.

Another form of 'variation' is exemplified by the still from *Ivan the Terrible* (Plate 15)—where the gap in the wall 'echoes' Ivan's shape, and the winding crowd the hang of his sleeve. The care behind the image is revealed by the way in which the 'twist' in the line of the crowd re-echoes in the 'twist' of Ivan's staff and to his sleeve and shoulder.

The next two stills, one from Murnau's *Tabu* (Plate 17), the other from *La Passion de Jeanne d'Arc* (Plate 16) show how otherwise very different visuals may have certain marked features in common—in this case, a vigorous organization of diagnosis and zigzags.

Often the composition is a matter of lights and darks. In the still from *Tabu* (Plate 19) the left and right hand sides are 'mirrors' to each other. Just as there is a triangle of darkness on the left, there is a triangle of light on the right. The image from *Ivan the Terrible* (Plate 18) is a *pointilliste* 'spatter' of lights and darks. (If one half-closes one's eyes, the chiaroscuro can be seen more clearly.) The shot from *Tabu* is more than a merely formal pattern: the contrast between the flesh of the man's torso, as he lies awake, and the girl's face, lost in the darkness of sleep, between flesh (on the left) and darkness (on the right), is part of the emotional impact.

A film may be built on a contrast of textures—whether of fabrics and objects as in *Les Yeux Sans Visages*—or of *photographic* textures. There is a beautiful run of colour contrasts during the credits of George Sidney's *Pal Joey*, where we cut from a 'hot', glittering shot of neon lights at night, to a 'cool', silver, metallic train, and then to the soft, creamy pastel white of a ferryboat. Somehow, this is more than mere technical 'dandyism'—it seems to be saying something about the blend of gloss and melancholy in American life. Freda's *The Terror of Dr. Hichcock* has an extraordinary funeral sequence. Black-clad mourners in black umbrellas walk under a silvery glitter of sunlit rain; they pass bright flowers; the grain of the coffin is warmly visible in the sun. The living wood. . . . As the procession passes a row of silhouetted, green-tinged cypresses, a shaft of sunlight pours down on them and for a split second is broken up by the camera lens into all the colours of the rainbow. 'Artificial' as it is—the human eye wouldn't see it—the effect 'fits', because it lifts to the level of paroxysm the tragic irony of sunlight at a young woman's funeral.

Although the photographic image has no 'line' (being only patches of light-and-dark) robes, swirling water or other objects may be used to create a 'calligraphic' effect. The folds and swirl of robes in Cocteau's *La Belle et la Bête* have a nervous linearity reminiscent of Cocteau's drawings—and not really very far from the calligraphy of robes in 'The Three Graces' by another tormented soul, Botticelli.

Film lighting is a primary factor in creating atmosphere—though very much at the mercy of a good print. For *Le Sang d'Un Poète* Cocteau asked Perinal for 'a debauched sort of lighting', but the film's quality of four-in-the-morning-blues is due to many factors. There is the stealthy, slithery, strained postures of the poet, whether he is crouching horrified over the lips bubbling in the palm of his hand, or sidling along the enigmatic corridor. The light, without quite *sculpting* his muscles, picks out their movement, caressively. There is the contract between his bare flesh and the drab, seedy wall.

51

A lucky accident helped the film's atmosphere. '. . . the sweepers were told to clear up the studio, just as we had started on our last shots. But as I was about to protest, my cameraman (Perinal) asked me to do nothing of the kind; he had just realized what beautiful images he would be able to take through the dust raised by the sweepers in the light of the arc lamps.'

All Cocteau's films are extremely sensual, and to consider them as a collection of merely literary symbols is to miss half of their power. The symbols themselves are sensual—snow, blood, opium, poisons, rubber gloves and suits, women in white fur against white snow, negroes with shining muscles, champagne served in a house with peeling walls, *les enfants terribles* sucking away at prawns in bed, bodies struggling and straining against the wind, or oozing along in reverse- or slow-motion, giving an effect of laborious sickliness. One can *feel* the lips bubbling under water in the poet's hand. And what could be more physical than the idea of mirrors which turn to water when you hurl yourself into them?

As Death (Maria Casarès) in his *Orphée* dons and removes her crackling rubber gloves, we are not far from the fetishistic sensations which upset Emanuelle Riva while she was making *Le Huitième Jour* for Marcel Hanoun. She testifies: 'The erotic scenes are intended to shock. . . . He found the putting on of rubber gloves particularly exciting, and made a great deal of the crackling noise they made and the vaguely sensuous idea of a second skin. . . . I had really a very unpleasant time making it.' When Orphée (Jean Marais), finding the mirror remaining glass, impenetrable, sinks down wearily against it, we hear his flesh squeak against the glass. 'Oh that this too too squeaky flesh might melt. . . .' Such sharp little details of physical realism give a hallucinatory power to the film's world.

The film director can sensitively orchestrate light. He can model, give or remove depth and contour, vary or contradict the shapes and surfaces of his décor. In café or ballroom scenes, the light is a prime source of atmosphere, weaving light and smoke into nets of chiaroscuro. By light, says Sternberg, 'air can be made to glow. Just as I spray trees with aluminium to give life to the dull green, just as one filters the sky to reduce its whiteness . . . the skin should reflect and not blot light, and the lights are to be used to caress, not to wipe out, what they strike. . . .' A character's 'walk . . . or movement through space should be made into an encounter with light . . . lifeless surfaces should be relentlessly treated to take light, and over-brilliant and flaring surfaces must be reduced to their order. . . .' It is plain that one has not fully felt a Sternberg film, whether in the 'dirty' key of *The Blue Angel*, or the 'glittering' key of *The Devil is a Woman*, or the mysterious gradations of *The Saga of Anatahan*, until one can share something of this painterly *sensuality* about light. The same is true of Murnau, of Leni, of many of the German directors of the silent era.

Particularly with colour-and-Cinemascope, it is possible to speak of 'décor' directors—one thinks of Minnelli's *The Bells are Ringing* and *Two Weeks in Another Town*, of Cottafavi's *Hercules Conquers Atlantis* and Bava's *Hercules at the Centre of the Earth*, and Kurt Maetzig's *First Spaceship on Venus*, at which we shall glance again later. At the other extreme, the harmony of cloths and furnishings in Renoir's *French Can-Can* isn't unlike Minnelli's films in its 'Mozartian' colour. But Minnelli seems to have difficulty in escaping from the academicism of a certain 'colour elegance', even if most of his films have admirable scenes. Décor directors are usually also costume directors—as exemplified by the 'echo' of robe and wall in *Ivan the Terrible*, where the cloak becomes part of an overall architectural structure.

Camera movements constitute an integral part of the cinema's visual repertoire. In Autant-Lara's *Le Diable au Corps* Gérard Philippe's first love-scene with Micheline Presle is climaxed by the camera tracking past a chequered bedshead to two hands clasping over the light-switch and each other. But later, as the heroine lies dying, in the same bed, giving birth to her lover's son, the camera repeats the movement—this time, though, her hand closes over her husband's, while she cries her lover's name. And her husband takes it as the name she has chosen for their child. . . . Without the repetition of the camera position and movement, we would feel much less sharply the irony of deception and misunderstanding, the immortal moment denied and reasserted. . . .

The same 'elegaic' use of camera movements is found in Ophuls, but developed to the pitch of paroxysm. As James Mason remarked,

> '*I think I know the reason why,*
> *Producers tend to make him cry,*
> *Inevitably they demand*
> *Some stationary set-ups, and*
> *A shot that does not call for tracks*

53

Is agony for poor dear Max,
Who, separated from his dolly,
Is wrapped in deepest melancholy.
Once, when they took away his crane,
I thought he'd never smile again. . . .'

The camera's movements through elaborate Ophulsesque décor carries an astonishing lyricism. Whenever camera movements depart from 'natural' lines of sight or of movement, the spectator becomes vaguely conscious of a certain uneasiness, or of exhilaration. Thus when in Clair's *Le Quatorze Juillet* the camera moves along the outside of a house from window to window, one has a mixture of feelings—of cheeky wit (we are 'Peeping Tom'ing in this Godlike way); of melancholy (we are *outside* the house); of intimacy (our partial exclusion emphasizes the privilege of catching them in secrecy); there is the absurdity of all these characters so near to each other, and so self-engrossed; and the curious feeling of superiority in our magic gliding through mid-air. Similarly, long trackings can create a kind of gathering excitement, as the landscape streams past us. Particular tensions are possible when the camera moves at oblique angle towards a 'point of intersection' with a moving centre of interest (a dancer, a rider, a train).

By his camera movements, Ophuls gives both visual life and emotional dynamism to the stuffy, hierarchicalized, static décor—and society—of Vienna 1900. His camera moves past screens, flunkeys, fans, candles, whispered conversations, much as a Henry James sentence winds its way through innumerable reservations, concessions and hesitations to its final rather tentative assertion. Ophuls' films are full of symbols of movement—staircases, spiral staircases, immensely long corridors, the can-can in *Le Plaisir*, coaches, the lovers waltzing in *Madame De. . . .* In *Lola Montès*, even the ship waltzed under the stars, and when Lola and Liszt live together, it is in two coaches, travelling.

Until Ophuls, technicians' lore had it that one must never, never bring a pan back to its starting point. But again and again Ophuls' camera performs *la ronde*. It moves as his plots move. *La Ronde* begins and ends with the same prostitute, for Viennese love is a merry-go-round which spins industriously and none too merrily. The plot of *Madame De . . .* is based on the jewels which keep *returning*. *Lola Montès* is a film of circles—the circus ring round which the ringmaster moves incessantly, Lola on a carousel. . . . Ophuls' way of telling stories in flashbacks is another form of 'circularity'—we are constantly returning to the past, and then returning to the present. Thus past and future are mingled—just as in *La Ronde* Anton Walbrook leads Simone Simon from 'now' to 'six months later', when, ironically, she will betray the soldier who betrayed her then. Ophuls' fondness for episodes is another form of his fondness for flashbacks —both suggest that human encounters are shapeless, indecisive, in a sense, pointless, leading to nothing in the future.

To over-simplify, perhaps, Ophuls' camera movements suggest a mellow 'fatalism'. Everything ends where it begins. The world is a maze of ironies, of impermanence, of nostalgias. If Ophuls' camera moves, it is *à la recherche du temps perdu*. But it isn't possible to separate the camera movements from the décor through which it moves, and which it shows to us, or the dramatic context in which it occurs. It has lately become fashionable to attribute to camera movements effects which are really due to décor and lighting. John Guillermin's (interesting, and cleverly styled) *Waltz of the Toreadors* has a track-through-a-dissolve-to-the-same-ballroom-years-before which Ophuls would have been pleased to have thought of. But the total effect is weaker because the lighting and staging haven't the Ophuls magic.

Similarly, movement *within* the frame may be 'carried' from one scene to another. The rhythms of Fellini's *La Dolce Vita*, are beautifully controlled in their very slowness. Quite exquisite is the way in which the curve of Anita's 'cardinal' hat, as it falls in the wind from the dome of St. Peter's, is continued by the movement of a saxophone in the next shot. I described Franju's *Les Yeux Sans Visage* as a metronome-and-protractor film, and King Vidor literally used a metronome to regulate the action climaxes in both *The Big Parade* and *Our Daily Bread*. 'I was in the realm of my favourite obsession, experimenting with the possibilities of 'silent music'. . . . When we filmed the march through Belleau Wood . . . I used the . . . metronome and a drummer with a bass drum . . . so that all in a range of several hundred yards could hear. I instructed the men that each step must be taken on a drum beat, each turn of the head, lift of a rifle, pull of a trigger, in short, every physical move must occur on the beat of a drum. . . . When the picture opened, I requested Sid Grauman to have the orchestra stop their musical accompaniment at the beginning of the sequence, and keep silent until its finish. . . .' Again in *Our*

Daily Bread, 'The picks came down on the counts of one and three, the shovels scooped dirt on count two and tossed it on four. . . .' Similarly, Greta Garbo's movements during the scene in Rouben Mamoulian's *Queen Christina* where she 'remembers' the furniture were timed to a metronome.

A film may be built on its sense of space, like *Entr'acte* (which is regularly credited to René Clair, although Clair acted mainly as a technical assistant to the dadaist painter, Frances Picabia). The film (whose title means 'Intermission') formed part of a dada ballet called *Relâche* ('No Performance Today'). Picabia's problem was to translate the ballet's flow of jokes into terms of screen action and movement.

The film was originally shown on a very large screen, giving a 'Cinerama' effect. It falls into two parts, the first rather static and full of arbitrary dada in-jokes. In the second a narrative crystallizes, and we have the celebrated sequence of a funeral procession rushing along at the double after a runaway hearse (which is drawn by a camel).

But amidst all the comment of the baffling *non sequiturs* of its 'literary content', only Bardèche and Brasillach point out that the 'continuity' of the first part is its play with sensations of space and balance—to link it with the surrounding ballet. The rooftop setting, and panning shots round the horizon, the tilt up a 'column' of windows, the theme of people *taking aim* from rooftops (with shot-guns or cannons, sometimes into the audience), the coconut bouncing on the jet of water, all are intended to create in the audience a kind of spatial uneasiness, indeed, giddiness. Interwoven with these are dislocations of movement—two men floating over a cannon, the unexpected angles on a ballerina, the visual echo between a worm's-eye-view of her knickered thighs and a pair of boxing gloves nudging each other, a slow chess game proceeding on the rooftops, which begin spinning crazily. The film becomes much more satisfying and 'logical' if one more or less forgets the 'literary content' of the symbols, concentrates on the visual-spatial sensations and jokes offered by objects and settings, and finds most of their 'poetic' meanings in these physical relationships.

In films like these the film's mixed-art status is confirmed. During the shooting of *The Big Parade* 'one British veteran wanted to know if he were performing in "some bloody ballet". I did not say so at the time, but that is exactly what it was—a bloody ballet, a ballet of

death.' Equally, 'I decided to treat . . . building this ditch in a manner
I imagined a choreographer would use in plotting out the movements
of a ballet. . . .'

Griffith was a master of counterpointing shapes-in-motion. There
is far more than narrative interest to the celebrated 'cross-cutting' in
his chases. The final 'movement' of *Intolerance* (1918), where pre-
parations for a hanging proceed while a car races a railway train
with news of a pardon, is built up out of story ingredients which
can't possibly carry conviction today. But the sheer sense of movement does. Griffith contrasts the steady, sweeping, winding curve of
the train with the car's bullet-like movement on a twisting, switch-
back-like road—meanwhile the three prison officials bob up the little
staircase to the scaffold with a petty, jagged, insistent movement, like
the meticulous ticking of a watch. The surging train, the yo-yoing
car, the brisk little movements in the condemned cell, all form a
choreographic 'whirlpool' of movements. The descent of Cyrus'
army on the Babylonians has some astonishing play with crowd
movements. Choreography rules even the intimate scenes—as the
Three Uplifters advance to seize the young mother's baby, all their
grasping arms and hands move like the tentacles of an octopus. As
the Huguenot girl is slaughtered by a Catholic mercenary, Griffith
asks us to *feel* the contrast between the soldier's spiky uniform and
sharp brutal movements, and the girl's slow slide in her flowing
nightshirt to the floor as she dies. Griffith broke down the 'semaphore' acting code of his time (outstretched arms for 'go', clasped
hands for 'please', jumping up and down for joy, and so on) and gave
it a choreographic organization. His sense of organizing movement
is at least as great an innovation as his narrative developments. It
inspired Lang's *Metropolis* (1926), and seems to me a more important
feature of Eisenstein's silent films than his application of theories
about 'intellectual' montage.

Such devices, in their mechanical forms, have become an integral
part of film technique, but are capable of more imaginative application—whether the tempo is *lento ponderoso* (as in Lang's *The Woman
in the Window*, Franju's *La Tête Contre Les Murs*), or allegretto
(Chaplin's little comedies abound in the sprite orchestration of
chases in every direction and dimension of space and shape of
obstacle), or whether in the sustained, symphonic structures of
Alexander Dovzhenko. A cut in Jules Dassin's *Thieves Highway*
serves to indicate other contrasts. A shot of a heavy fruit-truck

careering off a road is followed by a shot of the oranges showering all over the screen. The cut brings into play contrasts of shape, form, pattern, direction of movement, sensed texture.· . . . There is a fascinating effect in Kurosawa's *The Seven Samurai*. As they answer an alarm, we see, in quick, sharp succession, four shots, each showing one Samurai running, from right to left. But in each shot, the Samurai is further to the right of the screen than his predecessor was. Each is, so to speak, 'falling back'. In short—they're all running as fast as they can, straining at the limit of their strength, can't run at the superhuman speed they feel they need.

Our survey of visual effects has necessarily been summary and impressionistic, but will have served its purpose if it shows how extensively content is created out of details of style, and what sort of 'pictorial content' can work effectively on the cinema screen.

4 · Auteurs and Dream Factories

Questions of style bring us to the so-called *auteur* theory and the debates about it that sprawl through French, British and American film magazines. Our concern is not to discuss these controversies in all their aspects, but to concentrate on those which concern the issue of style and personal vision.

At the same time, it may be helpful to enlarge the field of reference a little, so as to see how, behind the specific disagreements, many assumptions have been operating which have confused what only seems a 'purely' aesthetic disagreement.

The *auteur* theory is the assumption that most films can be interpreted in terms of their director's artistic personality just as intensively as a novel can be interpreted in terms of its authors'. It is obviously true of, for example, Dreyer and Bresson, so that much discussion has centred on the question of how far, if at all, such an approach is relevant or adequate to Hollywood directors.

We may perhaps usefully contrast *limited* and *extended* applications of *auteur* theory. A limited theory was central to the tenets of what one may call the '30's school' of British criticism, running from Paul Rotha and John Grierson through to Richard Winnington, Roger Manvell and the *Penguin Film Review* (1946–49). Their *auteurs* were such artists as Griffith, Eisenstein, Pudovkin, Flaherty, Disney, Capra, Carné, Welles, Sturges, Huston, Lean and so on. But side by side with this appreciation of the artist, these critics generally had a special interest in a film's reflection of social reality, and a special antipathy to Hollywood 'glamour' (which was tolerated, or not, but generally felt to be antithetical to seriousness, with the occasional exception, as for Garbo). Thus the documentary movement was felt to be extremely meritorious, because it showed docks and post offices and all the exterior paraphernalia of 'social realism', whereas Sternberg's films with Marlene Dietrich were felt to be more or less meretricious (distinction between these and the Garbos was assumed rather than explained). The critics were very sympathetic to the *auteur* struggling to be individualistic and honest within the restraints of the Hollywood system (which indeed attained a peak of rigidity in the early 40's). Their lively awareness of the negative aspects of the Hollywood system constituted a powerful check to *auteur* theory. Another check came from their advocacy of the documentary *movement* and *its* themes and qualities. It was assumed that a director might make one or two good films, or come up with the brilliant fluke, then yield to pressures, or stray after false gods, and be lost to serious film-making. Even the films of obvious *auteurs* would be related to general aesthetic directives or social issues with little exegesis and less close linking with their creators' artistic personalities. All this constituted a *limited* form of *auteur* theory.

A new spirit appeared when a group of Oxford undergraduates, notably Gavin Lambert, Karel Reisz and Lindsay Anderson, founded their magazine *Sequence* (1948–52) which, without reacting against the older critics, moved a little way towards a less earnest tone, and to more probing exegeses, after the model of the undergraduate English essay. Lindsay Anderson's enthusiasm for John Ford's *She Wore a Yellow Ribbon* (1949) and Gavin Lambert's for Jean Cocteau signalled an increase in interest in what *Sequence* called 'the poetic vision', as against the documentary and realist virtues, which were in no way decried. Nonetheless Richard Winnington, who had initially encouraged these young critics, repudiated them, just before his death, for having regressed to a precious aestheticism.

Gavin Lambert, aided by the *Sequence* team, had by then become editor of *Sight and Sound* and of its sister-journal, *The Monthly Film Bulletin*, which had fallen into a dismal academicism. Lambert and Ken Tynan, who contributed excellent appreciations of gangster films and Tom and Jerry cartoons, looked like continuing the tradition of appreciative criticism that had been so positive a factor of *Sequence*. But Lambert and Tynan left, and the magazine began a period of slow stagnation, all the more marked by contrast with the convulsive transformations of French criticism. It maintained a sufficiently authoritative tone to be accepted both here and abroad as 'the' organ of English intellectual opinion, which is why we pay attention to it here.

The range of *auteurs* was scarcely widened from that which they had inherited from the '30's school'. Indeed, by the late 50's, John Grierson reproached the magazine for having neglected the discovery of new talent (it promptly discovered Richard Quine, and then left Hollywood at that for the next few years).

While the old-established *auteurs* were treated with consistent respect, and an uncritical adulation for Ford prefigured the excesses of extended *auteur* theory, there was a group of directors who were held to have had their time as *auteurs*, but to have lapsed into the Hollywood ruck. These included Fritz Lang, King Vidor and Alfred Hitchcock (*auteurs* for some of their pre-war films), Frank Capra (for his 'socially conscious' comedies of the 30's), Minnelli (for his flirtations with populism and for his musicals). *Red River* (1948) was the last Hawks film to have an enthusiastic review. Nicholas Ray, Robert Wise, Jules Dassin and Joseph Losey earned short-lived reputations for early films (*They Live by Night, The Set-Up, The Naked City* and *The Dividing Line*) which were in accepted traditions, but were dismissed when they grouped for new idioms and attitudes. Veterans like Raoul Walsh and Allan Dwan were as unnoticed as a relative newcomer like Otto Preminger, and none of the new directors to emerge in the 50's provoked enthusiasm comparable to the old *auteurs*. Thus Richard Brooks, Sam Fuller, Elia Kazan, Frank Tashlin and Budd Boetticher were scarcely distinguished from the Hollywood 'ruck'.

Interest in 'social realism' itself underwent a change. In theory, at least, a special importance was attached to 'social consciousness', whether documentary or neo-realistic in type, or inclining more to the 'poetic vision', like Ford's *The Grapes of Wrath* (1940). A tense cynicism and questioning was accepted, but only within certain limits of tone and topic. Thus Preston Sturges' edgy comedies were securely within the pale, whereas Billy Wilder's aroused a faint distaste. The 'Raymond Chandler' mood was welcomed for its lyrical astringency, but there seemed an increasing deprecation or resentment of those films which brought this astringent, questioning mood into relation with specific social issues, or with the American social climate as a whole, notably Fritz Lang's *The Big Heat* (1953). The idyllic, 'Ford' Western was still enjoyed, but not the new bitter tone of Sam Fuller's *Run of the Arrow* (1957) or Anthony Mann's *Man of the West* (1958). Now Richard Winnington's denunciation, which at the time had seemed excessive, began to justify itself as a shrewd insight. Films such as Richard Brooks' *The Blackboard Jungle* (1955) or Nicholas Ray's *Rebel Without a Cause* (1955) were damned with faint praise. Lindsay Anderson denounced Elia Kazan's *On the Waterfront* (1954) as 'implicitly, if unconsciously, Fascist . . . hopeless, savagely ironic . . . fundamentally contemptuous . . . without either grace, joy or love', but his vehemence was, in a way, more worthy a response than the supercilious shrug which greeted many equally 'concerned' American films. Unusually gracious was P.H.'s description of Nunnally Johnson's *The Man in the Grey Flannel Suit* (1955) as 'uneasily fascinating'.

But whether such films were condemned, tolerated, or adduced as evidence of symptoms of moral decay, their *auteurs* were credited with little ability to think about, or make any interesting comment on, either their topics in particular, or human nature in general. They were spiritually depersonalized, they were merely 'Hollywood', and the word 'Hollywood' was used with a quiet, but firm, dismissiveness. Hollywood had slickness, yes, but intelligence, never. The only exegesis of such films was destructive; Penelope Houston attempted to prove that Stanley Kramer's *On the Beach* (1959) made fallout glamorous.

Gradually, this derisive approach extended even to obvious *auteurs*. The first Bergman film to be shown here, *Sawdust and Tinsel* (1953), was dismissed as a neurotic throwback to the tricks of Germanic expressionism. Even after Bergman's increasing celebrity had modified this attitude, Peter John Dyer saw in *The Virgin Spring* (1960) only 'consulting-room horrors . . . exhibitionism . . . at its most pathological'. The same article dismissed Visconti too; his *Rocco and His Brothers* (1960) was 'the boldest example of fraudulent conversion since *Ossessione*'. It displayed 'self-indulgence' (a trait which this school of criticism was quick to notice, perhaps because it bears so close a resemblance to self-expression), and Eric Rhode, writing about Visconti's *La Terra Trema*, concurred in this 'hypochondriac' approach to the *auteur*: 'There is something wrong somewhere' (context implies: with Visconti's emotional health) 'when a nobleman makes a film entirely about Sicilian fishermen' (presumably we should each keep to our own class?). To the first Bunuel film to reach this country for several years, *La Mort En Ce Jardin* (1956), Dyer conceded 'a workable script' and some interesting ingredients, but concluded: 'What is missing is the barest competence in direction.'

Whatever one's opinion of these films may be (mine is that only the last three are anywhere near 'masterpieces') it was difficult not to be startled by the contrast between the brutal, summary tone adopted by the English magazine, and the thoughtful and complex exegeses characteristic of the wide range of continental approaches. The *Sight and Sound* team seemed unreflectively to identify the most concerned and vital American directors with an 'unhealthy' American climate, while castigating distinguished European artists for an equally unhealthy individualism. In England, only 'Free Cinema' (intimately connected with the magazine itself) earned more than token appreciation.

What seemed an attitude of complacent contempt set the tone for the bitterness with which *Sight and Sound* was attacked by the younger English critics, notably the 'new wave' of undergraduates who were associated first with the Liberal magazine *Oxford Opinion* and later with *Movie*, and who were generally felt to be English proponents of *auteur* approach.[1]

The main dispute was not whether a film had to be by an *auteur* in order to merit critical opinion, but, which directors were the *auteurs*. The younger critics accepted most of the orthodox 'elect', and the dispute centred largely on the status of directors whom *Sight and Sound* had consigned to the Hollywood 'ruck'. The *Movie* critics accorded particularly high places in their canon to the post-war films of Hitchcock, Hawks, Preminger and Ray. In America, Andrew Sarris, the most thorough Anglo-Saxon exponent of *auteur* theory, went on to postulate as *auteurs* some fifty Hollywood directors, thus, if not actually denying, at least sharply diminishing, the significance of traditional criticisms of the Hollywood system.

In this respect *Movie* and Sarris concurred with the 'second generation' (*ca* 1954–58) of critics of *Cahiers du Cinéma*. These critics, dubbed the 'Hitchcocko-Hawksiens', included such *Nouvelle Vague* directors-to-be as François Truffaut, Jean-Luc Godard, Claude Chabrol, Jacques Rivette, and Eric Rohmer. Thus, by the time the controversy came to England, they were possessed of immense prestige, for their stylistic and thematic innovations as for their international success.

The supposed indebtedness of the younger British critics to *Cahiers du Cinéma* gave rise to many a merry jest, though I doubt

[1] Not at all as rigid as that of *Cahiers* in theory, though most of their writing centred round *auteurs*.

whether *Cahiers* was much more to them than a signpost to some directors, and, otherwise, a flag to rally round. There was certainly little emulation of its approach or thought. *Movie* offered, instead of *Cahiers*' characteristically 'philosophic' approach to style (of which more later), something between 'exegesis' and 'functional analysis'. Its critics often restricted themselves to clarifying the relationship of stylistic details to the whole, and they generally refrained from judging the quality of the view of life in the films of their favourites. Ian Cameron wrote, coat-trailingly, 'To judge a film on anything other than its style is to set up the critics' own views on matters outside the cinema against those of its maker. This is gross impertinence.' This, surely excessive, limitation on the scope of criticism becomes more understandable when one bears in mind the cavalier dismissals which had become the rule in *Sight and Sound*. The younger critics, while capable of summary writing-off, wrote at length only about the films they had enjoyed.

There can be little doubt that this critical line, however controversial in detail, had the excellent result of extending critical interest and respect to the films of many interesting directors, who for decades had been relegated to the outer darkness. For as we have seen *Sight and Sound* had become rather more rigorous in its disdain of Hollywood than the 30's school had been. And incapable of extended *appreciative* exegesis, restricting itself to, not interpreting, but 'evaluating', a film in a rather piecemeal way (the acting was 'sensitive', the direction was 'imaginative', the film a 'poetic vision' and so on). Indeed *Movie* and *Film* both showed that many criticisms were virtually paraphrases of criticisms by *other* members of the team of *other* films—identical phrases recurred, no 'specific' points were made. The equivalent French magazines had never adopted such a 'negativity'.[1] From 1928 to 1931, and again from 1945 to 1950, *La Revue du Cinéma*, under the editorship of Jean-George Auriol, was devoting major reviews to such films as Dassin's *Brute Force* (1947), Charles Vidor's *Gilda* (1946) and William Dieterle's *Love Letters* (1945).[2] There was nothing specifically new, youthful or 'rebellious'

---

[1] Not, at least, on aesthetic grounds. *L'Ecran Français*, while dominated by French Stalinists, had embarked on a systematic denigration of Hollywood films, but the movies there were political, rather than 'supercilious'. The *Sight and Sound* attitude was of course helped by a confluence of two attitudes: a general sympathy for the left, and the cultured English disdain for vulgar Americana.

[2] During its earlier period, it had an English equivalent in *Close-Up*, which however, was much less interested in American films.

about *Cahiers'* responsiveness towards American films. Indeed, the majority of French magazines were also exploring Hollywood extensively. *Positif* (founded 1952), with its Marxist and Surrealist tendencies, soon asserted its predilection for, notably, Robert Wise, Richard Brooks, John Huston and Frank Tashlin. And Henri Agel, doyen of the Roman Catholic school of film criticism, had also been paying serious attention to such refreshingly unexpected films as Hawks' *Monkey Business* and King Vidor's *Duel in the Sun*.

Indeed, it is possible to regard the *Cahiers* version of the extended *auteur* theory as a 'dogmatized' degradation of this general tradition. To understand it one must refer briefly to the figure of *Cahiers'* 'senior wrangler' André Bazin.

Bazin was a left-wing Catholic, completely unpuritanical, broadminded and generous in his attitudes to the cinema. With his passionate responsiveness to the cinema as an authentic 'humanism', as an essentially 'impure' art, went a sensitivity to the cinema as a culture whose nuances and sensitivities could be as non-literary, as specifically cinematic, as those of music are specifically musical. He had two particular interests which were to be over-developed by younger writers. There was his concern with the philosophical implications of stylistic nuance, implications which he expressed in terms bordering on the metaphysical. This was partly a natural result of his Catholicism, partly because he often wrote as if style expressed mainly the *auteur's* attitude to the character's experiences (whereas I would argue that it more often expresses nuances in those experiences). Schematically rather than accurately, one may say that Bazin identified himself with the director, and the director with a very kindly God, who was blowing a kind of spiritual life into his subject-matter, much as God breathes life into Adam. A very kindly God, but also a rather vague one. For Bazin, in his very kindness, often dissolved the specific personal or social issues of a film into a spiritual generalization, rather after this pattern: 'Of course, *Bicycle Thieves* is, in a superficial sense, 'about' *this* workman in *this* society. But this predicament is only an image for something *deeper*: the *universal, human* predicament. . . .'

The, not so much flaws, as limitations, of such an approach must be evident. Soon, no film is felt to be 'about' its subject-matter. Its specificity, concreteness and consequently its richness of detail, dissolve into a sort of spiritual soup, which itself makes nonsense of all the differences between one culture and another, one person and another, one film and another. Without some sort of specificity *through* which any 'universality' can be attained, as a sort of none-too-important 'bonus', 'art' sinks back into something like religious-generalization-in-individualistic-metaphor. And much of Bazin's criticism is quite different from exegesis. It is about the relationship of an *auteur*-God to his creation. Bazin's 'collected works' read like one long stream of theological rumination, all the more amiable, perhaps, for centring on man rather than God. They sometimes read like tentative prologomena to *Honest to God*, and, however full of solipsisms, have, not only their own cinematographic interest, but a quite theological tension and flow.

Bazin certainly makes the point that in the films of a genuine *auteur* every detail can be taken as 'meant', and is neither accidental nor 'pure form'; and also that style 'is' content.

But some of Bazin's successors in *Cahiers* made of his approach a Procrustean bed. They sometimes denied that an *auteur*'s films could validly be related to anything other than its creator's attitudes. Once they accepted a director as an *auteur* (and only directors were *auteurs*), then he could no more be deposed, or fall below himself, than God. The *auteur* had a quality of 'efficacious grace' that enabled him to score repeated triumphs, down to the minutest detail, over the Hollywood system. If an *auteur*'s film was dramatically trite and boring, they shifted their interest to its 'allegorical' level. Or they felt that the *auteur* had, if not deliberately chosen, at least seized upon, so 'empty' a subject, so as to give *carte blanche* to his nuance-laden style, through which the critic could apprehend, by camera movement or other subtle means of stimulating reflection, the 'spiritual generality' of which the film was an illustration. Or, again: only so 'banal' a subject could enable style to be its own subject-matter; so that a trite film could be talked about in a jargon verging on that used of abstract painting (surprisingly, it never did more than verge on it, perhaps because the critics' real interest was philosophical). They occasionally argued that poor technical quality (e.g. of back-projection) showed a director was interested only in the 'deep' (allegorical, philosophical) aspects of his plot. Or he might be speaking to those connoisseurs who knew how to 'decode' the inner meanings of his films.

In itself, none of these principles is far-fetched or absurd. They are used every day in criticisms of the other arts. The much-ridiculed idea of *auteurs* speaking through an esoteric symbolism is relevant in the case of certain films, notably, of course, those which the *Cahiers* critics themselves went on to make. The idea of offering 'special' meanings to one's *amis inconnus* is common in all the arts, and quite compatible with the idea of the work of art communicating before it is understood. The idea of 'meaning through style' is very fruitful in the case of, for example, Max Ophuls or Joseph von Sternberg. This essay has advocated virtually this approach to the films of Bresson and Dreyer, by suggesting that the spectator understands them best when he 'plays the game' of assuming that every detail in a film is 'meant'.

But the application of these principles was often disquieting. What might seem that most sympathetic of critical aberrations, the 'delirium of interpretation', soon revealed itself as not at all generous. For it was used to rule out the film's differences from the critic's own sensibility. Thus Ophuls, Hitchcock and Bunuel were all mashed together as crypto-neo-Platonic-Catholics-despite-themselves. And Bazin's own 'generous' indifference to social significance hardened among his followers into something like resentment of it, with the implication that this aspect of a film could be only 'obvious' or 'banal', a 'party line', as it were. Thus a concentration on 'the philosophy of style' too often went with quick evasions or dismissals of a film's literary or dramatic components. A cabbalistic subtlety was attributed to films which showed no other sign of deep thought, or even of being more than entertainments of moderate competence. Since the 'esoteric' meanings weren't very profound either, there seemed neither a *prima facie* case, nor a reward, for all this complicated decoding. Indeed, many of the directors celebrated had made it amply clear that they were very rarely in complete control of their films, that they made many potboilers for 'alimentary' reasons, that compromises, concessions, unwanted scripts and stars, were forced upon them.

One willingly grants 'total meaning' to Bresson and Dreyer because they give ample evidence, internal and external to their films, of having achieved their extraordinary degree of control. But it isn't a dogmatic assumption made before every film, nor an assertion that every artist has equal control over his own experience, his medium, and his creative circumstances.

The attribution of 'secret meanings' to otherwise unremarkable craftsmen looked suspiciously like (*a*) a way of treating films as *objets trouvés*, rather than as part of a communicating situation (so distorting them), and (*b*) a way of enjoying the Hollywood film while giving it an apparent, but basically distortive, congruence to 'high culture' ideas about authors and creative personalities.

For all this, it would be misleading to overlook the more 'moderate' positions always characteristic of the best writing in *Cahiers*. It would be most inaccurate to equate French criticism as a whole with *Cahiers*, or *Cahiers* as a whole with all that was most extreme and limited in *Cahiers*. Unfortunately, this last was taken virtually for granted throughout the *auteur* controversy in Britain, largely as a result of *Sight and Sound*'s own, defensive reflex. Sarcastic as its own dismissals of Bergman, Visconti, Losey, Ray *et al*. had been, the magazine felt wronged when attacked itself, in exactly similar terms, by the rising generation, and replied in terms which seemed to aim less at a genuine understanding of the issues at stake than at a crushing polemical victory. Thus Penelope Houston and Richard Roud both chose to identify French criticism as a whole with the extreme trend in *Cahiers*. They seized on its repudiation of social significance, and on its acceptance of style as its own subject-matter, so as to contrast their own 'humanism' with the 'non-humanist aestheticism' which Roud presented as *The French Line*.

Penelope Houston even went on to equate the younger English critics with something like a 'hoodlum' view of life. 'To the generation which has grown up during the last few years, art is seen as something for kicks; films which stab at the nerves and emotions; jazz and the excitements surrounding it. . . . Violence on the screen is accepted as a stimulant. . . .' Not surprisingly, the younger critics disliked being called kicks-crazy when all they were asking for was for more directors to be treated with critical respect and for more attention to be paid to subtleties of style.

The *Sight and Sound* team proposed two solutions to the 'style *v*. content' issue. Miss Houston settled matters peremptorily: 'Cinema is about human relationships, not about spatial relationships.' But this rules out the possibility, surely obvious, since the cinema is a visual medium, that spatial relationships might themselves be metaphors for human relationships. Richard Roud's conclusion seemed more conciliatory. 'We would gain . . . by adopting . . . the firm belief that form is at least as important as content.' But the persisting separation of form and content which 'as important as' implies, reveals its consequences when Roud, commenting on the spatial relationships in *L'Avventura*, sees its visual qualities as only 'an addi-

tional, non-representative element for our pleasure; a formal choreography of movements which accompanies the films, providing a non-
conceptual figure in the carpet'. Yet this formulation itself falls into
precisely that 'non-humanist aestheticism' so derided in *Cahiers*: 'A
film's style is not about human relationships, but about its style.'

To criticize this non-response to the eloquent visuals of *L'Avventura* is in no way to deny the possibilities of visual abstraction in
films, nor of a possible layer in *L'Avventura* itself, of aesthetic
interest for its own sake (a layer to which I would myself attach little
'cultural' importance). But what is curious is the difficulty in seeing
that the spatial relationships might be connected with the story.

Also worth remarking is the hardening attitude towards the *auteur*.
The 30's school awareness of the Hollywood 'system' went with a
certain sympathy for the artist who was trapped within it; *Sight and
Sound* made little or no attempt to distinguish, in the current films of
Hitchcock, Lang, Losey, Hawks, and so on, anything that wasn't
'system'. The extended *auteur* theory, on the other hand, makes little
or no allowance for the 'imposed' aspects of a film. It is content to
'decode' meanings and experiences from cryptic hints, imaginary or
real, and, in so doing, to accept, for the full emotional picture of an
experience or attitude, a rather cerebral 'notation'. No distinction is
made, or felt, or respected, between the 'sign' for an experience from
the 'symbol' for it. But before we look at some consequences of this
non-distinction, its origins can perhaps be clarified.

The *Sight and Sound* critics were heirs to an upper-middle-class
climate of cultural habit and opinion exemplified, at its best, by the
novels of E. M. Forster, at its most mediocre, by the complacent
pessimism of the remarks on the popular cinema by Palinurus in
The Unquiet Grave, and, at its least pleasant, by disdainful assumptions of superiority over, and censorious defensiveness towards, the
'popular'. They brought to the task of film criticism a philosophical
infrastructure which, felt rather than stated, and certainly never
examined, included such axioms as that the civilized few must protect the humanism of a minority art-culture against an unthinking
and vaguely unpleasant world, which was exemplified by, variously,
'the moguls', the 'mass media', the 'undiscriminating public' or an
undefined, *sensed* 'ruck' of inferiority. Further, since art is a 'sensitive
individualism', then if a film isn't by an artist with an obviously
sensitive feel for the moods and nuances of human relationships,
then it is probably an insensitive, impersonal film; i.e. it is a product

of the 'ruck', unthinking, a specious substitute, and therefore unpleasant.

Now, these nuances are sensed only when expressed by literary and dramatic elements (because in Britain literature and the theatre are facets of general culture, whereas the appreciation of the visual arts is more specialized), and furthermore the critic can recognize quality and sensitivity 'intuitively'. He brings no ideological nor intellectual dogma to a film, he 'senses' whether it is true or not to his own experience of life. If there isn't this immediate 'recognition' effect, the film is probably untrue, therefore unthinking, therefore cheap and contemptible, like Kazan's, Bergman's, or Visconti's; it has *nothing* to offer.

Indeed, under the pressure of these assumptions, the stress on 'social consciousness' steadily receded throughout the 50's. Mere 'social realism' took second place to 'sensitive nuance', lack of which relegated, for example, John Frankenheimer's *The Young Savages* (1961), to the untrue-unthinking-contemptible category.[1]

However, this whole tradition had begun to lose hold on the younger critics. For them, the 'sensitive nuances' of relationships were only parts of human relationships, which were primarily determined by strong, basic drives and attitudes. Marxism, psychoanalysis, sociology, the war, the new social mobility, a general cultural requestioning, had shifted attention from 'nuances' to 'fundamentals'. Thus the 'sensitive nuance', though still a factor, had ceased to be the *touchstone* for a film's quality. From this view, E. M. Forster's novel *A Passage to India*, without in any way disputing its positive qualities, is uncongenial, in so far as it tends to present racial tensions, sexuality, national cultures, religious prejudices, and so on, in terms of 'nuances', rather than as strong, driving, insistent urges, and so we never get a clear, 'dynamic' view of their play and interplay. On the other hand, Nicholas Ray's film *Rebel Without a Cause* may be 'stylized', it may fall into rhetoric, it may be rather less sensitive in its study of mood and nuance than E. M. Forster's

[1] Hence in the mid-50's *Definition*'s young critics, taking their inspiration from the post-Suez New Left, attempted to reverse this trend, reproaching *Sight and Sound* for making vaguely progressive noises while rejecting all ideological interests. For this criticism Miss Houston denounced them as 'cultural gauleiters'. Lindsay Anderson, whose discovery of Ford in *Sequence* days had contributed to the eclipse of 'social consciousness', had, by the late 50's, become a champion of the New Left, and, enjoying prestige in both camps, was spared both their broadsides. He has now decided that he was a 'romantic' all along.

novel. But it is likely to be more congenial to those who see life in terms of 'basic' drives and their intricate relationships. For its (relative) lack of sensitivity, its rhetoric, its concessions to melodrama, are compensated for by the central place which it allots to basic tensions and their interaction: the relationships of mother, father and son (Freud), its complacent evasions (middle-class culture), the insidious blend of toughness and conformism in peer-group morality, which the hero gradually renounces as he comes to equate virility with tenderness (to the heroine) and moral responsibility (he adopts a paternal role to another teenager). Thus he is freed from the state of alienation and nihilism whose cultural origins are mediated through such lyricized symbols as the planetarium, the ruined house and so on.

This contrast between the limitations of E. M. Forster's novel and the structure of Ray's film is meant only to stress that the film has a quite direct and valid appeal to a new common kind of sensibility. But it is also arguable that the 'resonance' of these basic clichés makes Ray's a more sensitive and disturbing film than a study which, though more 'sensitive' ('truthful to conscious experience'), in a Forsterian way, has little or nothing to say on this more 'dynamic' level.[1]

The assumption that the critic is one of the cultured few who must defend his sensitivity against mass crudity has also undergone alteration. The younger critics have grown up with the mass media—films, comics, records and so on. They are used to picking their way through them, and for them the 'superficial' film is in no way a 'specious' substitute for an 'authentic' work of art; it is a 'fun' film that one sees once and enjoys, more or less: 'superficial' doesn't imply 'contemptible'. There are films to which one returns again and again, but no Manichean polarity as between the 'elect' and the 'philistine'. Nor is a film that criticizes society felt to be *ipso facto* more 'salutary' or true or brave than a film that accepts it.

There seems also to be a difference between the very quick and total dismissals characteristic of the 'sensitive nuance' school, and the perhaps more cerebral, but also more thoughtful and adaptable, responses of the younger critics. For the absence of 'dogma' on which

[1]There is a further twist to this in so far as people think in terms of psychoanalysis, sociology, etc., a film can refer to such 'dynamics' quite briefly and concentrate, again, on nuances (as Antonioni does in *L'Avventura*). My own feeling is that this procedure is often a pretext for a thoughtless and boring lack of thought; not always, of course. Either way it doesn't affect my point, that there is another kind of 'awareness', of 'dynamics'.

the 'sensitive nuance' school prides itself is not without its narrow-mindedness. After all, one may be very sensitive to the sorts of nuance that are relevant to the feeling-tones of upper-middle-class English liberalism (and its currently favourite 'exoticisms', notably, American sophisticated comedy of the 30's, Kurosawa, Ford Westerns, Satyajit Ray's India, Raymond Chandler); and yet be very insensitive to anything uncongenial to those feeling-tones. A film which is immediately 'plausible' to one's sensibility may be far less accurate in its picture of alien sensibilities, and far less rich in insights, than a film which one learns, almost against one's will, to trust. To take only one example: Lindsay Anderson attacked Kazan's *On the Waterfront* for its 'Fascism', using as his implicit standard of comparison either the attitudes of London dockers towards trade-union solidarity or nebulous notions that working-class solidarity must be the same all over the world. Yet Daniel Bell's account of the *specific* labour disputes on which Kazan's film is based convincingly vindicates it against most of Anderson's criticisms.

The issue is not so much one of the critic's knowledge of the world, as of the extent to which he is willing to try to lend himself to a film, on its own terms, *before* he decides whether to accept or reject it as a whole or in part. The younger critics have the advantage in that, adapted as they are to a time of cultural fluidity and change, they often find more relevance to their own problems in American or foreign films than they do in English tradition. In the same way, Belmondo in Godard's *A Bout de Souffle* turns, not as his father might have done to his age, to the novels of Gide, but to a photograph of Humphrey Bogart (who is of course an 'intellectual's' star). This very flexibility tends to go with a more 'cerebral' approach, an acceptance of 'sign' for 'symbol', of 'idea' for 'experience'. One may regret, as I do, that so many young critics reacted against a too-arrogant attitude towards the artist's vision of life into a refusal to criticize it, an opposite, if more amiable, excess. Yet for critics to think of themselves as artists' friends and accomplices is surely more responsive and constructive, a better beginning for eventual evaluation, than the assumption that a critic can judge works of art 'off the cuff', from some stratospheric impartiality of his own.[1] The difference, in the end,

---

[1] In the event of course the brutal tone had to be at least partly abandoned in the face, not only of European critical attitudes, and of the younger criticism here, but of the extent to which the English 'literary' and intelligent public became interested in films.

is less between 'humanists' and 'aesthetes', than between reviewers who feel it their job to taste and judge, and critics who try to understand and explore.

At any rate, it is not so much the French influence as the importance traditionally attached to a 'personal vision' in art, that has provoked the younger generation to feel particularly concerned to show that, for example, Hawks and Preminger are each valuable for their qualities of personal vision and style. But I should like here to question the centrality of this issue, and to reassert an attitude more like that of *La Revue du Cinéma*.

The *Concise O.E.D.* gives us another definition of the word 'style'. It signifies also the 'collective characteristics of the writing or direc-

The subsequent course of *Sight and Sound* was erratic. There were a few ventures into criticism in which philosophical terms were used freely, and sometimes incoherently, in an effort to sound as profound as Bazin was thought to be. The tone (exemplified by Rhode's feeling that Visconti must be mentally sick to be interested in the proletariat) lacked Bazin's generosity, and continued what was worst in the old, hostile complacency. At the same time, Pauline Kael was 'imported' from America to 'debunk' various sorts of intellectualizing about movies (one of her articles is cited later).

These destructive rearguard actions were followed by a general elevation of Hawks, Ray, Mann, Losey and others to the realms of critical goodwill, an elevation not extended to those *auteurs* who hadn't been forcefully pushed into the limelight by the younger generation. The influence of younger or French critics was never acknowledged.

There was a notable change in the attitude to 'pulp' movies. This the magazine's pseudonymous columnist, Arkadin (reputedly John Russell Taylor) asked, 'Why don't we take horror films more seriously—well, not seriously seriously,' as if unaware that the rest of the world had been taking them seriously for some years. Since then the floodgates have opened and for the last two years the magazine has been dabbling in an ostentatiously hedonistic acceptance of, for example, Don Sharp's *The Face of Fu Manchu*. One of the excellences which T.M. advances as evidence of this being 'a *really good film*' (my italics) is that 'when a sinister hand coils round the edge of her door, Karin Dor doesn't just scream, she very commendably slams the door on it'. John Russell Taylor is also staggered by such creativity: 'when the young heroine is threatened by a sinister oriental hand sliding round her living-room door with a missive, she wastes no time in helpless wails, but smartly slams the door on it. . . .'

It's hard to believe that people of these critics' culture and intelligence could really have been so impressed by such 'innovations' (which aren't), if they weren't forcing themselves to 'be jolly'. Yet the whole point of appreciating a good film which happens to be couched in the idiom of a pulp thriller is that you don't lower your normal standards an inch, you're no more indulgent to Bond than you would have been to Liberace or Rin-Tin-Tin. The partial *volte-face* from critical 'superiority' to uncritical acquiescence is more than an example of the general aesthetic upsets generated by the current confluence of 'high culture' and popular art. The nervous strivings to keep up with 'festival opinion' on one hand and high camp on the other are the vacillations of a stiffly classbound 'liberalism' in a cosmopolitan world.

tion or artistic expression or way of presenting things or decorative methods proper to a person or school or period or subject; manner exhibiting these characteristics'. In other words, a director's vision or style may be of great interest and sincerity even when it is shared by a great many directors—just as in architecture one speaks of collective styles—Norman, Early English, decorated perpendicular, Tudor, Queen Anne, and so forth. Similarly, in literature there are 'groups' of artists (just as there are groups of critics!) who have many opinions and mannerisms in common—the 'Metaphysicals', the 'neo-classicists', and so on. These writers can both be contrasted for their differences and compared for their similarities, the latter being no less significant than the former. For the purpose of art is not exclusively or even particularly to express the unique individual, but also to express feelings, attitudes and values of any kind, whether individual or communal. Indeed, the unique individual is often prized as an artist because he crystallizes, with unique strength and clarity, many of the tensions in a 'communal' climate. A film may be of considerable cultural significance even if it is quite anonymous—just as medieval religious paintings, stained-glass windows, certain poems (Beowulf) or buildings (the Taj Mahal) reveal little or nothing about any individual *auteur*. Most folk art is, by definition, anonymous, but none the less poignant and significant. A cathedral may be altered down the centuries, by one generation after another (certainly with no one mind in control!) but still be of artistic importance. In fact the very notions of 'culture' and of the 'spirit of an age' are arrived at by taking as significant those elements which artists have in common. *Kiss Me Deadly* isn't important because it tells us anything about an individual called Robert Aldrich. Aldrich is important because *Kiss Me Deadly* reveals something about America, and about us all.

The fact that a director has an 'individual' style doesn't of itself make his films interesting (except for those connoisseurs who collect odd styles like some people collect quaintly-shaped inkpots). To take literary parallels, Enid Blyton, Marie Corelli, Dean Farrer and Amanda McKittrick Ross all have 'individual' visions and styles, and are undoubtedly *auteurs*, but this doesn't make them great creative artists, or even readable, except for the relaxing giggle.

It is not denigrating the importance of personal idioms, nor of individualism as such, to say that there is also merit and significance in the 'collective' aspects of Hollywood style. It is fast, bold, terse, flexible and clear. Its sharp cuts and bold reverse angles express a philosophy of life as fact confronting fact, face confronting face, in a series of collisions and challenges, a philosophy of dynamic action-reaction, viewing life as a sequence of decisions tending to some purpose. It has the limitations, but it has also the meanings and merits, of any 'classicism'.

Another peculiarity of the *auteur* approach is that, in practice, if not in theory, all the *auteurs* seem to be directors, and little interest is taken in the many important creative personalities who are producers. One thinks of Mark Hellinger, and of David O. Selznick, who virtually directed some of his films 'through' his director, reputedly bombarding him with fifty-page telegrams telling him exactly how a given scene ought to be played. Selznick is an *auteur*, in that *Portrait of Jennie* is 1 per cent Dieterle and 99 per cent Selznick. Other *auteur* producers include John Houseman, Stanley Kramer and Hal Wallis. Several screenwriters are *auteurs*—Philip Yordan in Hollywood, Bryan Forbes in Britain, Carl Mayer in Germany, Jacques Prévert in France. As Renoir remarked, '. . . anyone that says that *Les Enfants du Paradis* is Carné's film is crazy. It's Jacques Prévert's. Prévert was the dominant personality. Not that Carné is not a good director—but I think he was born to be a good director of great writers.' Renoir continues, 'Sometimes it can even be the actor who dominates—take the Mary Pickford films, for example.' The mere fact that the public follows stars proves that a star is an *auteur*. So are 'undirectable' actors like George Arliss and Charles Laughton, certain personalities (Louise Brooks, Robert Mitchum), and, particularly, comedians like Jerry Lewis and Laurel and Hardy.

It isn't unknown for excellent parts of an *auteurs* film to be directed by someone else. Thus the chariot race of Wyler's *Ben Hur* and the land race of Anthony Mann's *Cimarron* were both handled by Andrew Marton, the exteriors of Corman's *The Terror* by Monte Hellman. *Gone With the Wind* has a consistent visual style through all its changes of director because it was master-minded by Selznick and storyboarded by William Cameron Menzies. Nominally an art director, Menzies created the visuals of many British and American films. His own directorial efforts suffer from a poor story sense and slightly stilted acting, but he is certainly an *auteur*, and many directors have enjoyed the praise for effects which were actually Menzies'.

Many films bear the marks of several *auteurs*. *Le Crime de Monsieur Lange* is 100 per cent Prévert, and 100 per cent Renoir—total

200 per cent. *Duel in the Sun* is 80 per cent Selznick and 80 per cent Vidor—total 160 per cent. But a good film is always a subtle balance of creative energies and ascendancies, especially in Hollywood where until recently the *auteur* was at bay against the production line system imposed by such studio chiefs as Louis B. Mayer and Harry Cohn (who, though the 'villains of the piece', also, occasionally, had first-rate ideas).

Some brilliant films have been made by directors who, for one reason or another, have not emerged as consistent *auteurs*. One thinks of, for example, Joseph H. Lewis's *Gun Crazy*, E. E. Reinert's *Quai de Grenelle*, or Norman Panama and Melvin Frank's *L'il Abner*. And who is the *auteur* of such weird and brilliant one-shots as *The 5,000 Fingers of Dr. T* (director, Roy Rowland), *Gilda* (director, Charles Vidor), *This Island Earth* (director, Joseph M. Newman)? In these cases the fullest list of credits offers little clue. As Renoir said, 'A good film is a miracle . . .' that is, a series of happy accidents.

Inevitably, a mediocre or bad film by a 'great' director will be of more interest to connoisseurs than a mediocre or even a good film by a mediocre director. Renoir's *Le Déjeuner sur L'Herbe* might have been the work of two men, containing as it does one beautiful sequence (the disturbed picnic) in a context whose dithering results (one hopes) from a wrong theory pushed to the limit. Any artist's inspiration results from a conflict, that is, a precarious balance, of attitudes and emotions, and there's nothing illogical in, for example, my own feeling that King Vidor's *North-West Passage* and *H. M. Pulham Esq.* are as nauseating as such films as *Hallelujah* and *Ruby Gentry* are inspiring. However moved we may be by the archaic charm and careful thought in the veteran Allan Dwan's *The Enchanted Island* it's no use pretending that *The Most Dangerous Man Alive*, by the same producer and director (Benedict Bogeaus—Allan Dwan) is anything but a stinkeroo. Conversely, Benedek's subsequent decline casts no reflection on his achievement in *The Wild One*. Often, film *auteurs*, like novelists and poets, die before their death—like Tay Garnett, Stanley Donen, Edward Dmytryk, Robert Siodmak.

A special form of *auteur* is the *anti-auteur*—the man who delights in adopting different themes and styles for each of his films—for example, Fred Zinnemann in America, René Clément in France and Alberto Lattuada in Italy. Ford has had two distinct styles—his 'open-air' style (*Stagecoach*) and his 'expressionistic' style (*The In-*

former), (it's a pity, maybe, that even in *The Long Voyage Home* he doesn't explore the region where these two tones and views of life meet and conflict). Many directors, cameramen and writers are, deliberately and cultivatedly, 'chameleons'—specialists in 'adjusting' their style to that of their directors or actors—giving the paradox that substantial contributions to a film's content and quality are made by artists who express another person's character rather than their own —a process which may be just as creative as a dramatist's expression of characters and views *not his own*, i.e., of the zeitgeist . . . *Ars est celare artem*; not all inglorious Miltons were mute.

Another kind of creative personality may come to dominate the cinema's history, not simply because of his own films, but because of his creative fertility—the German scenarist Carl Mayer, the Italian writer Cesare Zavattini, were both one-man mass movements, in that their scripts are often the salt that savours, and saves, the loaf. Creative too, to some extent, was Gregg Toland—whose deep-focus expressionism was used extensively in Ford's *The Long Voyage Home* (1940) *before* Welles took it up for *Citizen Kane* (1941). Not that Welles doesn't deserve credit; he does; but so does Toland; and Welles without Toland and Herman J. Mankiewicz (his writer) has never quite reached the same heights. Were these collaborators quite so 'passive' as we sometimes imply when we write, 'Welles. . . .'?

Although many of Hollywood's directors are *auteurs* it is quite possible to speak of an overall Hollywood 'style'—in that, whether the narrative is fast (La Cava's *Stage Door*, is surely a contender for some sort of world record) or slow (Henry King's *Snows of Kilimanjaro*), there is a certain tautness, a spareness of intention, a lack of distraction from the principal story points. There are none of the asides one finds in, say, Renoir or Becker, and which European directors generally are more inclined to entertain. Hollywood would never have invented such 'European' ideas as the *temps-mort*, or the stylistic potpourri of Truffaut. American films seem to be enclosed by their subjects, and the dramatic tensions are calculated with a Protestant rigour. European directors often deliberately relax the story so as to dwell on the sprawl and irrelevance of 'off-moments' (which after all constitute 80 per cent of life).

A notable limitation is the Hollywood tradition that it's cissy to pan where a cut would do—the latter being faster, smoother, tauter. The preference for camera-movements over cuts is primarily a European tradition (Murnau, Renoir, Ophuls) which Hitchcock's *Rope* reduced to a pedestrian *exercice de style*. In general it seems true to say that Hollywood directors show less variety of theme and approach than European ones, basically because Europe is culturally more diversified than America, dedicated as the latter is to the moulding of immigrants into one cultural pattern. None the less, a few directors, for example, Hitchcock (sometimes), King Vidor or Samuel Fuller (if only by his customary ferocity), show a 'European' extent of individuality, whereas, say, Hawks and Preminger don't.

Of course, one can group individualists, in America as in Europe, into 'schools'. After Preston Sturges 'died', his vein of sick humour was asserted by Billy Wilder, from whose failing grasp the torch was snatched up by Stanley Kubrick. In fact one can group and re-group Hollywood directors in all sorts of ways, depending on which points of style one finds interesting. There are 'soft' directors (Frank Borzage, Allan Dwan) and 'bleak' directors (Hawks, Jack Arnold, Boetticher), 'muscular' directors (King Vidor, Fuller, Richard Fleischer, Anthony Mann) and 'tight-lipped' directors (Lang, Mann, Hawks). There are 'women's directors' (Cukor, Minnelli), 'theatrical' directors (Cukor, Wyler), 'actors'' directors (Cukor, La Cava), 'novelist' directors (Mankiewicz, Brooks). There are 'TV' directors, whose visuals are often ragged (like Delbert Mann's, and Frankenheimer's, except when he carboncopies Hitchcock) but who have a powerful acting sense. There are 'plush' directors (George Sidney, Douglas Sirk, Quine, Edwards). There are the 'tearaways' (Don Siegel, Phil Karlson). There are directors whose *forte* is what we have called *mise-en-scène*—Nicholas Ray, Boetticher, Minnelli, Jack Webb. Douglas Sirk approaches a plush weepie like *Imitation of Life* with a dry calculation-in-excess, resulting in a sense of lonely alienation which to the style-sensitive eye is not unlike Antonioni's: the apparent dedication of a whole town to a coloured mammy's funeral isn't unlike the interplay of crowds and emptiness in *L'Avventura* (1959). This doesn't, to my mind, justify calling Sirk brilliant, or even lucid, though it justifies not ignoring him; but what is interesting to notice is that the commercial cinema, by curious processes of its own, is often ahead of 'art' films. There are essentially 'middle-class' directors (Wyler, Zinnemann, but with a pessimistic undertone). There are 'fake liberals' (George Stevens), 'flabby liberals' (Wyler) and the younger, tougher more courageous men (Wise, Brooks, Daves in his Westerns). There are even more bitter, virulent men (Aldrich, Losey). There are 'right-wing' directors (Leo McCarey,

John Wayne, Ray Milland). There are deeply ambivalent figures like Ford, Fuller and King `Vidor. There are the 'intellectuals'—John Huston (who, perhaps the most interesting moralist in the American cinema, joins Losey and Bunuel in the trio of screen moralists), Arthur Penn, Elia Kazan.

But none of these directors can be contained within such a classification. Cukor's *Heller in Pink Tights* reveals his affinities with Vincente Minnelli. Wyler's *Ben Hur* resembles Fleischer's *Barabbas* in its use of symbolism, its 'staging', its sense of physique. Raoul Walsh, lyricist *par excellence* of male exuberance, endows parts of *The Lawless Breed* with a soft, feminine delicacy (or is this the contribution of an art director?). One can almost describe Frank Borzage's *Moonrise* (1948), with Charles Laughton's *Night of the Hunter* (1956) and Allan Dwan's *The Enchanted Island* (1958) as Hollywood's tattered rearguard of Griffith-spirited films. Yet, with *Wild River* (1960) Kazan returns to a romantic lyricism not far in spirit from Borzage and Dwan.

Curious affinities link otherwise completely different films and directors. The use of depth and space by Budd Boetticher (a genuine *auteur*) in *Ride Lonesome* (1959) is very reminiscent of Roman Polanski's in *The Knife in the Water* (1962) (which could easily be transposed into terms of a Boetticher Western). G. Tchouhrai's *The 41st* (1956) is Russia's answer to *Duel in the Sun* (and vastly inferior), in climax (shotguns), style and love-hate theme. Kazan is the most 'European' of American directors—his *On the Waterfront* is the stylistic inspiration for Visconti's *Rocco and His Brothers* (1960), while the immigrant story of *The Anatolian Smile* (1963) is Kazan following, in turn, the immigrant story of Visconti.

The paradox is not that the various groups of *auteur* theorists accept the films that they do but that they reject so many films which would seem to be on their wavelength. Subtle, searching and courageous films like Ray's *Rebel Without a Cause*, Fuller's *Run of the Arrow*, Vidor's *Ruby Gentry*, Lang's *The Big Heat*, Aldrich's *Attack* or Kramer's *On the Beach*, arouse the ire, contempt or, at best, indifference of the older critics, who however lavish praise on the canny escapism of John Ford's potboilers. Conversely the younger theorists, priding themselves on their sense of style, all but pass by George Sidney's *Pal Joey* or his very beautiful *Jeanne Eagels*, or even of Corman's horror rhapsodies, while applauding every time such limited stylists as Hawks and Preminger manage to move the camera from

A to B.[1] Hitchcock and Preminger, two of the Hollywood directors whom they most admire as moralists, are, to my mind, sophisticated entertainers who carefully tailor their message so as not to offend their audience; while the films of Howard Hawks, charming as they are, rarely venture outside a range of agreeable cliché which almost any other American director can handle, and at some time or other has.

Yet one can understand why Hawks' films mean so much to French intellectuals. His very simplicity can have a tonic, and a real value, as a corrective to various debilitating concomitants of European culture ('confusionism', snobbery, contempt for decision, action, efficacy, simplicity). But it is as well to remember that Hawks moves on some of the easier and simpler wavelengths of his (mass) audience's responses. Even his 'deadpan', 'tough' way with emotion, though not altogether untrue to some aspects of the American attitude to emotion, is, at its best very near a favourite American cliché, and, at its worst, corn-and-ham on wry. If Hemingway's style is tainted by the same facility, it has an overtone of pain, of waste, which Hawks, more sentimentally ignores.

Hawks' films have shown a remarkable consistency (which is also a tedious monotony) throughout his long career, with the paradoxical result that though his films are full of American cliché they are also identifiable as the work of an *auteur*. He has all the insidious convenience of typicality; his individuality is in his flawless typicality. In his perfection, there is, undoubtedly, an authentic sophistication—if that implies that he has made decisions about the importance of human moods and meanings. Yet, if sophistication means humanity, variety and subtlety, then his films are generally simpler and more facile than their nearest comparisons. Thus his *Scarface* is simpler than Wellman's *Public Enemy*, his *A Girl in Every Port* is a sardonic counterpoint to Tay Garnett's *Her Man*, his 'satires' are innocuous compared to Wellman's *A Star is Born*, his *Gentlemen Prefer Blondes* is eclipsed by Wilder's *Some Like it Hot*. But if 'sophistication' means a sardonic attitude to humanity, a deadpan humour which, under the pretext of toughly controlling emotion, also all but denies it, then the very limitations of his films enable these tensions to emerge more sharply.

For much the same reason, his early films have 'aged' very well—

[1] Perhaps this is unfair, in that they are stressing the simplicity, economy and sobriety of Hawks's style.

or, more accurately, perhaps, they suit current taste. Wellman's *Public Enemy*, with its serious appeal to primitive sociology, with its complex counterpointing of sympathy and contempt towards its central figure, now 'creaks', in the context of our changed ideas and assumptions, whereas *Scarface*, with its complete lack of interest in anything except revealing that Scarface is not only a rat but a coward too, who cannot but destroy all his friends and then himself, is extremely naïve, but has a near-classical simplicity, of 'thrust', form and thought. Garnett's *Her Man* is now conspicuously vitiated by the sentimentality of Helen Twelvetrees, a latterday Dorothy Gish awkwardly 'framed' in a saloon: the point of Hawks' counterpart is the real cynicism of the equivalent character (Louise Brooks). The toughly cynical stoicism which Hawks adopted very early in his career avoids all dramatic exaggerations, and so suits, not only the modern 'deadpan' rhetoric, but our aptitude for debunking and de-sentimentalizing.

My own reaction is to find the other films *more* interesting than Hawks', just *because* they have dated, and so say, to me, something new; whereas Hawks' merely say, with a special deftness, what innumerable American films are interminably, and boringly, saying.

Even so, his films authentically express the streak of stoicism in the American character. The ruthless thrust of the categorical imperatives of the Calvinist conscience has been transposed into another set of values. It has been cut away from any belief in God, or even of reward, which is a bait, an inspiration, rather than an end. Hawks' 'buddies' are loyal, with a conscious purposelessness, in defeat and death. 'Fun' morality is accepted, but, more often than not, with a certain misogyny and masochism, as from a puritan residue, and from the feeling that pleasure is more of a threat to one's stoicism than pain. The overriding purpose is, in the end, the achievement of one's manliness, usually (and sentimentally) squared with a dour, cagey, wry moralism, in which puritan extremism ties with a sullen scepticism. These assertions enable Hawks' films to check their nihilistic trend, and to endow life with some sort of moral meaning. His tightlipped stoicism—nihilism—isn't altogether unevocative of an existentialist mood—even though the 'solidarity' is matched by a brutal competitiveness. Otherwise, Hawks' summary way with any philosophical issue is as far from existentialism as the Marine sergeant's taunting, 'Do you want to live for ever?' For much of its length, *The Big Sleep* admirably catches the Chandler mood. But the sadder implications of that mood are lost in a sort of spirited non-chalance, and one may, in the end, prefer Dmytryk's less perfect, but warmer and sadder, *Farewell, My Lovely*. Huston's *Treasure of Sierra Madre* and *The Misfits* are 'tragic critiques' of the Hawksian ideal, respecting it, fairly, but going beyond their tough conformism to a profounder humanism. Perhaps Hawks' best films are those in which, without losing the shock of his terseness, he goes some way beyond it; in *Sergeant York* (co-written with John Huston) and *The Big Sky*; while *The Big Sleep* and *Red River* have the virtues of a *petit-maître*.

Preminger is another minor figure with a, to my mind, inflated reputation in *auteur* circles. He is at his best in the 'modest' films made between 1944 and 1956 when he had emerged as a producer, but was still 'trapped' within the system—*Laura*, *Fallen Angel*, *Angel Face*, *The Man With the Golden Arm* and *Anatomy of a Murder*. All these films have a real feeling for the enigmatic quality (and the cynical undertow) in human relationships, and an authentic atmosphere of sordid anguish. But the ambiguity *in* these small-scale subjects gets into the treatment *of* the latter, bigger themes, which consequently become as boring as they are non-committal, Preminger carefully implying a cynicism which he equally carefully never crystallizes. If he makes *Saint Joan* there's Shaw's play for the respectful agnostics, Greene's screenplay for the Catholics, Jean Seberg as an identification-figure for the teenagers of the Middle West, Richard Widmark for the 'industrial halls', and Anton Walbrook and John Gielgud for the 'carriage trade'. This sort of calculation is common enough, in films, but Preminger's too often shows. His *Exodus* does for Israel what George Stevens' *Giant* does for Texas (nothing, in Cinemascope), while on the most controversial issues of all *Advise and Consent* and *The Cardinal* contrive to see all sides of the question, so disturbing everybody a little and nobody much; a mountain-size framework produces a mouse-size thought, and I don't have much hesitation in preferring to *Advise and Consent* Franklin Schaffner's *The Best Man*, to *The Cardinal* Richard Brooks' *Elmer Gantry*, to *Anatomy of a Murder* Wilder's *Double Indemnity*, and to *The Man With the Golden Arm* Wyler's underestimated *Carrie*. Preminger's best films are part of the 40's wave of 'tightlipped misogyny', notably, Vidor's *Gilda*, Hughes' *The Outlaw*, Stahl's *Leave Her to Heaven* and Welles' *The Lady from Shanghai*. Even his masterpiece, *Laura*, is one of a deluge of 40's films about portraits and missing women (such as

Hitchcock's *Rebecca*, Robert Siodmak's *Phantom Lady*, Albert Lewin's *Pandora and the Flying Dutchman*, William Seiter's *One Touch of Venus* and William Dieterle's *Portrait of Jennie*, the last a favourite of Luis Bunuel's). That most of Preminger's films show the mark of a definite artistic personality is beyond question; nor are his less satisfactory films devoid of interest. But I wouldn't see him as other than a minor Hollywood figure.

Given the Hollywood system, it's evident that few directors' names can be a guarantee of quality. For example, Lang's *The Big Heat* is a key film, in its atmosphere of bitterness and corruption; the attempt to repeat its success in *Human Desire* results in a limp, dull film, while *The Blue Gardenia* has none of the merits, and few of the mannerisms, of a Lang film. Similarly, Ray's *Party Girl* is as inept in its thought and feeble in its dramatic punch as his *Rebel Without a Cause* and *The Savage Innocents* are complex and moving. Donen's musicals are classics or near, with or without Gene Kelly as his collaborator, yet his later comedies are insipid. It may be just coincidence, but all Hitchcock's films for Paramount and Universal are at least interesting, while all his films for Selznick and (bar *Strangers on a Train*) Warner's, are below par. Indeed, Hitchcock's case is interesting. There has been a certain amount of controversy as to whether (as the '30's school' and the *Sight and Sound* team maintain) his early British films are by and large superior to his post-war Hollywood films (which are championed by *Cahiers*, *Movie* and Robin Wood, in his extremely interesting study). But the question seems to me awkwardly posed. There are certainly general differences between the periods (as well as underlying similarities), and, within each period, some films are richer than others. And my own inclination would be to ask which are the best films of each period (and which have merits which are typical of neither one period nor the other)? *Sabotage* (1936), *Strangers on a Train* (1951) and *Psycho* (1961) seem to me to enable the receptive spectator to live more fully through more challenging experiences than say *Secret Agent* (1936), *Notorious* (1946) or *Marnie* (1964).

And I don't see any reason to make of Hitchcock a 'consistent' *auteur* who never falls below his own best. It is possible to point to certain limitations which even his best films don't altogether transcend. It is arguable that, *Psycho* apart, Hitchcock has never unleashed the full weight of his irony, misanthropy and moral disquiet, and that he has too often too carefully tailored them, restricting himself to 'intimations' of what he thinks the public will enjoy without resentment. (Indeed he makes a point of it: so-called *Stories They Wouldn't Let Me Do on TV* appear in paperback anthology.) And yet, Hitchcock does say *some* things, not only *despite* the system, but *by means of* the system. When all the sad truths about Hollywood have been allowed, it is doubtful whether it cramps its best directors' style as much as the Victorian climate of opinion constrained our Victorian novelists. Indeed, if we allow the least literary status to, say, Robert Louis Stevenson, it becomes very perverse indeed to rule out even the 'middling' films of Hitchcock, Hawks, Ray and so on.

Quite apart from any question of exterior constraint, the greatest novelists may vary a good deal in quality, for purely personal reasons. In any case, even when an artist is exceptionally consistent, one may wish to acquaint oneself with only those works of his which have a marginal superiority over the others. Few readers would want to read every play by Samuel Beckett, for example, not because they're not good but because each is a corollary of the other.

Every spectator will of course have a greater temperamental affinity with some *auteurs* than with others; and to a great extent the broadening and mellowing quality of art comes from adapting oneself, so as to take on the sensibility of those *auteurs* who are least congenial to one's own responses. Further, the minor films of a major artist will naturally attract more intensity, more awareness of response, from their context, than the best films of minor artists, even when these, in a one-for-one comparison, are more interesting or true than a great man's failures.

Yet perhaps the best way of 'valuing' Hollywood—or any category of films—is not by selecting certain *auteurs* as 'in' and others as 'out', but by picking out the best films of (for example) Aldrich, Arnold, Boetticher, Brooks, Cassavetes, Daves, De Mille, Donen, Dwan, Ford, Fuller, Hawks, Hitchcock, Huston, Kazan, Kubrick, Mankiewicz, Mann A., Mann Daniel, Mann Delbert, Minnelli, Ray, Sidney, Sirk, Tashlin, Wilder, Wise, Wyler, Zinnemann *et al*. Thus one's canon of 'great', or 'key', or 'interesting', or 'useful' films has vastly greater variety, and one is also saved from having to see the dreary, pusillanimous, or repetitive films which all these directors have perpetrated from time to time. In just the same way, novelists can fall below their own best standards, without literary critics feeling obliged, either to rally to their defence, or to write about them with contempt.

5 · Caligari is Dead—Long Live Caligari

'Expressionism' is as undefinable a category as 'realism', which it resembles in being not only a classification for certain works of art but also an urge which underlies all art but becomes particularly obtrusive at certain times and places. Our concern here is not with tracing the history and development of screen expressionism, but, first, to replace some of its stylistic traits in their context, so as to further our understanding of style in the cinema, and second, to suggest the relevance, to the present, of a critically still unfashionable mode.

In their *Dictionary of Art and Artists* Peter and Linda Murray describe expressionism in painting as, 'The search for expressiveness in style by means of exaggerations and distortions of line and colour; a deliberate abandonment of the naturalism implicit in Impressionism in favour of a simplified style which should carry far greater emotional impact. In this general sense of emotional force Expressionism is a feature of non-Mediterranean art in general, Grünewald being the standard example. . . . In the more limited context of modern art, the Expressionist movement may be said to spring from Van Gogh's use of drastically simplified outline and very strong colour . . . the principal exponents . . . were mostly German (or at least 'Nordic', like the Norwegian Munch). . . .'

From this angle, a characteristic of Expressionism is that the feelings portrayed invade, swallow up the 'otherness' of the outside world. English romanticism knows this impulse, and uses it, without actually abandoning itself to it, restricting itself to what is, for all the rhapsodic use of the 'pathetic fallacy', a conscious search for the soul of man, for *his* harmony with the world, rather than for any 'Music of the spheres' in itself. Wordsworth and Shelley consciously make of every realistic object and element a sounding board for their own personal feelings. But German romanticism went further into transcendentalism; the artist feels that he is expressing the 'inner soul' of Nature, of the outside world. Cooler, more sceptical souls will value such art for its picture, not of the outside world, but of introverted sensibility, so 'reducing' it to a more 'English' romanticism.

From 1830 on, English romanticism gradually ebbed, vitiated partly by the English blend of puritanism, compromise, snobbery and general anti-emotionality, and partly as the more extroverted problems of social realism became increasingly obtrusive on the literary scene. But German expressionism, whether consciously subjective or avowedly transcendental, struggled to portray complex social problems as if they were metaphysical issues or 'extroverted spiritual states' through which the artist-spectator-hero must make his 'way of the Cross'. Sometimes, as with the playwright Ernest Toller, the realistic awareness prevailed over the 'Messianic' spirituality; other playwrights, more conscious of spiritual angst than of social problems, remained mystics; a few found it easier to come to terms with Nazism than with the democratic rationalism underlying social realism.

Sometimes the expressionist artist portrays 'real' objects, which are lyrically 'convulsed' by formal style—as the sun and sky in Van Gogh are dissolved by the slap and slice of brushstrokes. Sometimes he concentrates on the emotive effects of abstract forms (though arguably all abstract art is either abstract expressionism, in that the gestalt of forms suggest tensions and therefore feelings and often ideas, or it is nothing. From this point of view, tonalities of sturm and drang are simply more easily recognizable as 'abstract expressionism' than, say, the paintings of Piet Mondrian). Sometimes the Expressionist uses passionately heavy symbols, blurring the idiomatic and spiritual frontier between expressionism and Surrealism.[1] Of course many artists use several methods, at different times or all together.

[1] The rigorous anti-anthropomorphism of Robbe-Grillet is thus at the opposite end of the literary spectrum to expressionism, which has however this advantage over the more sceptical literary genre currently fashionable: an artist who endeavours to tell us everything about everything is more likely to say something interesting than an artist who aspires to tell us almost nothing about almost nothing. That said, the *nouveau roman* has a certain lyrical charm, in carefully chosen extract, and by its very pedantry creates a mood of nihilistic solipsism which is not unexpressionistic itself.

The parallels with cinema expressionism immediately present themselves. It is notably a German movement. There is a similar heaviness, symbolism, and sense of *haunting* about such Nordics as Sjostrom and Bergman. (We might also speak of a Slav expressionism, ranging from the Czech Gustav Machaty's *Ecstasy* to *Ashes and Diamonds* by the Polish Andrzej Wajda, *The Crime of Dmitri Karamazov* by the Russian Fedor Ozep, and even Eisenstein.) The starved, haggard, nightmarish quality of so many German films of the 20's is prefigured by Munch's *Abend Auf Dem Corso Karl Johan* (1892). The turning away from naturalism is paralleled in the German preference for huge studio sets and elaborate technical effects rather than location photography. There is a similar 'simplification of outline'. In such films as Paul Leni's *Waxworks*, Murnau's *The Last Laugh* and Joe May's *Ashphalte* the storyline is very simple (so simple that the films can move very slowly). The relationships of the characters are all reduced to broad, primal attitudes and urges. The acting concentrates, not on the ebb and flow of people's behaviour, but on broad, forceful postures and gestures. Thus the film is reduced to a series of *basic* moments each of which is then emphasized and 'accordeoned out'—giving the characteristic 'heaviness' of German silent films. But this 'exaggeration' is meant to express the basic, the key, attitudes and emotions, in all their vehemence and purity.

Even the décor is subordinated to the lyrical surge. Leni's *Waxworks* is a fascinating example. A fairground showman asks a poet to write three stories round his collection of wax figures, notably Haroun el Raschid, Ivan the Terrible and Jack the Ripper. The episode of Haroun and the baker's wife is an orchestration of soft, doughy, round shapes—turbans, bellies, ovens, rings, minarets, chessmen, spiral staircases which coil like intestines. The Ivan episode is stiff with sharp, dark, iconic shapes—Ivan's angular form and jutting beard, an arrow slanting from a stiffly slumping back, bars across windows, low, heavy roofbeams. The Jack the Ripper episode is a slow drift through the mysterious land of photographic superimpositions. Not only are the *forms* of the décors different, so is the *texture*. Those in the Haroun episode are soggy and flabby, like the Caliph himself; the Ivan the Terrible sequence is in the key of carved wood. Jack the Ripper is a world of dim, celluloidy transparencies.

There is more expressionism in realism than we usually realize. When Carol Reed tilts his camera in *The Third Man* he is superimposing 'expressionism' on a realistic setting. Background music, most acting, is expressionist, in the sense that it endeavours to 'express' emotions. In this sense, the difference between 'expressionism' and 'realism' is simply the degree of 'poetic licence' which the former allows itself in its handling of the visual appearance of things. If Robbe-Grillet's 'new' novels seem extreme it is because they attempt (unsuccessfully) to purge realism of any expressionist element. Where there's emotion in art, there is expressionism, of a sort. The beautiful smokescapes of Flaherty's documentary *Industrial Britain* are as subjective and visionary as the sheerest expressionism, though idealistic rather than tormented. But we can usefully contrast *realism* and *expressionism*, or speak of a battle between magic (Méliès) and daylight (Lumière), studios (Méliès) and location (Lumière)—so long as we remember that each style derives its meaning only from the implicit presence of the other.

Between them, Siegfried Kracauer, in *From Caligari to Hitler*, and less moralistically, Lotte H. Eisner in *L'Ecran Démoniaque*, have studied the social implications, the aesthetic origins, of expressionism in German silent films. Our purpose here is rather different: to see expressionism as a particular kind of 'style', as well as an often ignored, but ubiquitous, tradition, a constant, if unnoticed, diastole to the systole of realism.

We should perhaps make some sort of rough distinction between 'expressionism' proper and mere elaborateness of visual organization. Dreyer's *La Passion de Jeanne d'Arc* is visually very expressive, but Dreyer does not *distort* reality. We feel an emotional weight and angst which may remind us of expressionism, but it is created by very careful selection of reality, rather than by overriding it. In *Caligari* on the other hand an emotional shudder runs through everything—the streets, the doors, the windows, stagger and totter, just as if 'the time is out of joint'. Paths and fields are broken up into spikes and shards, roofs become mere huddle of splinters, while the asylum has an oppressive, massive solidity and order. However, *Caligari*, like *Waxworks*, asserts an extreme of expressionism—and exactly when the use of light, shadow, and objects becomes 'expressionist' rather than 'realistic' is impossible to define. In the end it's a matter of the spirit. An 'expressionistic' film has a more dreamlike feeling, a sense of blurring and vagueness, of heavy but undefined emotion, which *looms* oppressively without being analysed or explained.

By 1925 'pure' expressionism is virtually ended: from then on the films of Lang, Murnau and Pabst use the full range of expressionistic devices, and retain something of the expressionistic mood, but reconcile them with a more or less realistic framework and surface.

Thus Murnau's *The Last Laugh* relates to social circumstances of the time as concretely as *Bicycle Thieves*—with a lost uniform instead of a stolen bicycle. However, the film's visuals owe everything to expressionistic emphases. These are not a matter merely of 'heaviness', but of sensuousness. The porter's shiny tower of a uniform contrasts with the drab, deathly whiteness of lavatory linen stacked in a cupboard. The light has a grey, dusty, dispirited quality. Like Lang, Murnau loves to show characters puffing at fat cigars, and then showing the smoke drift and swirl up into the lamplight, glinting, diffusing and darkening, creating an ominous atmosphere. The sprightly, glossy twirl of the hotel's revolving doors is matched with the scurrying past of dark pedestrians and cars on the murky street beyond, and echoed later in the heavy, fateful closure of another pair of doors, down in the lavatory catacombs.

Equally *physical* is Jannings' acting. Expressionistic theory (as highly developed as 'Method'ism) required its actors to aim above all at simplification—catching the *one* important stance or gesture— and then intensifying it. It's not intended to show 'how people react in reality', but to evoke the full emotional surge, as it is 'at heart'. It's not so much to be 'looked at' with the eye, coldly, as 'felt with', by empathy, in one's body—the sense of strain, alertness, abandon in the posture transmit the subtleties in the emotion. (Plate 22.) Looked at as 'realism', it's easy to find Jannings' performances ludicrous— one eye narrowed to a slit, the other glaring like a soup-plate—just as it's easy to find 'rhapsodic' poets like Keats and Shelley ridiculous if one reads them without sympathy. But it has its own authentic, pantomimic power. Jannings allowed himself to stray as far from 'realism' as comedians do—one can speak of 'slow' expressionism, like Jannings's, and 'fast' expressionism, like Chaplin's (or Jerry Lewis's). The middle term between them is exemplified by Catherine Hessling in Jean Renoir's *Nana* (1926), where she gives what is both the best and the worst performance in the history of the French cinema. With her petal-light limbs flung out into Napoleonic postures, her bee-sting mouth pouting in her heart-shaped face, her eyes narrowed till the pupils disappear under a palisade of lashes, her fluttering precocity and jagged stances, this awkward blend of Chaplinesque quicksilver and marionette fixity comes, if only the spectator will adapt his response, to make at least as much sense as modern 'Method'ism.

Similarly, the expressionistic fondness for 'symbol' owed nothing to a code of dry meanings, everything to what René Huyghe, speaking of the painter Rouault, calls 'the emotional reverberation of sensation'. Just as the acting is based on *physicality*, a sense of *the body as pure emotion*, so the symbol acquires its meaning from sensuality. In Paul Wegener's second version of *The Golem* curving ceilings with their coracle-like domes make one's spine hunch up, the huge, claw-shaped hinges on sinister doors are like cruel fingers—it is through this physicality that the symbols have meaning.

In modern American films, on the other hand, objects pick up their symbolism by their role in the story—thus both *Rebel Without a Cause* and *On the Waterfront* have 'jacket' motifs—Dean 'inherits' Sal Mineo's, after his suicide, Brando that of Eva-Marie Saint's brother, for whose murder he is partly responsible. Ingmar Bergman's films mix both techniques; as Peter Harcourt has pointed out, the opening sequence of *Sawdust and Tinsel* with its emphases on cannons, clothes and the sun, endows inanimate objects with an enigmatic significance and a tempestuous energy.

Many of the German silent directors had in fact a visual rather than a literary background. Lang trained as an architect, Murnau was an art historian, Leni a painter. The soul of the films is always *in* the surface offered to the eye. *Metropolis* with the variously dulled and frantic movements of its factory-slaves, its crowds pouring like a torrent through narrow spaces, its lights flashing round the uneven rocks of a narrow catacomb, its floodwaters first seeping, then trickling, then hurtling, with an almost 'musical' development, is a metronome-and-protractor film, like *Intolerance*. Lang's American films have a 'realistic' appearance, but are just as 'visual' as his German. He is a master of so arranging his characters in space that a kind of nameless, fatalistic suspense palpitates between them. Slow, intermittent, dragging movements are his speciality—whether of trains in *Human Desire*, or of doors and people in *The Woman in the Window*. *Tigress of Bengal* has a careful colour symbolism (spoiled in the wretched English prints); good is a matter of dull buffs and plain whites, evil is mosaics of rich, glinting patterns. The beauty of evil and the colour-poverty of good connects with his tragic-ironic view of life. Lang's story sense may be shaky, even his orchestrations of movement less inventive than they were in the 20's. Perhaps only those of his films are masterpieces which combine their visual richness with a satisfying dramatic line. But his consistently expressionistic idiom is suggested by the similarity between these two scenes, one from *Metropolis* (1926), the other from *Fury* (1936).

Expressionism in France seemed less successful than in Germany, and one can even say that, after lying quiescent during the socially-conscious 30's and 40's, it doesn't come to fruition until Truffaut's *Les 400 Coups* (1959). In the 60's as in the 20's, the French movement would be more aptly described as an impressionism, or at least as an attempt to turn an impressionistic sensibility and idiom to romantic and expressionistic aims. The procedure is possible, as the paintings of Van Gogh demonstrate. But when, in the early 20's, Delluc, Dulac, Gance, L'Herbier, Jean Epstein and the other intellectuals who were faced with the task of artistically and economically reconstructing French film art from its wartime collapse, they constituted a sort of 'new wave', usually called 'impressionist', because they were very concerned with lyricizing psychological, subjective 'impressions', whether of the outside world, or of mental reality (a 'stream of consciousness' in opticals). Instead of the Germans' slow, heavy mime and architecture, their films disintegrated into a mercurial flurry of optical distortions, superimpositions, first-person shots ('the camera becomes a snowball' wrote Gance proudly) and hectic montages. As Jacques Brunius remarks in *Experiment in the Film*, 'In *Le Diable dans la Ville* (1926) Germaine Dulac doubled the image to indicate violent emotion in one of her characters. I do not know whether my eyeballs are peculiarly stable and unemotional, or simply whether I have never been sufficiently moved, but no such affective diplopia ever effected me, and a vision of this sort on the screen conveys nothing to me at all.'[1] Other pests described by Brunius include 'crick-necked camera', soft-focus, gauze, and 'cubist' décor. 'Fortunately at this time the trucks in French studios all had square wheels, and the impossibility of moving them spared us for another few years the annoyance of irrelevant tracking shots.'

---

[1] The concentration on the 'perceptual notation' prefigures the 'solipsistic-nihilistic perceptual pedantry' of Robbe-Grillet. This French screen impressionism lacked that careful exploration of visual sensation that was the procedure of an earlier impressionism—in fact it was too careless even for its own slaphappy lyrical purposes, lacking also the strong emotionality of Van Gogh. It was an aesthete's mode. Godard today has a similarly 'darting' eye for visual details, 'cool' rather than emotional; at its worst, a 'flip aestheticism', at its best authentically lyrical, in a solipsist-nihilist key.

Epstein's *La Chute de la Maison Usher* (1927) is an interesting, if finally only spasmodically successful, attempt at combining intensely lyrical location-shots (the dank, gloomy winter countryside, all mud and bare branches), impressionism *à la* Dulac (a plethora of 1st-person shots and 'arty' super-impressions—a forest of white candles 'walking through' a forest of black trees), and expressionistic décor (the House itself). It is a fascinating potpourri of the bad and the brilliant—in one slow-motion shot, a stack of books falling forward from a cupboard seem to be sagging, crumbling like a very old corpse. . . . The comparison with Corman's version is fascinating, especially since both films combine two Poe stories into one.

By about 1931 the French had given up such impressionistic-expressionistic cocktails. The great French films of the 30's are all in the tradition of a slightly literary realism. One director alone, in two films, achieves the perfect integration of the three idioms: Jean Vigo, with *Zero de Conduite* (1933) and *L'Atalante* (1934).

By the late 20's German expressionism and realism had reached the compromise exemplified by E. A. Dupont's *Variété* by Pabst's *Pandora's Box*, Joe May's *Ashphalte*, Fritz Lang's *M*, all of which, more or less acceptable as 'realistic', use a visual language derived almost entirely from expressionism. Streetscapes straight out of silent German films (huddled roofs, twisted windows) turn up even in British films—Dupont's *Piccadilly* (1928), Hitchcock's *Murder!* (1930). But though expressionism sensitizes and strengthens the camera's language, it can't be said that expressionism as such infiltrates world cinema. In the early talkies words seemed to discourage the lyrical simplicities of the silent film. They enabled plots to move much faster, and moved the acting and the whole 'tone' steadily towards the underplaying which passed for realism in the 40's.

The main exception is the out-and-out horror film, which flourished during the Depression, and which, by definition, rules out 'common sense', so as to unleash nightmarish emotion. In painting too, there is a general connection between expressionism and nightmare, that is, the primitive, morbid, uprush of subrational emotion, and this link characterizes the German silent cinema. In its storyline, *Caligari* is pure penny dreadful. Murnau's *Nosferatu* (1922) was the first screen adaptation of Bram Stoker's *Dracula*. American Depression-era horrors retained the germanic bestiary (*Dracula*), its trickwork (*King Kong*) and studio-sets (Frankenstein's tower and crypt); even the flashing of machinery during the Monster's resurrection is pre-figured in the creation of the robot in Lang's *Metropolis*.

The acting is often a dreamlike pantomime (Karloff, Lugosi). There is a procession of 'tyrant figures' like that which Kracauer notices in German silent films (for Haroun el Raschid, Ivan the Terrible and Jack the Ripper read Count Dracula, Count Zaroff and the Frankenstein Monster). There is a similar interest in tortures (Zaroff and Fu Manchu) and waxworks (*The Mystery of the Wax Museum*). But all these films are only just beginning to return into critical fashion. . . .

Nor have critics been very appreciative of those directors in whose works expressionism led a subtler existence, as a visual style. Of Joseph von Sternberg it can safely be said that if expressionism hadn't already existed he would have invented it. If his storylines incline to be a little too glib, his visuals are so impeccable, so rich, as to poeticize both the most arrant artifice (Marlene in 'Morocco' trotting out into the desert on four-inch heels . . .) and the most casual detail (a candle on an unlit stove, a boy poking his head round the side of a wooden mannequin). Straight from German expressionism is his sense of fate (suggested by the menacing dredger in *The Salvation Hunters*, the maze of nets in *Macao*) and of moral ascendancy and humiliation (Jannings, pompously: 'I am the professor of English at the local school!' Marlene, coolly: 'Then you should know enough to take off your hat.') His décor is completely controlled: its grotesque, suffering masks, its cages, its animals, are as expressive of the characters' souls as the expressionistic distortions of *Caligari*.

Near the end of *The Devil is a Woman* a train emerges from a tunnel; only Von Sternberg could make of its appearance a little poem. The sun is behind and above the tunnel, which forms a squat black mass far away down the line. First we hear the train approaching. Then we see the white smoke jet out amidst the framing blackness. Abruptly its grey-white pillar billows up into the sunlight. At last the black square mass of the locomotive itself slides out into the glare of sun, towards us, and blacks it out. These tonal reversals in and round a steadily thrusting-out object are quite hypnotic. Some of the visual jokes are admirable. Marlene dons insolent white to visit her lover in prison, and, to visit him in hospital, funereal black. As Lionel Atwill enfolds Marlene in his arms, she holds in her arms a goose in a cage.

The heavier, foggier aspects of expressionism inspire the lighting of Lang's *Fury* and *You Only Live Once*, Ford's *The Informer* and *The Long Voyage Home*, and Welles' *Citizen Kane*. Perhaps the last burst of Hollywood expressionism is the heavy shafts of light in the condemned cell scenes of Siodmak's *Phantom Lady* (1945). By the early 50's, expressionism seemed altogether exhausted. *Citizen Kane* and *Ivan the Terrible*—two studies in megalomanic solitude—seemed like whales stranded on the shores of fashion.

When the cinema wanted to be 'expressionistic', it had to find a location which gave the psychological effect a realistic 'pretext'. And it did (for the expressionistic urge can never die). The maze of mirrors, the clammy aquarium in Welles' *The Lady from Shanghai*, the empty fairground in Kubrick's *The Killing* (with the loudspeaker booming, 'We—the dead—welcome you . . .'), the planet Metaluna in *This Island Earth*, the blitzed church, the huge crucifix hanging upside down, and the rubbish dump on which the hero dies kicking and writhing in Wajda's *Ashes and Diamonds*, the complex symbolism of Ingmar Bergman (in *Summer Interlude* a woman walking on a windy, rainy path suddenly resembles Death . . .), the glossy clinic of *La Notte*, the children's downriver drift, watched by forest animals, in Charles Laughton's *Night of the Hunter*, all, in different ways, draw attention to themselves as overpowering mood, as whirls of intense emotion.

Two technical developments of the 50's pushed the pendulum of style slowly back from the 'realistic' to the 'expressionistic'. Magazine photography was controlling and exploiting such effects as blurring, grainy texture, out-of-focus, 'bad' light, 'wrong' exposures, and all the 'mistakes' which have vastly increased the camera's repertoire. For the movie camera too faster emulsions, simplified lighting, in or out of the studio, and smaller cameras permitted far greater variety, nuance and subtlety in location photography and movement.

The change can be seen as far back as Dassin's *Du Rififi Chez les Hommes* (1955), where the crazy streaming of trees reflected in a car windscreen mirrors the delirious, the *internal*, world of its dying driver. The director no longer has to *create* an effect, as did Wiene, Lang and Murnau. Now he has only to *spot* it. The 'camera stylo' is nothing new; a walking camera *à la* Coutard is used in Epstein's *La Chute de la Maison Usher* (1927), in Vigo's *A Propos de Nice* (1930) in Dreyer's *Vampyr* (1932), and many other places besides. What is new is the ease with which the director's visual *impressions* can be caught. At last his personal world can easily become a subjective, an expressionistic, world. American *avant-garde* had been developing such effects consistently for many years, but in the popular cinema the most useful milestone is perhaps the opening sequence of Truffaut's *Les 400 Coups*. The camera glides past blind brick walls, desolate warehouses, glimpsing intermittently, the Eiffel Tower stalking far away, like a pale ghost against an iron sky. Paris is suddenly chilled to one boy's feeling of utter desolation and solitude. The boarded-up windows become gouged-out eyes. This is a dead planet, one man's Metaluna. The visuals are one long, desolate wail. But the music is mildly sprightly, the music doesn't care too much, there is a discontinuity in the feelings—a discontinuity which comes closer to the surface in the 'cool' mode, the 'flip tragic' mood, of Charles Aznavour in *Tirez Sur le Pianiste*. The scene where a lover's-eye-view panning-shot round their bedroom is superimposed over a shot of the two lovers lying in bed is the consummation of the white candles-black forest effect in *La Chute de la Maison Usher*. At last such effects have emotional relevance.

Simultaneously, in America, Roger Corman and Floyd Crosby develop a colour expressionism, at its most dazzling in the delirium sequence of *Tales of Terror* (1962). Certain Saul Bass credits (like the prowling cat in *Walk On the Wild Side*) point the way to an expressionism based less on traditional 'painterliness' than on the newer idioms of graphic design.

The contemporary audience which accepts the 'false-time' jump cuts of Godard's *A Bout de Souffle* and Desmond Davis' *Girl with Green Eyes* is an audience which will take the cinema screen as, not a *literal* reality, but a 'mental world'. So with the 'puzzle worlds' of Resnais' *L'Année Dernière à Marienbad*, Fellini's *8½*, of Welles' *The Trial*, all of which are, in some sense, expressionistic films. Again 'realism' becomes merely a means to an end, a convention which can be accepted or ignored, whichever the artist prefers.

Still untapped possibilities loom. The difficulties are less of *inventing* and *controlling* effects, than of making sure that they have some emotional relevance. One can distort colour by using tungsten stock by daylight and daylight stock by artificial light. One can alter hues and shades by over- and under-exposure. One can throw backgrounds slightly out of focus to produce a 'dreamlike haze' (an effect already abused in magazine advertisements), or throwing images completely out-of-focus so as to create evocative patterns (corresponding to semi-abstract expressionism). Thus in *Lueurs* (1950), Dr. Thévénard let the camera dwell on a convict's cigarette smoke as he languished in his cell, and evocative music gave the smoke fleeting resemblances to blurred memory-images—a fairground, a girl. . . .

Colour commercials have developed a new sensuousness which the artist might well take up, deepen, and use in a disturbing or sinister way. There's no reason why one shouldn't re-explore certain silent 'effects'—masking, shooting through thin cloths. One might alter photographic textures by reshooting scenes projected on to suitably textured or uneven surfaces—thus in Michael Powell's *Peeping Tom* a film-within-a-film is seen on the hero's Harris Tweed jacket, and a face blurs into a skull. Losey does something like this in his use of a convex mirror in *The Servant*. Its bulge distorts the space it reflects, and therefore not only the relationships but the bodies and postures of the people in the room. Different colour stocks might be used in adjacent sequences or even shots. And as Von Sternberg has remarked: '. . . still photography as distinguished from motion picture photography has one enormous advantage which one day will cease to be: that is the treatment of the surface of the photograph. Choice of grain in the paper, paper, manipulation of the negative, the enlargement of an interesting detail, can salvage otherwise uninteresting work and make it effective. It is only a matter of time when such manipulation will be incorporated into our work.'

The greater the range of possibilities at the artist's finger-tips, the greater the importance of disciplined selection, of exact control. Effects must never be used in a random or pretentious way, that is, so that by drawing attention to themselves they disrupt instead of reinforcing the overall emotional substance. But that problem is a perennial one, it exists in one form or another with the simplest techniques—pencil on paper. Meanwhile the cinema stands on the brink of another leap forward in its artistic development.

1, 2. The two inquisitors: *La Passion de Jeanne d'Arc*

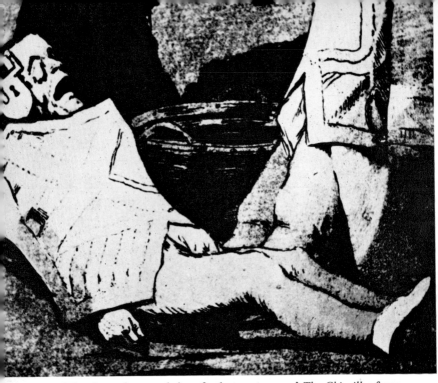

3. 'The sleep of reason brings forth monsters . . .' *The Chincillas* from Goya's *Los Capriocios*, 1797

4. Face as landscape: *La Passion de Jeanne d'Arc*

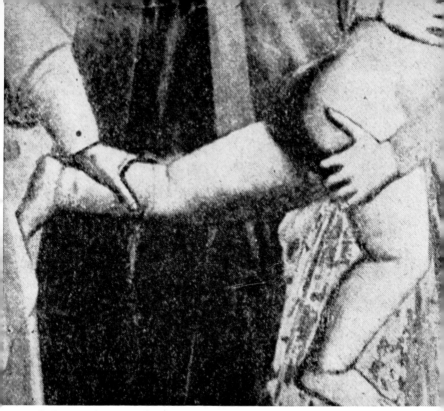

5, 6. Two close-ups: from Luciano Emmer's *Il Dramma di Cristo* and from *La Passion de Jeanne d'Arc*

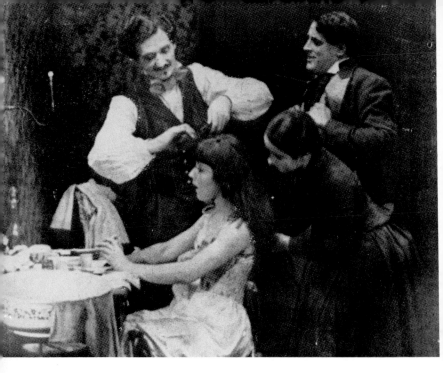

7, 8. Movement and informality: *Nana* and *Fires Were Started*

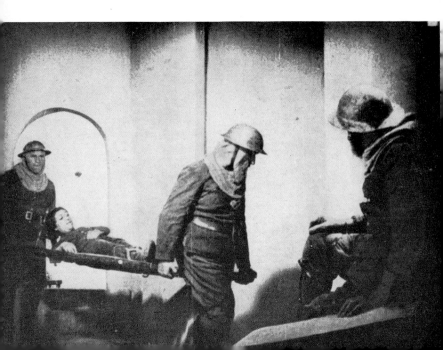

9, 10. Studies in depth: *Day of Wrath* and *Vampyr*

11, 12. Choreography and space: *La Passion de Jeanne d'Arc*

13, 14. Two compositions: *Alexander Nevski*

15. Echoes: *Ivan the Terrible*

16, 17. Echoes: *La Passion de Jeanne d'Arc* and *Tabu*

18, 19. Structures of light: *Ivan the Terrible* and *Tabu*

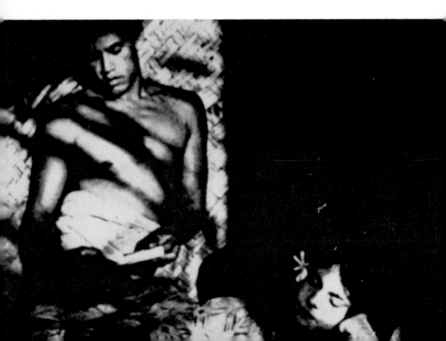

20, 21. Bodies and poses: Emil Jannings in *The Last Laugh* and
Jennifer Jones, Robert Sully, Gladys Cooper in *Love Letters*

22, 23. Two deserts. Orphée and Heurtebise in slow-motion in 'la zone';
below, Metaluna. *Orphée* and *This Island Earth*

24. Out on a limb: Harold Lloyd in *Safety Last*
25. Chester Conklin in *When Comedy Was King*

26, 27. While Hollywood dramas daydream, slapstick peeps in at the everyday cramped quarters and rustic plumbing: Laurel and Hardy in *Bonnie Scotland* and Keaton in *The General*

28. Charlie Chaplin and Paulette Goddard in *Modern Times*
29. Betty Hutton, William Demarest, Eddie Bracken and Diana Lynn in *The Miracle of Morgan's Creek*

30, 31. Lofty sentiments in ivory towers, and low cunning below the Plimsoll line: Fields and Dumont in *Never Give a Sucker an Even Break* and The Marx Brothers in *Monkey Business*

6 · Architecture in, and of, the Movies

A. The Rape of Architecture by Drama

Carl Dreyer has argued that the cinema's closest relative is architecture.

It may seem paradoxical to compare the most mimetic (photographic) of the arts with the construction of a new reality, and a dramatic art with a 'Utopian' one. Equally unexpected is the *rapprochement* of the most fluid of all visual media with the most solid and static.

Yet the paradoxes hold. For, by its nature, the cinema is a *beau monstre*. Like the theatre, it centres on actors. *But* its tempo-spatial flexibility approaches the novel's. *But* it is predominantly visual—flat, like painting. *But* its visuals exist in *movement* and *time*, so that its plasticity has musical components. *But* its photographic quality precludes music abstraction, suggesting a very literal realism. *But* seeing a film is notoriously a dreamlike experience. . . .

This blend of realism and onirism provides the clue to Dreyer's meaning. The cinema's mimetic fullness (photography, movement, sound) permits the creation of a *self-sufficient* world. Like the architect, the film director weaves diverse media into a 'new' reality.

The traditional division between the 'dramatic' and the other arts is only part of the story. Dramatic ugliness and tensions, even the tragic end, occur within aesthetic 'distance' and form part of an ultimately agreeable existence. The character dies, but author and actors enjoy our enthusiastic applause. Through vicarious experience, katharsis and enhanced understanding, drama, like architecture, improves the world.

And architecture, in its way, implies drama. There is the possibility of displeasure. An effective building, like a circus acrobat, might be graceless, but flies through the air with the greatest of ease. Its 'suspense' is non-representational, but exists as intensely as that of music. As Keats and Freud agreed, there is no beauty without melancholy, no thrill without anxiety, no elegance without the remembrance of pain. Creativity treads a tightrope between complacent 'good taste' (too little 'danger') and bad taste (an emotional 'unhappy end').

Architecture's immobility makes it the natural complement of the movie-camera. The basic architectural experiences—standing in a space, looking around, and walking along a corridor—find their equivalents in the screen frame, in the panning shot (the camera turns its head), and the tracking shot (the camera walks forward or backwards). Though the screen is flat, the camera's reticulation of movements in space confer on the succession of images (the sequence) a quality of space-in-depth, controlled and orchestrated.

Architecture has been described as 'frozen music'. When the camera moves, the roofline flows past us like a river. The camera tilts rapidly up, and banister and staircase cascade down. The cinema is 'unfrozen architecture'.

In the opening shots of Thorold Dickinson's *Overture* the swooping camera counterpoints the inner lines of the U.N. building at Lake Success with the opening theme of Beethoven's *Egmont* Overture. Space becomes time, balconies and musical phrases leap out together. The cinema *is* an architecture (and is the best medium for recording architecture).

B. How to Make a Building Omelette

But the film hurls form into a melting-pot of its own. It abducts, reforms, deforms, all it shows. Above all, as we shall see, it perverts its emotional sense.

When in David Lean's *Great Expectations* Pip as a boy calls on Miss Havisham her room is huge, cavernous. When Pip as a man (John Mills) calls on her it is stuffy, cramped. The room is the same. The camera lens is different. The camera is a born liar.

It commits every conceivable offense against the human scale. It is the anti-Modulor. The cloak of a foreground figure rears up over the palace beyond. Cut—and that monumental figure now becomes a tiny dot stranded in the forecourt, dwarfed in its turn by a foreground vase. The cinema's mobility *explodes* architecture.

The camera glides up the outside of a wall, and swoops from window to window. It glides 'through' walls from one room to another, creating a sense of magic ease, of liberation from gravity and mural impenetrability. In Jerry Lewis's *The Ladies' Man* the camera tracks back from an ordinary two-shot to reveal an entire mansion in cross-section. It doesn't reduce the house to a dolls' house; it makes the spectator feel he has become God's right-hand-man. Or empty rooms may be barricaded with shadows which appear as beams of black light. . . .

Films may convert space into time. Roger Corman's *The Man With the X-Ray Eyes*, is one of the 'pulp' films that fascinate pop-art addicts. The guilty scientist (Ray Milland) runs down a fire-escape, and superimposed over a 1st-person-shot of his feet hurrying down the steps, endlessly, endlessly, appear newspaper headlines announcing his escape. A mere 'metaphor'? But it shows that, in the spectator's mind, space was 'merging' into time. In *Hoven Zo* (*Steady*), Herman Van Der Horst's documentary on the reconstruction of Rotterdam, the camera, identified with a steam-drill, plummets down past tower blocks, which conversely seem to be thrusting up into the sky with a phallic indomitability; or like intention directly translated into fact. Thus camera style becomes metaphysics.

Jean Cocteau's *Le Sang d'Un Poète* opens with a factory chimney beginning to fall. Seventy minutes later it concludes with the chimney hitting the ground. This 'time-split' establishes the onirism of the intervening story (for back in the 30's dreams were thought to be all-but-instantaneous). But it harnesses also the thrill and awed chill we feel watching demolitions. We hold our breath, because as the chimney falls, we fall. That crumbling chimney is the spectator's own body 'dissolving', and through kinaesthetic empathy it triggers emotions of failure and death.

Louis Feuillade's *Les Vampires* (1915) is a pulp serial celebrated by the Surrealists and latterly revived with great success at the National Film Theatre. Perhaps its most beautiful sequences show criminals clambering about Paris rooftops, clad in black catsuits and Ku Klux Klan hoods (as to be completely inconspicuous). Their presence, akin to Chirico's geometrical figures, transforms the real, shot-on-location roofscapes into a world as hallucinatory as Chaval's Dream Palace at Hauterives. The roofs become moon dunes, the chimneystacks a cubist vegetation or lunar cacti.

C. Architecture as Metaphor

At the other extreme, architecture is a favourite image for social pressures, for society itself. The camera needs visual metaphors; and architecture is a man-made landscape, a man-made environment. Elia Kazan's *On the Waterfront* concludes with the dockers returning to work, strengthened by their new-found spirit of 'one for all, all for one', which will make an authentic unionism possible. But a grim steel shutter closes down on them. The docks in which they work are a prison. Their next fight is just beginning.

More subtle and evasive is the meaning of an extreme long shot in a John Ford Western, *My Darling Clementine*, showing three masses echeloned against the desert. Nearest us, the half-built church; beyond, the saloon; beyond again, a craggy massif. The formal echo summarizes the nascent West: the Protestant ideal; its brawling antithesis; and, over and above these, *their* antithesis, silent, sullen nature. The finest is the most 'fragile' of the three. Civilization seems a raft bobbing on vast sea, the third 'block' being—a tidal wave....

A fundamental equation of the cinema's is: landscape=state of soul. Architecture may constitute an X-ray photograph of the heroes' minds. If in *Rocco and His Brothers* Visconti stages a quarrel, between a newly urbanized peasant and a *dolce vita* call girl, on top of Milan cathedral, and then cuts and cuts jaggedly, hectically, it is because that cathedral, like the moral framework of their lives, is a giant ship keeling over beneath them. Christendom 1960 is a *Titanic*, sinking fast.

In Claude Chabrol's *A Double Tour*, Antonella Lualdi lives in a house one of whose glass walls lets a green field with poppies into the room. Between us and the picture window is an aquarium, and tropical fish slowly drift across the scenery, like living gems. The strangeness of all this transforms physical beauty into a spiritual power: the flesh (Lualdi), a *fin-de-siècle* preciosity (fish-gems), and nature-merged-with-structure (or, a new classicism) which has room for the romantic urge.

In many ways, the cinema deprives architecture of its autonomy, makes of it a symbol whose meaning alters with content. The concept of *objet trouvé* isn't inappropriate, for directors currently depend on finding buildings with emotional possibilities. The vast complex of rooms in Orson Welles' *The Trial* is not the studio construction it may seem, but the derelict Gare d'Orsay in Paris 'merged' with a Yugoslavian exhibition hall. The supernatural 'zone' of Cocteau's *Orphée* is the ruins of L'Ecole Militaire. It is not photography *per se* which makes these fantasies so convincing, it is the concrete specificity of their sustained architectural metaphor. Here architecture takes a thoroughly creative role. Eisenstein didn't think of a massacre on some steps and then select the Odessa Steps; the Steps inspired the staging. Carl Dreyer, while searching for a visual style for his *Vampyr*, came across a flour mill and derived from it the idea of a vampire film in the key of white.

D. The Rise and Fall of Expressionism

When photography was less sensitive than it is now, the director could control his environment only by building it in a studio. The facility of exaggeration led easily to expressionism.

Weine's *The Cabinet of Dr. Caligari* (1919) was not the first expressionist film (contrary to academic myth: its principal predecessor was C. A. Bragaglia's *Perfido Incanto* (Italy, 1916). But Weine's film initiated the screen's first concerted attempt to emotionalize architecture, along principles derived from Max Reinhardt's stage décor and the theories of Edschmidt. Seen through the mind of its madman, the streets and façades of *Caligari*, painted on intersecting back-cloths, were shattered into spikes and shards; ceilings warped and drooped, buildings were paper scraps. In Weine's *Raskolnikoff* (1923) the guilty student slept under a clutter of black beams which seemed to be pressing down upon his head like a vice. As he climbed the rickety staircase to the murder room, its tottering banisters were so many needle-like shapes, hysterically pointing the way. But as he backed hysterically out of the room, they seemed to be falling away behind him, letting him fall into the horror. . . .

Expressionism soon revealed two tendencies, the *paroxystic* and the *decorative*. In contrast to the flimsy, staggering structures of the madman's vision, the asylum in *Caligari* is a cool, heavy, immovable, three-dimensional structure. The enigmatic Dr. Caligari himself is awaited. From which of a row of three dark arches will he enter? The suspense turns the arcade into a labyrinth concealing the minotaur of authority. The asylum architecture has a strong, but slightly barbaric, feel, and one's feeling that its symmetry is hierarchic to the point of feudalism is confirmed by Fritz Lang's two-part *Nibelungen* film. There medieval orders of chivalry are associated with halls of chessboard patterns and a brutal solidity. Thus these apparently 'decorative' designs reveal their emotional tensions, and, as Siegfreid Kracauer suggests in *From Caligari to Hitler*, points to the house style of the Third Reich.

The madman's flat confusions oppose a brutal order; their linking term is the *maze* from which issues *tyranny*. Mazes, mirrors, the interplay of spotlights and drifting smoke on architectural forms, the tension and mystery of winding staircases, the squalor of crooked streets, are among the visual motifs which dominate German expressionism, whose inspiration is the reaction to the economic instability of post-Versailles Germany by a profoundly Junkerized *bourgeoisie*.

Abandoning expressionism in the late 20's, German directors transposed these visual motifs into realistic settings and subjects. The ominous atmosphere characteristic of all the films of Lang (who trained as an architect) is created by his feeling for small, slow movements isolated in empty, rectangular spaces. The films of Pabst are built on the motif of a sharply angled passage flanked by dark masses. The passage may be a mineshaft along which flames are leaping (*Kameradschaft*, 1931), it may be lorries driving out of a barrack square (*Jackboot Mutiny*, 1955), it may be tunnelled out of an enigmatic chiaroscuro by spotlights, but the implied or stated Z, with all its tensions, gives all the films of this celebrated 'realist' an emotional undertow as powerful as expressionism's. Lang's colour *Tigress of Bengal* is another of the 'pulp' subjects whose formalism has enraptured the writers of *Cahiers du Cinéma*, critical seedbed of the New Wave. In her white, almost *bleached*, clothes, the European girl, wanders through the Maharajah's Palace in search of her lost brother. First, by daylight, she strolls past vivid, coloured mosaics, orderly and rectangular. Then she strolls past dark, purplish murals —the colours are rich, but sullen, brooding, the forms more confused and hectic. At last, leaving daylight behind, she ventures into the catacombs, the palace corridors now yielding to a rocky irregularity of form.

Architectural forms strike off bodily motifs. In the temple, dwarfed by the gigantic statue of a goddess, Debra Paget dances, with lubricious legs-astride movements of her torpedo-shaped thighs.

Meanwhile the exploring architect clambers up a catacomb-chimney, his straddled legs 'rhyming' with hers.

In Dreyer's films architecture plays a major role. The hero of *Vampyr* arrives at an apparently deserted inn. He hears a voice and seeks its source. The camera tilts up one corner of the house, pans across the diagonal slope of the roof, and discovers a woman in an attic window. The camera moves along the edges of the building, which we always thought of as a volume. The house becomes a collection of edges, a set of blades, a slice of the sky stolen by man to live in.

Later, the hero dreams that his corpse is being carried past the church in a glass-windowed coffin. As if through his eyes, we see the sky and trees above us—and then the front of the church rears over us, turned on its side, quivering slightly as if with the movements of the coffin. It moves slowly over us, and away off the screen, and we, the not-quite-dead, destined for burial in unconsecrated ground, feel as forlorn as men in a lifeboat when the great ship they have attempted to hail moves steadily away.

By contrast with the human eye, the camera has 'tunnel vision', and Dreyer uses this visual concentration to render structures *unsteady*. The camera looks down across a room so that the far skirting is an uneasy tilt across the top edge of the screen. The furniture, or such floor-coverings as a heavily-patterned carpet, emphasize the floor's climb 'up' perspective hill, and it is as if the room were heaving under strange pressures. Wide-angle lens permit a whole web of such effects, involving also the angles of furniture and the human body. Degas' *Le Tub* (1888) anticipates them, but in Dreyer the effect is specifically of a building under the torque of disturbing spiritual forces.

The house in *Vampyr* is *also* a matter of flat planes. A door in a near wall opens to reveal a further wall beyond; the house has a Whistlerian flimsiness, even preciosity. 'Safe as houses?' No, a house is only a maze of planes, partitions between which the uncanny emanations freely flow—the fluidity suggested for us by a gliding camera.

Dreyer's *Day of Wrath* (1943) emphasizes *bourgeois* love of property as a spiritual evil. Heavy shadows, emphasizing solidity of form, an immobile camera, and 'rectangular' placings in space, render buildings and furniture dark and massive. In their stiff puritan clothes, the people themselves seem rigid as oak or teak. But when the flames are lit round the foolish old woman who has become the scapegoat for repressed hatreds, the hot air rising from the pyre makes the stone church beyond *tremble* and *shudder*. . . .

Despite the achievements of such lonely souls as Dreyer, the 30's saw expressionism in eclipse. In the popular cinema, almost its last stronghold was the American horror film. James Whale's *Frankenstein* (1931) and *Bride of Frankenstein* (1935), for whose lyrical power even the documentarist John Grierson had a grudged respect, are glorious specimens of what one can only describe as 'slaphappy Gothic.' There are among those artistic hybrids found only in the popular arts, the result of sophisticated people working for a hick audience, now subverting the formula with private parody, now hitting on a unique blend of subtlety and popular myth.

There are architectural jokes. In the middle of a deliriously cobwebby sepulchre, Dr. Praetorius warns Baron Frankenstein to, 'Mind the step.' As a laboratory, the too-audacious Baron uses a dilapidated stone tower on top of a hill. The Freudian symbolism of this topography (a phallic erection on testicle hill) is duly enhanced by the details of the process of carcass-revivification. The corpse, laid out on a stretcher, is hoisted to the top of the tower, preceded by an electrical 'pylon', which screws itself up into the nocturnal storm, whose energies are further tapped by a flotilla of kites. The thunderstorm, the lifting of the 'unborn' body, the erection of the spire, the floating of the kites, the crackling and sparking, introduce a plethora of classic orgasmic symbols. The reference is not only Promethean (stealing fire from the heavens), it is also to a gigantic, monstrous, erection—the megalomaniac 'hubris' of the scientist, creating life without the aid of God, or of woman. Grand finale: the Monster (Boris Karloff) is scorned by his Bride (Elsa Lanchester), who is an improved model, and only loves her maker (Colin Clive). Vengefully the lumbering old Mark I pulls the wrong lever, whereupon Tumescence Tower literally blows its top.

E. A Lyrical Realism

The 40's and 50's are under the sign of realism, and, predominantly, architecture 'is' society. Many young critics, preoccupied with screen aesthetics for their own sake, find it hard to respond to such films of de Sica's as *Bicycle Thieves* (1948) and *Umberto D*, whose style seems so cold and plain.

But 'cold and plain' is the key. The streets down which the work-man searches for his stolen bicycle have a bland, callous indifference to the desperate individual. In endless successions, skeins of terrace houses, lofty apartment blocks, become symbols of a society built out of privacy, indifference and a human 'absence'. De Sica's sense of Rome reflects his curious blend of Franciscan sentimentality and Marxist hard-headedness. And the 'coldness' of his films prefigures Antonioni's, whose evocation of 'alienation' transposes this critique of capitalism from the proletarian-economic sphere to the *bourgeois-*spiritual.

In the films of de Sica, Visconti (and of their Indian disciple, Satyajit Ray) architecture plays an interesting syntactical role in articulating the image. All three have to deal with poor people living in very crowded conditions. Continual close-up would abolish the sense of *man in his environment* so essential to the films' theme; so individuals are isolated by creating within the frame smaller frames by walls, windows, railings, or other spatial 'vignettes'. Often the character isolated is an unimportant one—a lonely grandfather shaving—while the story proceeds 'round' him, in terms of movement and dialogue. And we become aware of the loneliness in crowds, of lives proceeding beside lives, of individuality everywhere.

Neo-realism died, briefly, around 1953, killed partly by audiences' dislike of its drabness, partly by government dislike for its picture of an Italy where people were poor and it rained all the time. Around 1960 the 'economic miracle' and a governmental 'opening to the left' presented it with a new battery of themes, and it could call on the talents of the 'school of Visconti', a bunch of very highly cultured young Marxists. One film must stand for many (by Bolognini, Paso-lini, Patroni Griffi, Rosi, Olmi, *et al.*). In Lina Wertmuller's *The Lizards*, long white lines of sun-baked stone houses evoke all the harsh torpor of Southern feudalism. A boy dares outrage tabu and address a girl, unchaperoned, in the street. A God's-eye-view camera looks down on the boy as he overtakes the girl and walks alongside her. The pan continues through its 90° so that street and houses keep slowly over, and 'up' is slewed to some indistinct area to the left of the screen. The lovers walk on in a disordered, strange, *weightless* world—the effect is so uncanny that we know they will just let the matter drop.

F. The Architecture of Alienation

Richard Smith remarked in *Ark 19*: 'In *Little Caesar* (1930) Edward G. Robinson's set-up as a minor monster was straight from the Bauhaus stable. . . . Later, modern styling became associated with a new bogey man in the communist agent who, while obviously living in the same world as we, could not have settings impinging on the audience's dream world. So the as yet unacceptable modern was called into service, along with the use of modern art galleries and modern music as front organizations.'

An overt anti-egghead bias operated too. But it's less the heroine than the vamp who wears next year's clothes and keys next year's behaviour. So modern stylings gradually percolate from the villain to the hero-villain, and, via the psychiatrist, to the hero, and from the snooty hotel to the cosy home.

But a curious thing has happened to what the man-in-the-street thinks of as 'modern' architecture. Just as curtain-walls and tower-blocks are becoming familiar, so the screen portrays them as cold, remote, bland. Tati preferred the unfunctional ramshackle home of *Mon Oncle* (1958) to sterile *bourgeois* gadgetry. In Marcel Camus' *Orfeu Negro* (1959) a steel-and-glass office-building becomes a silent, shining sepulchre, past which winds the joyous snake of a Brazilian native carnival. In Louis Malle's *Ascenseur à l'Échafaud* (1958) a modern office-block evokes the larger trap, which is society. Seen through its glass walls, the windows in the block opposite are rows and columns of eyes staring at the hero as he murders his unscrupulous boss. As he escapes in the lift, a power cut traps him between floors—another image for *the system*, and an aesthetically pleasing converse to the sinister of open space. In Resnais' *Hiroshima Mon Amour* (1959), the new buildings, the glittering neon streets, past which the heroine wanders, are not just the cynical will-to-live of the Japanese people, shaming her 'idealist' clinging to her martyrdom in a cellar. They also represent a schizoid obliteration of the pain of Hiroshima, of the past.

In all these films the equation architecture=society is dominant. A world of rapid moral and spiritual change is a world of 'alienation'. Joan Littlewood's *Sparrows Can't Sing* (1962) half-domesticates current styles. A block of shiny flats rear over us imposingly; a feckless young Cockney gadabout (Barbara Windsor) leans over her balcony and yells down to her sort-of-husband, 'Don't forget to get us some lemons, love.' Not even modern architecture can awe the Cockney soul.

Occasionally architects' Utopianism can shade over into what feels like totalitarianism. One can still talk to people in the L.C.C. Architects' Department who want open-plan apartments imposed on people for whom one of the nicest things about quitting their over-crowded old slums would have been an orgy of privacy. There's no easy answer to such clashes of taste, involving so many factors. In Antonioni's *La Notte*, a man is dying in a cancer clinic, whose sleek, lavish lines are, somehow, an outrage—that is, an architectural metaphor for the way in which our optimistic, utilitarian rationalism smooths over human pain, therefore emotion, therefore communication. In this context, its elegance, like the charm with which Plato invests his totalitarian visions, is as sinister as a title like 'The Ministry of Peace'.

It's almost as if human nature prefers a slightly messy, random environment, not too ugly, but full of holes and corners and accidents and possibilities of ugliness, to suit its essential ambivalence. In films like *La Notte* we see the human mind making 'Utopian' architecture 'sinister', i.e. congenially ugly.

The animus is not against modernity specifically, but against the manner in which society dwarfs the individual, while uprooting (by rapid change) and manipulating him. It is with a seething hatred that King Vidor's *The Crowd* (1927), Billy Wilder's *The Apartment* (1960) and Orson Welles's *The Trial* (1962) show us a vast open-plan office —for its 'sociability' is an imposition of routine and of what David Reisman in *The Lonely Crowd* calls 'false personalization'.

In the films of Antonioni, architecture and landscape are inseparable. Throughout *L'Avventura* (1959) one broad, flat landscape after another drags itself wearily up the long, slow haul to the horizon. Limp roads lead the eye to clutters of irrelevant shacks. Buildings, cars, squares, are arranged with elaborate casualness, in unsettled snips, fragments of a jolted jigsaw, some of whose pieces are tracks and pans. They are linked raggedly. A slow motion earthquake is on. The perspectives are a web of emptiness.

We first see Claudia (Monica Vitti) waiting for Anna (Lea Massari) outside Sandro's house. She peers in through the doorway at a cold white corridor, hesitating before entering the labyrinth of his cold doubts. There are many such corridors in the film. The search for Anna after her disappearance is a *narrative* labyrinth, whose horror is that it dissolves into a grey mist of guilt. There is the corridor of the train in which Claudia and Sandro first toy with the idea of flirting. There is the long corridor down which Claudia runs in panic as the once-spontaneous Guilia and the sex-obsessed young painter make love. Her final search for Sandro, takes her down corridor after corridor, towards one vanishing point after another, until the pursuit becomes a dreamlike motionlessness. She is on the nightmare treadmill of their life together.

The strangely-deserted town of Noto, we remember, was completely destroyed by an earthquake in the eighteenth century, and reconstructed—as Sandro, an architect, would have liked to reconstruct Italian society today.

Resnais' *Muriel* (1963) translates modern deracination into architectural terms. Boulogne, like Hiroshima, is a 'rebuilt', that is, an amnesiac, town. A stranger asks for the town centre and is told, 'You're already there.' So much for civic spirit, for society as an organism. The heroine (Delphine Seyrig) lives among the antiques she sells—her home is a *musée imaginaire* in a shop, exemplifying all our cultural confusions. Her son lives in a rickety adolescent 'den' on a farm—as if all that wasn't complacent suburbia was banished to the periphery of consciousness. Nature—Pan—is only a desperate old tramp among the bunkers, vainly seeking a mate for his goat, while the human characters, with Proustian sterility, chase their memories, revealed mainly as illusions and lies except for the shameful secret of torture in Algeria. Neons and plate glass create a maze of reflections amongst which the peripatetic characters intermittently fragment. Only in the rusty iron lacework of an old railway station does there linger any romance, any magic. We are told about a block of new flats which capsized before they were occupied—an absurd accelerando of 'planned obsolescence'. Images of new white concrete blocks suddenly outcrop on to the dialogue, irrelevantly. In a haphazardly decorated flat, the windows become glassy spaces, unfinishednesses in the walls. If *Hiroshima Mon Amour* was, in essence, one long tracking shot through a maze of distractions, to the minotaur of a past trauma, *Muriel* is *pointilliste*, a mosaic of short, static shots catching a clutter of trivial, nervy, notations, movements, moments.

By the same token, *L'Année Dernière à Marienbad* is a lattice of dislocations and contradictions. One thinks of the x-dimensional architecture of M. C. Escher. For Dilys Powell its theme was 'time, memory and love', for Eric Newton it was 'place', and the terms are tautologies. This—clinic? hotel? limbo?—is the apotheosis of the 'amnesia' themes of *Hiroshima* and *Muriel.* Perhaps the palace dreams the people? . . . or perhaps they, elegant and lovely, and it, are the potential fullness of our lives: remote, frozen and two-dimensional because they are only wish-fulfilment images of ourselves, with no more substance than the nostalgia of 'if only. . . .' Thus they can exist only on the *brink* of freedom.

With its chessboard parquets and chandeliers like dream blossoms this intellectual structure is an Enchanted Palace whose Sleeping Beauty, instead of lying in a glass coffin, dances the icy minuet of schizoid grace. Similarly, under the ideal turbulence of the Trevi fountain, Marcello in Fellini's *La Dolce Vita* is about to embrace his dream princess (Anita Ekberg) when—the fountain dries, dawn descends, like a shutter.

G. The Pathos of the Baroque

'Baroque' is a conveniently vague and distended word to describe the sumptuousness of these films. Laurence Kitchin points out that in Carol Reed's *The Third Man* (1949), Viennese baroque seems 'a pompous gesture from the past' by contrast with the frenzied squalor of contemporary intrigue (which, we might add, climaxes in the architectural negative—a sewer). I don't see, with Mr. Kitchin, that its use of formal architecture makes *The Third Man* a dominant influence on the 60's: it derives from the formula of 'incongruous settings' beloved of the 40's melodrama; its director's stock has been plummeting for years; and the exquisite attention paid to the niceties of architecture by Visconti and Antonioni evolves from Italian film traditions. In fact the Italian films reverse the irony of Carol Reed's film. Baroque turbulence seems suddenly energetic, confident, everything the contemporary characters aren't, with their indecisions, their routines.

Fellini's delicate sense of open spaces and masses goes with narratives drifting from encounter to encounter and apply a *mise-en-scène* opposing continuous, indecisive movement to homes and palaces. The travelling entertainers of *La Strada* (1954) carry their motorized shack like a snail's shell. Restlessness is imparted to the 'closed circles' of *La Dolce Vita* and *8½* by the camera's surging, stabbing movements round characters who walk as they think. The peripatetic becomes nomadic. The most imposing architectural mass in $8\frac{1}{2}$ is a scaffolding surrounding a gigantic rocket which is only a film set, for a film which isn't made. Illusion of an illusion . . . Orson Welles' *The Trial* offers a prime specimen of paranoiad baroque. Using in some sequences an incessantly roaming camera, in others a flurry of quick cuts, Welles makes all space fidget. Taken on the diagonal, the rectangular jut of concrete balconies outside K's flat becomes a double lightning flash. Apparently separate locales—the bank, the tribunal, the lawyer's suite, the Ministry of Justice archives, the cathedral, the painter's 'cage'—are revealed as one agglomeration—the system in metaphor. K has long been in the whale's belly. Welles simultaneously 'explodes' space (cutting), shuffles (fidgeting) and 'agglomerates' it.

Any incongruities are happily exploited. The columns of the Gare d'Orsay appear incongruously in the cathedral, and in the lawyer's suite, among the forest of candelabra.

There exists a curious tension between the efficiency of the system (one thinks of *1984*) and its dilapidated architecture (evoking prewar European bureaucracies), a contrast underlined by K's modern equivalent. The dilapidated, peeling architecture gives the system an 'Oedipal' quality of which Welles is presumably aware, for the dialogue abounds in Freudian puns ('oval/ovular', 'phonograph/pornograph'). Thus the film links the '1984 syndrome' with the *bourgeois* conscience and love of law and order—an accusation characteristic of Welles's Nietzschean streak. The hollow grandeur thus implied is also a favourite architectural and thematic motif of his, reaching its apogee in *Confidential Report* (1955). His wide-angle lens and low angles enable tycoon Arkadian to dominate us; but also turn the walls and ceilings of his castle into converging, unstable, tottering affairs, a house-of-tottering-cards. Such shots are Welles's 'signature'.

H. Expressionism Rides Again

During the 40's Xanadu in Welles's *Citizen Kane*, the palace in Eisenstein's *Ivan the Terrible* and the Beast's castle in Cocteau's *La Belle et la Bête*—where living arms held candelabra from the walls— seemed the last bastions of screen expressionism. Less individualist directors compromised with realism by setting their stories in poetic locales. *The Third Man* might be subtitled 'Tales from the Vienna Sewers'. Welles's *The Lady from Shanghai* is famous for its love-scene set in a sombre aquarium (so that the silhouettes of shark and octopus would comment on the courtship), and for a final gunfight in mirror-maze (a superb perversion of architectural space which Welles remembered in *The Trial*, with the camera racing past alternate mirrors and spaces so that K sees Romy Schneider beyond her face; and his own image, alternate at machine-gun tempo).

Fast emulsions and pistol-size camera have vastly facilitated what we may call a 'flip expressionism'—subjective effects 'imposed on' reality simply by juggling with exposures, movements, and so on—as we saw in the case of Truffaut's *Les 400 Coups*.

Directed by Jacques Doniol-Valcroze (editor of *Cahiers du Cinéma*), *L'Eau à la Bouche* (*The Game of Love*, 1960), commits one of the most creative outrages ever perpetrated on architecture by a film director. Its very uniqueness is my excuse for recurring to an example I have cited elsewhere. Its story is a little piece of bittersweet, about three pairs of young lovers switching round during a week-end in a Perpignan castle. The castle is a real treasure of nineteenth-century *bourgeois* pretention, blossoming neo-classical statues, tapestries and paintings galore of Greek Gods up to their various amorous adventures. Their fullblown flesh and gestures contrast deliciously with the cool ways, the tight trousers and relaxed sambas, of the modern girls. Throughout the film an ever-moving camera rises to a crescendo of vivacity in two visual climaxes where the camera weaves itself round staircases. Up the grand staircase the pompous butler, teased beyond endurance, pursues the provocative maid, frantically tearing her clothes off one by one as she flees. And later, when the most sensitive girl, a loser in love, is missing, and her friends fear suicide, a *concierge's* knowing little daughter (actually the director's), gravely bouncing her yo-yo, leads the anxious adults along the ups and downs and ins and outs of an iron fire-escape that twists and bends across the roof to the little corner where the girl has hidden herself to weep. And there is a quite stupendous sequence where the camera thrice races round the castle, in whose huge bulk, set suddenly spinning, three lighted windows signify that three couples are revelling in the delights of the flesh. That intoxicated castle is the castle of worldly delights. . . .

The renewed popularity of fantasy, at all intellectual levels, has offered screen architects several unusual problems. In Roy Row-

land's *The 5,000 Fingers of Dr. T*, the prisons of the malicious Dr. T
include a staircase every one of whose steps is of a different, and in-
convenient, height. (Dungeon architecture would be an interesting
new field; after all, a 'good' dungeon reverses most of the usual
functional architecture, e.g. it should drive its occupants mad.)

In film studios, the current horror-cycle ensures that more ruins
are being built than at any time since the Gothic revival, and some
essays in science-fiction architecture are looked at in more detail in
our last chapter.

But in this necessarily incomplete survey we have limited ourselves
to the *dramatic perversion* of 'normal' architecture rather than to
sheer fantasy, or, on the other hand, the screen *presentation* of existing architecture. As it is, we can only lament our failure to dwell in
appropriate detail on such films as Eisenstein's *Ivan the Terrible* and
Jacques Rivette's *Paris Nous Appartient*, two vastly different essays in
paranoiad architecture; or the tormented baroque of Wajda's *Ashes
and Diamonds*.

7 · The Founding Fathers

Slapstick, like so many other things which we now think of as 'characteristically American', e.g. the Western, the gangster film, Pearl White serials and Cinemascope, was a gift to America from France. Years before Mack Sennett, French comedies swarmed with comic stuntmen called *cascadeurs*, who, in Nicole Védrès's words, 'really did perform the plunge from the third storey into a tub of washing; and at the exact moment that the floor of a room fell through, each man knew precisely where to leap—one on to the piano, another on to the aspidistra—silk hats still in their hands, lorgnettes dangling, beards a-quiver'. There was even a comic Emergo; 'one saw the *cascadeur* on the screen of the old Gaumont-Palace pursue his unfaithful wife from cab to cab, arrive at the door of the Gaumont-Palace itself, be refused entrance because of his disorderly dress, and resolve to get in over the roof. The screen darkened, the lights went up, and there, in the auditorium, shinning down on a rope from the ceiling, in person, was the very same *cascadeur* . . .'.

In 1907 Nonguet set a flotilla of nannies racing their prams across Paris rooftops (prefiguring the London–Brighton pram race in Michael Bentine's *It's A Square World!*). A charming little film starring Little Moritz had the very Mack Sennett idea of an entire house cascading into ruins under the energetic efforts of two irate men, one tugging away at the inside of a wall with his chest expanders while the other simultaneously hauls irately at a jammed bell-rope. The floors flap like so many trampolines, the walls stagger groggily and the chandeliers bob about like cutglass yoyos. From Italy came the equally inspired films of her Mad Mafia, André Deed (Foolshead in Britain), Tontalini, Polidor, Tweedledum and Bloomer.

Thus the Latin cinema broke through into the freedom of destructive absurdity, while American comedies were still 'cabin'd, cribb'd, confin'd' by the framework of the music-hall sketch. Mack Sennett studied the early French films, which were triumphantly cascading through American cinemas. Being a true genius, he not only acclimatized their style, he went on to intensify it. By 1912 he was beginning to establish the unholy trinity of American screen comedy: parody (of other films), ridicule (especially of noble virtues and lofty sentiments) and visual knockabout (which he lifted, by insistence and inventiveness, to the level of poetic fantasy).

Originally, the taste of crazy comedy was a speciality of uneducated, proletarian audiences. The French cinema abandoned it as its audiences became more respectable, and it continued its development in the U.S.A., with its vast city audiences of illiterate immigrants. As, in the 30's, American audiences in their turn became 'middle-class' (in aspiration and ideas, if not always in fact), crazy comedy, as we shall see, faded there too (or changed character), only to stage a comeback in the 60's, when affluence brought with it a more general feeling of being thoroughly at sea amongst all sorts of social, spiritual and sexual absurdities.

The mainspring of crazy comedy seems to be an awareness of quick, crazy tensions between man and man, man and society. Hence, perhaps, it has always been a shared taste between the proletariat and the intellectual. It seems to go with individualism, but with that individualism which feels lost in a crowd. So slapstick is soon identified with the land of immigrants, not only from all over the world, but those who poured from all the log cabins into the big cities.

Since 1914, French comedy has generally found its inspiration in the human touch, in interplay between people. The dominant mood of René Clair, long the nearest French artist to slapstick, is of a wistful loneliness. The slapstick element is a counterpart to this mood. But American slapstick traditionally drew its inspiration from the interplay of people with things and tasks. In France not only does Paris constitute a huge hothouse of emotional sophistication, but, via education, it profoundly influences a peasant and *bourgeois* nation. Instead of Paris, America had a rustic puritan past (with its simple-minded emphasis on industriousness and success), the rough and ready cultural melting-pots of the cities, and a middle-class ethos which was stiff with its conformist, rationalist, optimistic ideals. Thus American comedy continues to derive its poetry from coupling simple and violent human attitudes with a delirium of physical and mechanical knockabout.

Even within the actual sphere of physical action it's possible to point to a difference of emphasis between French and American physical humour. The French films were about chaos caused by people, Sennett's about people caught up in chaos. In the Little Moritz film, the house is pulled apart because people keep pulling. Though catastrophic rage isn't exactly unknown in Sennett still the name Sennett recalls speed gone mad, fandangos of disintegrating flivvers, spraying Keystone Kops to right and left as they swerve between converging streetcars, of jalopies stuck on level crossings as expresses charge nearer at supersonic velocity, of a crazy world, of a ballistic nightmare. An archetypal scene occurs in the Larry Semon comedy *Kid Speed*. A tired sheriff snores contentedly in bed (his badge pinned to his nightgown, naturally) until woken by the back-firing of Larry's 8-h.p. Snoozenburg being garaged next door. Larry promises to start her up quietly, but unfortunately starts her up in reverse. His car crashes through the wooden wall into the sheriff's bedroom, and hooks its back bumper over the sheriff's brass bedstead, which is soon being hauled along the public highway at 60 m.p.h. The rudely awoken sheriff leaps around on his bed waving his fists, only succeeding in getting tangled up and stumbling about in his sheets.

Much of Sennett's comedy is about the shock of speed, its insult to man. Again and again he turns the human body into a projectile, or into a package to be manhandled by physical laws—gravitational, ballistical, geometrical. Trees, cars, people alike are analysed down into objects whose fates become matters of weight, mass, trajectories, momentum, inertia, fulcrums and other impersonal qualities. Man's limbs become so many bars or levers, his body a cannonball. Even his skin becomes a flexible envelope, as when an over-zealous anaesthetist gives Ben Turpin so much gas that he swells up like the R101 and floats slowly around the room.

Sometimes slapstick makes domination of man by the machine even more marked. In an early Chaplin, *Dough and Dynamite* (1915) the human body is all but reduced to an apparatus for punching, kicking, ducking and dodging. It becomes a none-too-intelligent piece of protoplasm which has made a slap-happy adaptation to a civilization of crankshafts and flywheels. As Charlie's mate staggers under a sack of flour five times too large for him, and his legs begin to buckle, no one, not even the sufferer himself, thinks of so much as removing the sack from his shoulders, or helping him with his burden. They just push his legs back into the perpendicular, as if they were pit props. Often Charlie moves according to the most rigorous mechanical laws. If he wants to turn a corner at speed, he has to stick one leg out by way of counterbalance. If he wants to run away he has first to rev up by running on the spot. This, by contrasting with his desire for haste, gives us a curious impression that he's going backwards, like a car whose brakes are released. These things are based, of course, on physical experiences (the ballistic problems involved in running fast round corners), but the very stress on the physical problems of running has a materialistic tinge. We are not so far from the preoccupations of Muybridge and Marey. And the sharp, curt, pat, staccato movements of so many Sennett comics are vastly more machine-like than any form of comedy that had existed before.

Only a few years earlier the French philosopher Henri Bergson, in his famous essay on Laughter, had couched his view of comedy in the very terms which were to inspire Sennett. 'The attitudes, gestures and movements of the human body are laughable in exact proportions as that body reminds us of a machine . . . comedy arises from something mechanical encrusted on the living.' He was writing in 1900, before slapstick was so much as a gleam in Mack Sennett's eye, and said, 'On two occasions only have I been able to observe this style of the comic in its unadulterated state.' He found it in the most lowbrow medium of his day, the routine of two circus clowns. Clown wasn't then the respectable word it is now and Bergson describes their act with so sharp and friendly an eye that one can only hope he subsequently found his way to cinemas to enjoy his fellow-philosopher Mack Sennett's extraordinarily literal application of his theories.

Not that the mechanical is the only source of Sennett's humour. In the course of his thesis Bergson extended his notion of the 'mechanical' to include any maladjustment, any inept, inapt, or subadult response. Similarly the personages of *Dough and Dynamite*, amoeba-like, respond promptly to a prevailing stimulus—a beautiful waitress, a kick up the behind—but as abruptly recover from it after it has been removed, whereupon they await the next stimulus to prod them into action again. Affection and irritation spring up and die down, in split seconds, in a twinkling of the reflexes. There's certainly a reference to childhood impulsiveness, but the absurdity is so drastic as to go beyond that. It reduces man to the status of a mere package of

116

conditioned reflexes. Pavlov's dogs are masterminds compared to those nippy little knockabout monsters, dashing about the screen with the rapidity of jumping fleas. As Bergson said, 'We laugh every time a person gives us the impression of being a thing.' Such a formulation, like Sennett's humour, is inconceivable before the materialism of the nineteenth century. Isn't the depersonalizing humour of *Dough and Dynamite* a reflection of the mental climate that produced Pavlov and Behaviourism? The harsh, callous indifference of the slapstick world is softened only by our laughter.

The shift in stress, by Sennett, from the music-hall's older comedy of character to the comedy of mechanized man, parallels the invention, not many years before, of time-and-motion study, by Frederick W. Taylor. Daniel Bell's fascinating account of the birth of 'Taylorism', since become the keystone of modern industrial culture, leaves us with the pleasant reflection that this apostle of American super-efficiency was himself a raging obsessional neurotic, who, even when he went out for a walk, compulsively counted his steps, so as to ascertain the most effortless stride (he was also a lifelong martyr to nightmares and insomnia—irrational nature taking its revenge?). His first triumphant demonstration of his method was in 1899, and Henry Ford established his assembly line in 1914. Thus Sennett's films register not only the shock of speed but the spreading concept of man as an impersonal physical object existing only to work rapidly, rhythmically, repetitively. But Sennett parodies the conception, to concoct a universe where authority, routine and the monotony of factory days are shattered, as cars burst into bedrooms and beds race down the highway. Comedy, by exaggeration, veers towards revolt, an orgy of disorder, a Saturnalia of chaos.

Bergson applied the concept of the mechanical also to the influence of habit—beautifully parodied when Chaplin, in *Shoulder Arms*, gets into his waterlogged bunk with short sharp movements as if he were still on the parade ground. In *The Idle Class*, Charlie plays a dual role, as a tramp, and a rich playboy constantly befuddled by alcohol. Much of the humour depends on his bringing the reflexes of the tramp into the role of the aristocrat. This humour of misplaced habit, as distinct from humour of character, is not absent from earlier humour, but has a special emphasis in twentieth-century comedy, as if we moderns are more conscious than previous generations of a gap between what we feel, what we do, and what we seem, between our hearts and our acts.

Vast sectors of Sennett slapstick are, of course, not centred on the mechanical at all. Indeed Bergson's use of the word begins to show severe signs of strain when he tries to extend it to include, not only childlike behaviour, but even dreamlike atmospheres. For what could be less mechanical, more organic, than childish impulses or dreams?

The extraordinary richness of Sennett slapstick comes, perhaps, from the juxtaposition of these various 'mechanism' jokes, with jokes depending on such un-mechanical things as childlike impulse, infra-dig feelings, dream fantasy and visual poetry. The bakery in *Dough and Dynamite*, whose denizens are all constantly being stuck, bogged down, or trussed up, in tubs or swathes of dough, becomes a nightmarish netherworld. The generally infernal atmosphere is reinforced by the red-hot oven wall on to which the characters keep backing. What could more closely reproduce the common dream situations, of peril or embarrassment, than the sheriff in his nightshirt behind the Snoozenburg; a ghost, by daylight, at 60 m.p.h.? or Ben Turpin and his bride in *Wedding Yells* aboard an automobile which, deprived of all four wheels, keeps getting parked on level crossings while express trains suddenly materialize out of hitherto empty horizons? or, in *A Laugh A Day*, a man running away from his neighbours while the barrel which surrounds his modesty, explosively disintegrates, back and front?

And, always, slapstick comedians are childlike, and in consequence act out the impulses which as adults we suppress. Hal Roach put it, 'Actually the great comedians are representing or portraying children or the things that children do . . . Chaplin's . . . hitting himself in the back of the head with his cane and looking around to see who hit him is the action of a child.' And accordingly they are as indecent as children. When Ben Turpin hangs out of a window with his breeches hooked over a turned-on tap, until his trousers swell up to a huge size and finally spurt little jets of water from twenty or thirty holes, the overtones of wind and wee aren't too hard to see. The latter are confirmed by a similar scene. Charlie Chase is about to empty his waterlogged plus-fours in the street, until, scowled at by a passing cop, he hurries quickly away, as if he had been about to commit, if not a crime, at least a nuisance.

Silent slapstick could reduce to utter absurdity any human activity whatsoever, from politics to the very processes of consciousness. Snub Pollard plays El Presidente of a bomb-happy South American republic, where bombs with smoking fuses materialize from under cops' helmets, in socks and in street-urchins' footballs; one is even placed in its target's outstretched hand as he signals a left turn. For American audiences the real moral of this delirious burlesque of foreign politics is that all foreigners are absurd; but, even if, as satire it's smug rather than subversive, it becomes something rather more than satire, for its atmosphere is quite demential. James Agee has beautifully described the expressionism with which Sennett comedy presented its basically rather cruel vision of man's thought processes. 'When a modern comedian gets hit on the head, for example, the most he is apt to do is to look sleepy. When a silent comedian got hit on the head, he seldom let it go so flatly. So he gave us a . . . vision for loss of consciousness. In other words he gave us a poem, a kind of poem, moreover, that everybody understands. The least he might do was to straighten up stiff as a plank and roll over backward with such skill that his whole length seemed to slap the floor at the same instant. Or he might make a cadenza of it—look vague, smile like an angel, roll up his eyes, lace his fingers, thrust his hands palm downwards as far as they would go, hunch his shoulders, rise on tiptoe, prance ecstatically in narrowing circles until, with tallow knees, he sank down the vortex of dizziness on the floor, and there signified Nirvana by kicking his heels twice, like a swimming frog.' The angelic smile, the beatific trance, the frog's Nirvana, all due to a bonk on the cranium, exhibit a sweetly ruthless irony about the human soul. Chaplin's *The Champion* has a similar joke about individuality and le style, c'est l'homme. Each of the burly pugilist's sparring partners comes at him with an elaborately different style of boxing—and each gets knocked out in about two seconds flat by exactly the same, nonchalant, crude swing.

Although Sennett slapstick registers the shock of speed and mechanization it is by no means a protest against them. On the contrary, it accepts them as children accept them, as conditions of life, and it makes of them a source of festive disorder, a revenge which is a brief mental liberation from its oppressive aspects. It hoists the 'enemy'—the system—with its own petard. Yet the frequency of disaster in Sennett is, by a paradox common in comedy, an expression of zest, energy and ruthlessness of, in short, the American virtues which Sennett himself possessed super-abundantly. In a sense, their message is the opposite of that of the feeding-machine sequence in *Modern Times*. Not, of course, that Chaplin's and Sennett's attitudes are incompatible. Chaplin takes slapstick to the point of protest and tragedy, so as to remind us that the consequence of mechanization can be an outrage to the dignity of man. Sennett reminds us that, like his pin-men, we may be lucky, and survive this hectic world better than we sometimes fear. Even so, the fearsome bouncers, the punches, the kicks, the quick thefts and confidence tricks, the split-second utter lack of emotion, aren't as innocently childlike and stylized as the often only too sheltered critic may assume, and it's Chaplin who leaves us in no doubt that the usual inspiration behind slapstick is a stylization, not so much of childish innocence, as of the shifts needed to survive in a city jungle which, for immigrant and offspring, was an extremely chaotic and heartless one.

That mixture of confidence and callousness which enables Sennett to make his nightmares so outrageous and so funny, and which only an American could have taken so far, is beautifully summed up in the grand finale of MGM's *Hollywood Review of 1929*, where Buster Keaton, Marie Dressler, Bessie Love and the entire MGM roster of stars, all clad in yellow oilskins, cheerfully render 'Singin' in the Rain' while the rain pours down—before a backcloth, showing, on a mountainside, Noah's Ark. It's also neatly crystallized in the lyric Crosby and Sinatra sing at a party in *High Society*:

> *'Have you heard? It's in the stars,*
> *Next July we collide with Mars.'*
> *'Well, did you ever?'*
> *'What a swell party this is.'*

Only that spirit could dream up a scene where a series of cars roar into a one-track tunnel and a second later an express roars out.

Anyone can laugh at such a joke, but only an American like Sennett (or perhaps the odd Parisian) could have invented it, and hundreds of others like it. The art of slapstick lies in knowing (to hijack a phrase of Cocteau's) just how far to go too far. For however naïve slapstick seems, it isn't a naïve art-form (as innumerable British attempts at it only too lugubriously prove). Sennett repeatedly stressed the importance of some sort of possibility, of visual logic, in even the absurdest happenings. Lewis Jacobs records how Sennett had gags and scenarios explained to him verbally (never in writing), and, 'Often, during the telling of a story, Sennett, trailed by the writer, would go to the corner of the studio where his locales—lakes, rooms, fire escapes, etc.—were chalked out, and there work out the plan of the film. . . .' Clearly the mechanics of set-ups and things were more suggestive than those of character. Sennett himself said that he thought in terms of an idea rather than of individual personalities, 'Having found your hub idea, you build out the spokes; these are the natural developments which your imagination suggests. Then, introduce your complications that make up the funny wheel. . . .' He continued ruefully, 'We have tried famous humorists and I can say with feeling their stuff is about the worst we get.' One can't help feeling that this was not simply because of the screen's requirements, but also because of the newness and lowness of Sennett's humour, based as it was on a social stratum, on an experience of life, and a view of man, quite different from that of men-of-letters.

Not that his films are devoid of human interest. Even if his gags sprang from ideas and action rather than from character, Sennett knew the importance of gags not being out of character. His comedians passed gags on to one another, as more suitable for another's screen personality.

The best slapstick gags, however impossible, always have a kind of poetic rightness. Buster Keaton said, 'Nothing is worse than an ill-suited gag.' Larry Semon, thrown out of his car, which is leading the race, picks himself up and runs after it with such doggedness that he overtakes all the other cars and leaps into his driving-seat again. Larry defeats impossibility by running with all the 'I think I can, I tnink I can' earnestness of childhood. The impossible we do immediately: the inconceivable takes a little longer. Thus the 'gag' becomes a miracle deserved, indeed, compelled, by his sublimely dogged foolishness. Napoleon asked, before promoting an officer, 'Is he lucky?', and, similarly, Buster Keaton's aquiline gravity has the power to 'compel' luck, to turn it into fate. For poetry, even comic poetry, and superstition are profoundly connected, arising from the same springs of the imagination.

Speed isn't the only string to Sennett's bow. Much of the knockabout depends on a pigsty, barnyard, errand-boy, cabbage-patch, handyman frame of reference, vastly more meaningful when so many Americans had built their own homes, scratched a frugal living from dusty patches of soil.

With their variety of inspiration, Sennett's films have the richness to gain, rather than lose, from the sea-changes of time. To all their other charms, they now possess, not simply nostalgia, but a stranger kind of period charm. The tenderest absurdity now imbues Sennett's grotesque parodies of fashions and furnishings that no longer exist, parodies often far more delicious than the real thing. Particularly poignant, because of the slapstick context, is the grey, sober beauty of orthochrome and fixed-focus (in effect, almost deep-focus), which adds such an elegiac detail to the backgrounds of the action. There is that famous sequence of one tired old man pushing, not only his own stalled Model T, but a whole train of jalopies, forlornly up a gradient, not noticing they are dropping, one by one, over the edge of a precipice. The backgrounds of these comedies record a rustic America, of bleak shacks, of dusty hills, of flat horizons broken only by telegraph poles, of bare roads, of stores bulging with barrels and stoves. How poignant the contrast between this harsh, lonely world and the pranks and tricks performed by the human fleas—tricks sometimes less interesting than this vanished world, and setting it off with a soulless irony that's like a bitter elegy. . . .

The dreary slum frontages of *Easy Street* plunge us straight into the harrowing atmosphere of Arthur Morison's *A Child of the Jago*, and the very simplicity of the settings in *It's A Dog's Life* breathes a hopelessness no less terrible than the tragically bare workers' homes in the Tsarist Russia of Pudovkin's films.

Far from being a limitation, a sign of second-rate status, the (relative) absence of characterization in Sennett's films is of their essence. Depersonalization is part of their comic shock. In a sense, Sennett's humour is a preview of *Modern Times*. But it was his pupil, Chaplin, whose extraordinary eloquence restored a full humanity to slapstick and so made it simultaneously comic and tragic. You don't just laugh till you cry, you also laugh to keep from crying. And so, of course, your emotional defences collapse utterly. . . .

Chaplin wasn't, as is sometimes said, alone in bringing character into slapstick. But where lesser comedians had characters as simple and predictable as melodrama, Chaplin's reactions were a quickfire of nuances, shooting in a second from guttersnipery to romance, from fear to bravado, from brutality to pathos. His very walk gave the impression of being both mincing and bowlegged. His pantomimic skill must have owed something to the English music-hall (from the beginning his American colleagues admired his falling technique), as well as to the Frenchman, Max Linder, who, in turn, owed something to the Boulevard farces. The English music-hall comedians generally would seem ripe for revaluation; Bob Monkhouse, an authority on silent comedy, argues that there has been an unjustified neglect of Linder's foreign contemporaries. The French intelligentsia was quicker to appreciate such infra dig art forms as the music-hall, slapstick and Westerns than their English counterparts, who passed in silence over the equal or superior subtleties of, for example, Will and Fred Evans in *Harnessing A Horse*, 1912. Linder not only admitted to 'learning as much from Chaplin as he ever learned from me' but named Dan Leno and Bill Ritchie as 'the best masters of finesse to visit the Varieties'. Certainly the film sequences from the early 30's, of old troupers like Gus Elen singing 'It's A Great Big Shame' or of Lily Morris singing 'Don't Have Any More, Mrs. More' combine an immense verve with many subtly observed traits. It would be interesting also to explore the connections between the early screen comedies and the diverse music-hall styles in France, England and the U.S.A. After all, Bud Flanagan remarks in *My Crazy Life* that British music-hall artists had become heavily imitative of American as early as 1900, so one can't altogether rule out the possibility that much of what Sennett took from the Europeans was a development out of American ideas in the first place.

8 · Aimless Odysseus of the Alleyways

Chaplin may have derived a prop or two, and aspects of his character (the would-be dandy), from Linder, but psychologically his 'Little Man' is far richer and more complex (and, by 'realistic' standards, far more impossible). He is at once a tramp trying to be a dandy, and a child trying to be an adult. Despite his incessant failure, the delicacy and finickiness of his gestures are far more than a dandy's. They reveal a genuine, painful sensitivity, not at all unegoistic, that one can fairly call soul—a soul at the mercy of the cuffs, the cops, the bullies, all the gutter bestiary, and fate. It's an achievement to create such a character, but Chaplin not only created him, and in comedy, but contrived to gear in a tragic weight of nuance with the gross velocity of Sennettalia. Chaplin's short films are probably the only works of art ever created which can spin the spectator from laughter to tears and back in a *few seconds*. One wonders whether, if it weren't for the Mack Sennett forcing-house, Chaplin would ever have risen to the height he did—and have virtually re-created the art of mime.

While Sennett's slapstick is an art of objects, props, places and people-made-objects, Chaplin crosses it with that pantomimic virtuosity that delights in dispensing with objects altogether—as in his miming of David and Goliath in *The Pilgrim*. A fascinating example of cross-breeding props, mime and puppet-show is offered by the Dance of the Rolls in *The Gold Rush*. Two forks, stuck into rolls, parody legs executing ballet-steps. Sometimes they read as the left and right leg of one person, but sometimes they suggest two people. But if forks are legs and rolls are feet, then what huge feet the dancer has (recalling the huge boots Little Tich wore in the halls before the turn of the century). Moreover, the Little Man, seated at the table, also mimes the dancing with his face, head and shoulders—so that we

124

have a huge head, no body, tiny legs and huge feet, a grotesque caricature made out of both 'puppets' and puppeteer.

Here, as so often, a good joke includes all kinds of sub-jokes, that the conscious mind doesn't notice, but that the laughing mind does. . . .

Chaplin stands at a confluence of traditions. His pathos, and richness as a character, has its roots in nineteenth-century emotionalism whereas the cool callousness of Mack Sennett is more twentieth century. His sensitivity and his quixotism are as poignant as they are only because blended with scurrility, cynicism and all the comic vices.

Indeed, his films, the early ones in particular, abound in satire directed, bitterly, at pity and pathos. In *The Pawnshop* Charlie shamelessly exploits his boss's streak of tender-heartedness. He in turn is fooled by a ham actor whose sobs and groans make Charlie put an outrageously generous valuation on a ring—for which the customer then gives change from a vast bankroll.

Finally, when a lank, scrawny, mental defective brings in an alarm clock Charlie (once bitten, twice shy) examines it so thoroughly that he destroys it, and hands its debris back with a curt shake of the head, emphasizing the point by picking up a hammer and hitting his (completely inoffensive) victim smack between the eyes. If these early films had themes, that of *The Pawnshop* might be defined as *Beware of Pity* or, more scathingly, *Never Give A Sucker An Even Break*.

Raymond Borde points out that in certain scenes in *The Property Man* Charlie exhibits a cruelty rivalling anything in Bunuel. 'Charlie has to carry a very heavy trunk and doesn't fancy the task, so he approaches a colleague, a pitiful old man with an utterly humiliated expression. He loads the trunk on to the back of this human wreck. The man staggers forward, leaning on his cane. Charlie beats him like a mule, and the other collapses altogether, to lie, crushed under his burden, on the ground. To get him going again Charlie leaps up on the trunk, thus adding to the burden of the old man, who now resembles nothing so much as a pathetic beetle pinned to the ground by some sick wit. And *The Property Man* is no exception. In his short films, from 1914 to 1922, Charlie's sadism is incessant. . . .' And, one might add, no less serious, here, and in these terms, than thirty years later, in the verbal terms of *Monsieur Verdoux*.

Maybe this sadism is, by implication, excused by his pathos, but it's also true that Charlie's pathos enables him to be easily the cruellest of Sennett's comedians, with the potential exception of Fatty Arbuckle, whose face is rather more heartless than his actual acts.

So heavily has the stress been laid on Chaplin as a waif, as a sentimental clown, as Don Quixote, and so on, that criticism has all but lost sight of the complementary pole of his inspiration, a disconcerting matter-of-factness about basic, physical things. In *It's A Dog's Life* he hungrily tussles with a dog for a bone (if this isn't sick humour it's hard to see what is). In *The Vagabond* he not only washes the little waif's face, he searches in her hair for fleas, and he finds them. Chaplin remembers those vermin in *Limelight*, where Calvero has two performing fleas, called Phyllis and Henry.

Such humour may be charmingly 'picturesque' nowadays, but it must have had a much more realistic edge for the slum-and-immigrant audiences of the time—as we may have been reminded by the excellent Granada TV documentary, a montage of contemporary photographs evolving the extreme harshness of life for immigrants in the New York of the time, and their exceptionally high death rate, testifying to the traumatic shocks inflicted by the realities of New York's tenements and sweatshops.

Similarly, we tend to remember most of all the 'romantic' love-theme of *The Gold Rush*. But most of the film is concerned with more basic, physical problems of survival—food, warmth and feet. Whether by accident or design, feet acquire a Surrealist enormity. They blend with the theme of food when Charlie cooks and eats a shoe, and with that of warmth when, while he is entertaining Georgia, the rags wrapped round his foot go up in flames, giving him a hot foot and Georgia a (literal) hot seat (Charlie is never too busy for a scurrilous reference. Brushing himself down after being rolled in the dust in *Mable At the Wheel*, he pays particular attention to the seat of his pants, just as in *Limelight* he puns, 'What can the stars do but sit on their axes?').

Although Charlie appears as a gold-seeker, he, essentially, just wanders around the frozen North foraging as aimlessly as along the gutters and doorways of the slum alleys. The prevailing impression left by *The Gold Rush*, far from being, as, in view of Charlie's left-wing sympathies, one might expect, an indictment of gold-fever, greed and capitalism generally, is of tiny figures rushing about in empty spaces. The film's narrative may be about survival, but its visuals are about loneliness. This mood goes with innumerable trance-like situations: dreams (alone, Charlie dreams Georgia is applauding his Dance of the Rolls), hallucinations (starving Big Jim dreams Charlie is a giant chicken), amnesia (Big Jim has found a mountain of gold but can't remember where it is), and confusions of identity (millionaire Charlie dresses as a tramp for the news photographers and so not only meets Georgia again but can be sure her love isn't just a gold-digger's). Although the use of the 'double personality' isn't rare in Chaplin (in *City Lights* and *The Great Dictator*), *The Gold Rush* becomes a special meditation on loneliness, on who-am-I?, on am-I-real? The indefiniteness is enhanced by the featureless white wastes, by a scene where a hut is filled with slowly falling white feathers, and by another showing it being blown miles across country by a high wind, to end perched on the edge of a precipice, balanced on a knife-edge, like a seesaw, such that the slightest movement sets it swaying and tilting into the void.

There isn't a feeling that 'Nature' is the enemy. Nature, here, seems only part of a bad dream from which the characters are all trying to awake. More perhaps by a sure intuition of Chaplin's than by conscious design, *The Gold Rush*, with its loneliness, its confusions of personality, its universal indefiniteness, recalls the feelings of alienations in Kafka (albeit *vis-à-vis* an American chaos instead of a European bureaucracy).

It's interesting too that the *City Lights* idea of a rich man who's only amiable to a poor man when he's drunk was taken up later by the magpie Brecht for *Mister Puntilla and his Valet Matti*. Chaplin links the alienation theme to the greed theme very loosely, as loosely as Antonioni relates Monica Vitti's lonely-city-blues to his Marxist critique of the capitalist system and its gradual chilling of the soul.

It's interesting how often crazy comedy, in its general mood, precedes 'highbrow' message films, presumably because, offering irresponsible exaggerations, it has a fair chance of anticipating the eventual development of current trends.[1]

Modern Times is more 'topical' in its time. Again, one might expect it to be a message film, about the need for workers' solidarity, but it's nothing of the sort. Charlie gets arrested for waving a red flag at the head of a militant mob, but he was only trying to attract the attention of the lorry-driver who'd dropped it. The mob fell in behind him entirely of its own accord.

The film's spirit is thoroughly anarchistic. Its theme of unemployment is subordinate to that of deliberately contracting-out of society. Certainly there is the subsistence theme (food), but here it's not in short supply. On the contrary it's there in abundance for those who

[1] Those exaggerations which are non-prophetic come to detract from the comic's appeal, or have a nostalgic effect, or aren't noticed.

will accept the grotesque postures forced on them by the machines. Charlie is put in a feeding-machine. His mate gets trapped in another machine during lunch-break, and has to be fed by Charlie. Charlie later becomes a singing waiter who, caught up in a mass of dancing couples, can't get his food over to his impatient customer.

The theme of home is more agonized, expressing security and independence rather than survival. Charlie and Paulette camp in the luxury 'rooms' of a department store, then make do in a rickety old shack (which he dreams is a country cottage), and finally do without a home altogether. But this time there are two of them to walk off down those long, silent-film roads, towards hills, as bleakly grey as coketips, but lightened by a few shafts of sunlight. Even on the road, two people are—home.

In *Modern Times* the Little Man's berserk revolt is against being spoon-fed or mechanical shovel-fed. It is as anarchistic as Harpo Marx's and indeed, resembles it. Just as Harpo would have done, Charlie spreads disorder among his workmates, and he menaces a passing woman with a disquietingly sadistic eroticism (brandishing his spanner like Jack the Ripper's knife and threatening to twist the buttons off her clothes). Even when society sends, not cops to arrest him, but ambulance men to care for him, he, and we, revolt against them, just as the Marxes revolt against kindly Margaret Dumont, because, through our comic heroes, we sense the smothering quality of such 'niceness'.

Some critics of the time reproached Chaplin for seeming to blame the machines rather than the system that misused them. But by doing so, Chaplin attacked the enslavement of man to dogmas of productivity, whether under a profit system or a Stakhanovite one. *Modern Times* is now more modern than ever, for it anticipates that anarchistic faith in the couple, that semi-militant beatnickery, that is increasingly prominent, not only among the Anglo-Saxon young, but also among the youth of Communist countries. *Modern Times* is a layabout's manifesto. . . .

To over-idealize Chaplin into an inoffensive Little Man, all pathos and lovable mischief, a sort of Saint Chaplin, is not only to miss half of his humour and meaning, it is to make nonsense of all that really can be called Chaplin's comedy of the misplaced soul. To be misplaced, it has to be perched in someone who's incongruous and unworthy, who's infra dig, who has a guttersnipe's reflexes and lack of scruple. The mainspring of Chaplin's genius is, in a sense, the spiritual vividness which he gives to the basic, undignified physical things, fleas, feet, sausages. His one semi-failure, *A King in New York*, is also the one film that cut loose from these basics and lost itself in generalizations *about* society. Deep thinkers are two a penny nowadays; but guttersnipes like Charlie are worth their weight in gold.

Although Chaplin's psychological complexity is unrivalled among the 'Sennett school', many other comedians had a real, vivid presence. Marvellous indeed is that startling squint of Ben Turpin's and the dervish fanaticism with which it imbues its possessor. His eyes seem permanently rolled in paroxysmatic emotion, while their violent dislocation endows him a kind of utter helplessness. Hence Turpin was the ideal parodist of high-flown romantic characters, like Valentino and Von Stroheim. Every squint has its own soul, and Ben Turpin's was completely different from James Finlayson's. While Turpin's was both wild and endearing, Finlayson's was as mean and dour as a Scottish dominie's. Fatty Arbuckle was that rarity, a fat man who was neither pathetic nor a bully, but, among all the usual slapstick stupidities, alert, aware and cool.

9 · Self-Help with a Smile

Where Buster Keaton and Harold Lloyd were 'doers', Harry Langdon and Laurel and Hardy were the helpless ones (not that these are hard-and-fast categories, of course : comedy is based on contradiction as much as on consistency). The most cherubic and passive were Harry Langdon and Stan Laurel. Oliver Hardy was a 'tackler', or at least a bungler, so incompetent that he's an honorary member of the helpless club. But Keaton and Lloyd often came off best in their bouts with chaos, and much of Keaton's humour, particularly, is about the neatness of his gambits *vis-à-vis* the impersonal objects amongst which he gambolled. His humour depends on the combination of extreme bungling and extreme skill. His famous 'impassivity' is truer in the spirit rather than the letter. For his craggy, doleful face does change expression, his staring eyes are as eloquent as Eddie Cantor's, and his body is flexible and eloquent—indeed in moments of panic his limbs shoot out all over him like porcupine's quills. In his quiet style, he can be surprisingly versatile—*Sherlock Junior* has a beautiful shot of Keaton, as a suave detective, pressing an electric bell with a fastidious delicacy worthy of Dorian Gray fingering rose-petals.

Keaton said, 'I just concentrated on what I was doing.' This seriousness is a very different thing from the deadpan, and only apparently akin to a clown's mask. Rather Keaton's 'Old Stone Face' seems to blend the traits of America's original inhabitants—the silent solemnity of the Red Indian brave, the gloomy persistence of the Calvinist pioneer. Bleak and woebegone, his countenance holds at once a dour hopelessness and an undaunted never-say-die. He has a kind of childlike promptitude in performing his duty, and brings an almost ecclesiastical solemnity to the outwitting of machinery, to, as it were, redeeming it from its fits of Original Sin. His solemn face conceals the whirring gyroscope of inner-direction.[1] Buster brings a zany genius at lateral thinking to such obsessional tasks as chasing runaway locomotives, becoming a trapezist (in *Blue Blazes*) or trying to sign on for the Confederate Army. Of all the American comedians, he has the most one-track mind. Many of his mistakes spring from it, e.g. he keeps shovelling sand under the locomotive's skidding wheels even after it's moved off. He's as rural-American as the Model T, and has the calmly glum seriousness of the Abe Lincoln generation. He has a log-cabin loneliness and persistence. Yet in his general air of being *too busy* to feel emotion, he oddly anticipates the matter-of-fact dedication of Howard Hawks—which also seems to be modern, cool, derivative from American pioneer puritanism.

Keaton, in action, brings to knockabout both a balletic grace (he is the Fred Astaire of slapstick) and a Euclidean wit. He's a geometrician —in his own words, 'After all, to be able to scratch your ear with one of your toes requires a good dose of discipline, and all discipline boils down to mental discipline. . . .' All his epic battles between man and machine—whether a balloon (*The Balloonatic*), a deserted ship (*The Navigator*) or a locomotive or two (*The General*)—seem built around an *idée fixe*. It's not that they work their way through every comic corollary of a given proposition, for as Montaigne remarked, 'L'art de bien écrire est de sauter les idées intermédiaires.' But only Harold Lloyd, matched with skyscrapers, could find as many 'gag-gambits' in a given object. *The Navigator* has been called a '*Robinson Crusoe* in reverse', and it's also the story of Jonah in a mechanical whale.

Keaton virtually directed most of his own films; all have an ascetic, yet dashing, beauty. Perhaps *The General* is the most beautiful, with its spare, grey photography, its eye for the racy, lungeing lines of the great locomotives, with their prow-like cowcatchers, and with its beautifully sustained movement (notably Keaton, astraddle his locomotive tender, chopping away frantically, obliviously, as his locomotive steams through the battlefield, past a contrapuntal pattern of drifting smoke, retreating Confederates, and advancing Federals). In spirit it's not unlike a John Huston film—the young civilian earning his 'red badge of courage'—and it's amusing to imagine what Keaton would have done with the situations of *The African Queen*.

---

[1] Inner-direction is the name which David Reisman in *The Lonely Crowd* gives to that old-fashioned conscientiousness which asks no reward but that of doing what conscience bids. He contrasts the contemporary trend to other-direction, a concern with popularity and conformity to the consensus.

Perhaps his strangest film is *Sherlock Junior*, where he plays a cinema projectionist who scrambles into the film, so getting caught up in (to borrow Jeff Keen's phrase) the movies' space-time warp. He tries to step into the film drawing-room and the door is slammed in his face. As he leans on a pot in the peach-spangled garden, cut, he falls into the middle of a desert. Just as he's picked himself up and is beginning to adapt to that, cut, he's marooned on a spray-soaked black rock. He dives bravely into the angry ocean, only to end stuck head-down in a snowdrift, out of which his black legs kick forlornly. Keaton's aquiline solemnity gives such *Hellzapoppin'*-type gags a quite different atmosphere, more reminiscent, perhaps, of the *Ficciones* of Borges.

His face, as mysterious as the statues of Easter Island, hints at his inner realms of dream, and of the emotional reserve suggested by his name in France, Frigo. Bernard Stora comments that, 'His procedure consists in protecting, at all costs, that portion of reality which immediately surrounds him. . . . In this perspective, the sequence of *The Navigator* concerning his subaquatic expedition reveals its full meaning. The liner's propeller being damaged, the young girl who accompanies him on this weird voyage persuades him to don a diving-suit and examine the damage. Having arrived on the ocean-bed, he immediately tries to control this new element by strictly applying the laws which rule that which he has managed to control. He meticulously puts out a sign, "Danger—Men At Work" and carefully washes his hands in a pail of water—which he then empties—under the sea.' The hero has freed himself from his rich youth's maladjustment (no practical sense), only to adopt another maladjustment (a plumber's habits, underwater). Stora sees in Keaton's constant 'trying to reduce life to a structure of habits' a stiltedness of the heart, springing from the same root as his awkward reserve with women. For the virtuoso with machines is a gawk with girls (indeed with people generally). In *Sherlock Junior* he finally treats the screen love scene as an instructional, imitating it move by move, baffled only when it cuts from a passionate kiss directly to the arrival of twins. At the end of *The General* he has to turn his right arm into a saluting-machine so as to kiss his girl undisturbed. But it's also as if part of him is trying to sneak off and become as robotized as the machines which obsess him. Keaton's achievement is to move into this territory, as strange as science-fiction, yet never for a second lose his startling intensity of feeling. Against all these spaces and processes, he acquires all the desperate simplicity of an everyman; as poignant in affirmation, more genial in invention, he becomes as basic an archetype as Beckett's tramps. The New York avant-gardist Alan Scheider built his version of Beckett's *Film* round Keaton's silent eloquent back, and, as Robert Benayoun remarks, 'I don't know if Beckett thought of Keaton in writing this *Film*, but it's unthinkable that any other actor could have played this role, so adapted is it to his physique, his legend, his essential themes.' But perhaps Keaton's real swansong is *The Railrodder* where he traverses Canada on a diesel runabout, as pure, as worried, a totem at seventy as forty years before. This extraordinary sense of time passed, yet revived, of experience marked in this man's face, is, of course, laceratingly part of the film itself, for, by recording personality as it does, the movie medium possesses an aesthetic dimension with which theories relevant to literature, music and painting, are ill-equipped to deal. Cold as he may seem, Keaton's presence is strangely barbed with a quality of stoic elegy, and surely he's not so much the second genius of silent slapstick as the poker-faced compliment to the quicksilver Chaplin.

If Keaton, with his lean, knobbly, mule-face, always has something of the log-cabin loner about him, Harold Lloyd is slapstick's small-town Samuel Smiles. Lloyd played many different characters, from chefs to professors. He might be basically shy and he might be brash; but all his characters have the bounce and pluck of the self-help generation. 'Step right up and call me Speedy' he brags, to cover his shyness. He's a small-town Pollyanna shaping up to all the hectic opportunities of the roaring 20's, and is almost a comic variation of Douglas Fairbanks, who, at the same period, owed his popularity, not to the expensive swashbucklers with which he's now associated, but to his eupeptic playing of unstoppable guys next door. If Keaton is fired by duty rather than ambition, Lloyd is the eager-beaver with pasteurized hopes.

Lacking any hint of introverted depths, he offers less fertile ground for criticism, which has, perhaps, underestimated the resonance of his complete identification with the aspirations of his time. *A Lifetime of Comedy* offers snippets from a fascinating film in which Harold applies time-and-motion-study tricks to his morning journey to work. Darting back into the house for something he's forgotten, he leaves his car circling the lawn; running into a flock of sheep, he leaves the car creeping forward while he scrambles out over the bonnet to shoo them out of the way.

Occasionally a sense of strain becomes predominant, as in *Safety*

Last. Harold, whose trip to the big city has ended in failure, wants to impress his girl with his success. He sets out to win part of a 1,000-dollar prize for climbing a skyscraper. He plans to climb the first few storeys after which his more agile pal will take over, and they will split the reward. But a baleful cop and other bystanders force Harold to complete the climb alone. True, he's thus entitled to 1,000 dollars instead of only 500 dollars. But he only wants 500 dollars and with every floor his chances of death increase. It's a good symbol for the rat-race: you have to risk everything for big success, you can't settle for a modest reward and safety.[1]

Like Buster Keaton, Harold Lloyd made movies almost through to World War II, and he briefly emerged from a prosperous retirement when Preston Sturges concocted a characteristically disenchanted comedy about hearty hopeful Harold, twenty years on. *Mad Wednesday* is almost a slapstick equivalent of *Death of a Salesman*. Its first reel is the last reel of *The Freshman*, one of Harold's silent hits, and shows milksop Harold winning the match for his college. He is offered an executive position by an excited businessman who, by the next morning, has sobered down, and tells him, 'I'm going to give you a chance to succeed in the good old American way—right from the bottom. I was unfortunate, my father left me the business, ah well. . . .'

Twenty years on finds Harold, despite all the optimistic mottoes and slogans on his walls, still a lowly clerk, who has loved, and lost, each of seven beautiful daughters in turn. His boss, in yet another two-faced speech, 'retires' him. Realizing that all the homely small-town virtues have betrayed him, he goes 'mad', and does everything condemned by the small-town spirit (whence the film's American title, *The Sins of Harold Dibbledock*). He falls in with some city slickers, he blows his savings, he drinks hard liquor, he bets on horses, he buys loud check suits, he bullies bankers by storming into their offices with a lion on a chain, and at last becomes a success. The inner-directed ethos of diligent, self-help is ousted by a more cynical outgoing parade of irresponsibility, trickery and bluff. The release delays often associated with Howard Hughes productions, Sturges's not always successful blending of Runyonese and slapstick (e.g. too many quick-cut changes of angle spoil the flow of physical action), and a slackening of spiritual tension in the second half, took the edge off a nonetheless fascinating film.

[1] It's interesting that his cheating isn't felt by us to disqualify him for the reward.

10 · I was a Middle-Aged Water-Baby

Of the dreamers, Harry Langdon is the arch-apostle, with his wryly delicate mouth, his apple cheeks and moomin eyes. Bursting out of his suit like an overgrown baby, this sleeping prince is as virginal as Lillian Gish. By contrast Stan Laurel is a city slicker. And whereas Buster, especially in his moments of scarecrow limbed panic and jejune gawk, has something of the wizened timidity of a child that has experienced hurt, Langdon's childishness has a tremulousless, as if he'd always been too afraid to be hurt. Perhaps his complement is Fatty Arbuckle, the hard, energetic, cynical fat boy. To Buster's and Fatty's songs of experience, Harry pipes up his songs of innocence, 'I am not yet born, Oh hear me . . .'.

Whether in the guise of a small-town adolescent, a *City Lights*-type tramp or the only American sentry who doesn't know World War I ended a week ago, he seems, by some dogged self-abstraction, to have retained an embryo's immunity from the outside world. That strange blink of his eyes, the shy, quick dawn of a smile, imbues all he sees with the insubstantiality of a dream. And dream he constantly does. He takes too many pills in *Tramp Tramp Tramp* and thinks he's dreaming his way through a cyclone which devastates a town; he dreams he is still in his seat as everyone else leaves the theatre in *All Night Long*; in *Three's a Crowd* he tries so hard to watch over his sweetheart and her baby that he falls asleep, and while dreaming that he's putting his rascally rival to sleep with a monster punch, he sleeps through the gentle, prodigal father's return. But the swathes of dreaming sleep through which he has to perceive the world are only a special form of conscious bewilderments, which, progressively, become not only absurd, but tragic, and archetypal, man's inalienable

135

alienation from reality. Our consciousness is a dream from which we don't know enough to awake.

The theme of innocence versus experience, of dream versus disillusion (and of its social metaphor, small-time niceness versus urban corruption) had long been a central motif of American literature, and Harry's mere presence intensifies it into paroxysm. It's paroxysmatic because it's complicated by his curious sense, pervasive, but unstated, of the perversities at the core of innocence. His invisible innocence wouldn't be even faintly tragic were he merely a cherub in man's clothing, a Little Lord Fauntleroy who'd flown off with Peter Pan to Never-never-Land. But there's no real absence of evil intent in Baby Face Langdon. The small-town Master Bovary in *Long Pants* is longing to slough off his innocence, to which end he locks himself in his parents' attic and reads Byron's *Don Juan*. Dazzled by the city vamp, it is with blissful serenity that he plans the murder of his sweet fiancée, and lures the unsuspecting girl out into the woods. There she closes her eyes and puckers her rosebud lips for a kiss, while he gets the pistol stuck in his pocket, loses it in the autumn leaves, can't aim because his hand's shaking, gets his hat jammed down over his eyes, falls into a barbed-wire fence, and catches his ankle in a man trap, from which he has to be rescued by his intended victim. Of course the comic, typically, acts out the impulses which only cross our minds, and of course accident, i.e. fate, plays, as in this scene, the role of our moral repressions. But of all American innocence, funny or serious, in any art form, only Langdon comes so near an adult's recreation of that *absolute state* of baby greed, baby gloating and baby blandness in selfishness. The Surrealists are quite right to claim him for their own, for there's never any real reason why he shouldn't, if it suited him, perpetrate the archetypal Surrealist act: taking a revolver and firing at random into the street. There's something so irresponsible it's almost evil when, dressed as a (monstrously tiny-headed) baby at the end of *Tramp Tramp Tramp*, he shakes himself until the giant cradle in which he's lying loops the loop. At those moments when he is a half child, if half adult, in an adult situation, his surprised, passive eyes set up complex reverberations of erotic hysteria. When, in *Long Pants*, the city vamp crawls maternally, treacherously, over him, not unlike Marilyn over Tony Curtis in *Some Like it Hot*, he is stunned into a wide-eyed immobility which simultaneously suggests (*a*) a total intellectual blankness as to any possible reason for such puzzling behaviour, (*b*) an arrested development whose other name is impotence, (c) a delicious paralysis, as at dawning awareness of ecstasy, and (d) the uneasy suspicion that a treat so sudden must have an ulterior motive, and be as dangerous as it's nice.

The world confronting Langdon's dreaming, milk-white countenance is often his accomplice in poetry. Seen from a bird's-eye view the small-town hero cycles slowly round the automobile in which the vamp sits. She looks straight ahead of her; he performs his small-boy cycling tricks. *Three's A Crowd*, perhaps less moving than *City Lights*, has no less magic. Its sense of a slum district is chokingly bleak and the long-flighted staircase leading up to Harry's drearily sagging and lurching cabin is worthy of *The Salvation Hunters*. In *Tramp Tramp Tramp*, a short-cut takes him up to a fence marked 'Private. Keep Out'. Briskly scaling it, he turns around prior to descending the other side, without even noticing that when he drops to earth he'll plummet straight down a 500-foot precipice. The man who put such a notice on such a fence had a demoniacally pedantic sense of private property, and an extraordinary viciousness infiltrates what is in any case a virtuoso passage of gag logic.

In *The Chaser*, which Langdon directed, some elaborate tracking shots, of rare formal beauty, astonishingly anticipate Renoir's in *Boudu Sauvé des eaux*. Keaton's sense of railroad rhythms is paralleled by Langdon's flair for slow, wavering movements, with their hallucinatory poetry. His period of stardom was cut short by sound, though he continued a prosperous career concocting gags for Laurel and Hardy and many others. In a sense, his intelligence had a wider range than his screen *persona*; if his stories are less moving than Chaplin's, it is because his screen self couldn't always provide a holding, a linking, centre for his pathos and his gags. There seem, now, odd jumps, gaps, lacunae, rather than smooth transitions, between his other-worldly aspects and his this-worldly entanglements, between his pathos and his immunity, between his lunar, his adolescent and his adult responses. He lingered just a little too rigidly, perhaps, within his baby register. Stan Laurel occasionally capsizes into his crying act but most of the time he thinks like a man, or like a boy.

Yet Langdon, like Chaplin, like Keaton, like Stan and Ollie as a pair, bears the stamp of comic genius. His gestures, vague, yet clipped, brightly hopeful yet squidgily inept, sketch, vividly, a baby attitude untranslatable into any adult code, a strange condition of being pampered and lost, expectant and malicious. In pace, he anticipates

W. C. Fields (whose mind, more disgusted with reality, plunged right out of this world, to appoint its owner dictator of Klopstockia, or to hurl him headlong from an airliner washroom on to the ivory tower of Mrs. Haemoglobin). Harry Langdon gropes, from some virginal limbo, over the threshold of our mad, half real world, opening up weird spaces and emptiness all around himself, and within us. If Langdon was in some ways Stan Laurel's *alter ego* (he once replaced him as Ollie's mate) he also anticipates Jerry Lewis, even though his hysterias are silent and slow motion. In *Tramp Tramp Tramp*, he carries placards of the star (Joan Crawford) whom he adores, anticipating the Anita Ekberg-crazy Jerry in *Hollywood or Bust*, as surely as Harold Lloyd's Freshman ages into Harold Dibbledock.

Langdon's slow *tempi* remind us that slapstick and speed are not at all synonymous. If Sennett's *accelerandi* tend to fantasy, many silent comedies dwelt on bucket-and-ladder jobs whose homeliness was intensified by Sennett's great rival impresario Hal Roach. While Sennett piles one fandango situation on to situation, a Hal Roach two-reeler puts its characters in one simple plight and watches them, methodically, not get out of it. While Sennett's characters are well on the way to being pin-men, the slower Roach pace goes with a genial relish over reactions and character. Thus Sennett's semi-abstract Keystone Kops contrast with Roach's individualized Our Gang. If the 20's are Max Sennett's years, the talkie brings the Hal Roach idiom to full bloom. Though so many Laurel and Hardy films were made during the 30's, they had found their style by the coming of sound. Indeed, their talkies have a quality as of silence into which dialogue of sub-title simplicity is interjected.

11 · Beau Chumps and Church Bells

Mr. Laurel and Mr. Hardy are the simplest, the homeliest and the great, exponents of the Hal Roach style. Not that their career isn't diversified by such flights of fantasy as *Swiss Miss* and *Flying Elephants*. But even their absurdest moments are firmly anchored to our heroes' actions and reactions, which are essentially plodding and homely.

And never more so than in psychological paradox. How absurd yet how strangely persuasive are those 'tit for tat' sequences, where Stan, Ollie and an antagonist or two, often James Finlayson, each take it in turns, and irately allow the other, to rip off his clothes, tear his jalopy to pieces or ruin his shop or his home. Each lets the other do his worst before retaliating—perhaps in obedience to some strange relic from the Code of the West; perhaps deliberately stoking up his own indignation and therefore strength; perhaps out of bravado; perhaps out of obedience to some streak of masochism which, if Laurel and Hardy films are any guide, must be more compulsive in human nature than unaided common sense would have us believe. The ungentle art of self-destructive escalation was worked out by Stan and Ollie long before Herman Kahn applied its logic to nuclear war.

Laurel and Hardy must number among screendom's greatest gluttons for punishment (even including the soap-opera queens). Stan suffers because he's timid and inoffensive, Ollie suffers because he's pompous and rude. Stan is the 'child', Ollie is the 'parent'. But Stan's meek awkwardness is regularly more destructive than Ollie's irate bungling. It's possible that, if children predominantly identify with Stan and think Ollie rather fierce, parents identify predominantly with Ollie, surprisingly patient victim of Stan's childlike 'helping'. Not of course that Mr. Laurel is without any means of defence. He

can, on occasion, when pressed too far, or when the wind is blowing
from the right direction, be both adamant and violent. When, in
You're Darn Tootin', Mr. Hardy keeps punching Mr. Laurel in the
stomach, Mr. Laurel retaliates by kicking Mr. Hardy on the ankle
rather hard, so that our two friends come to perform between them a
species of stooping-and-hopping ritual, further diversified as tensions
mounted, by trouser-ripping. This spreads compulsively, from one
passer-by to another, like an Artaudian plague, until the whole street
is thronged with ducking, hopping and ragged-trousered misanthro-
pists. Their natural level is proletarian, and even their mayors have
the minds of bottle-washers.

A kind of quiet fruitiness, bringing music-hall 'presence' back into
screen comedy, makes Laurel and Hardy perhaps the supreme screen
practitioners of the *temps-mort*.[1] One of the funniest moments in
County Hospital (a gem of sick humour) has Stan, simply, swallowing
a hard-boiled egg. The duo loved to combine such inanities of detail
with dramatic ironies. Thus, in *Brats*, we know that Stan and Ollie
(filmed child-size) have left the tap on after being given their bedtime
bath by Stan and Ollie (filmed parent-size). Ollie, overflowing with
sentimental fondness (irony 1) sings the dear children a lullaby, 'Go
to sleep, my ba-ha-by'. Ba-ha-by asks, 'Can I have a drink of water?'
(irony 2). Stan, helpful as ever, says, 'I'll go,' (irony 3), to which Ollie
replies sternly, 'No, I'll go, you'd only spill it' (irony 3). None of these
ironies on 'flood' would be half so funny if Mr. Hardy didn't speak
weightily, and complacently, and pause. Not that their slowness is a
mere device for milking three audience laughs out of the gag. It is
psychologically right, it establishes the obliviousness of their innocence, pompous in one case, meek in the other, and dim in both. It
inflates every moment of time to the strange distensions of childhood's subjective clock. Typically, the most catastrophic events (like
Stan reducing Ollie's house to a smoking ruin in *Helpmates*) ascend
from the little slips and forgetfulnesses to which children are especially
prone.

The inexorability of disaster has a poetic quality of its own. *The
Music Box* takes a simple labouring job (two men carry a piano up a
long flight of stairs), and makes it a perfect little epic of monotonous
futility, ornamented with odd little lyrical moments (as when the
manhandled music box seems to mutter to itself, melodiously, sul-

[1] *Temps-mort* is a *nouvelle vague* term for moments when nothing at all is
happening, story-wise, and nothing much emotion-wise.

lenly, or when, having fallen from a balcony, it sways gently in the shallow waters of a little pond). It's the myth of Sisyphus in comic terms, a little hymn to the uselessness of work, a study in absurdity that one has not the slightest hesitation in ranging alongside the few best examples of the theatre of the absurd.

So strong is this aspect that certain images, from Laurel and Hardy films, qualify as visionary crystallizations of the human condition. Thus the plight of art is summed up by the scene where Laurel and Hardy, as street musicians, patiently render 'In the Good Old Summertime', while the snow falls, and falls, and falls. On human respectability: as a jealous husband fires a shot at our (innocent) duo, a jump cut shows every window in the street fly open while a horde of nightshirted lovers leap into the street below (*We Fall Down*). All the inadequacies of human friendship are summed up by the muffled anguish of Ollie's cry in *County Hospital* at the delicacies thoughtfully brought for him by Mr. Laurel. 'Hard-boiled eggs and nuts! Mmm-mmm!'

The gap between the ultra-high-brow 'theatre of the absurd' and these ultra-low-brow comedies is narrower than it may seem. When Kafka read his stories to his friends, he and they used to roar with laughter at the ridiculous conduct of his heroes. Samuel Beckett obviously derives a great deal from music-hall techniques. Perhaps it takes the atmosphere created by the high-brow pieces to make us so fully, so uncomfortably, aware of the strangeness or sinister aspects occluded by our hilarity at these 2-reel comedies. But the obscurity, and complacency-in-despair, of many *avant-garde* plays needs, in turn, completing by the crazy comedies, whose blend of disquiet and reassurance, of absurdity and homeliness, confers a tone which, while other, is no less satisfying than, that of the *avant-garde*. And it may be that the low-brow form is, in the end, less petulant, more mature, truer of the general run of humanity. For Laurel and Hardy, whether they're street musicians or mayors, life isn't, after all, devoid of all meaning or feeling, as it is for Beckett's tramps. However obscure their goals, however brief their satisfaction, however petty their (in)dignity, life goes on, and it's a sign, not of their escapism, but of their truth, that Laurel and Hardy were never simply laughed at by their fans, but loved by them. In his biography, John McCabe quotes Stan's account of the pair's arrival at Cork in 1953, 'There were hundreds of boats blowing whistles, and mobs and mobs of people screaming on the docks. We just couldn't understand what it was all about. And then something happened that I can never forget. All the church bells in Cork started to ring out our theme song, and Babe looked at me, and we cried. . . .'

12 · Suckers and Soaks

Mae West and W. C. Fields came to the cinema from the regions where theatre interbreeds with vaudeville, and top the bill among the early 30's influx of vaudeville and radio comedians. Ken Tynan described Wheeler and Wolsey as the only American cross-talk comedians whose films will never have a season at the National Film Theatre, but it would be interesting to see more of the comedies of Joe E. Brown and Jimmy Durante (almost the last of the race comedians, indifferently Jewish, Italian, or East European), which may well possess consistently what they possess in extract: the kind of zany fidelity to grass roots reality which one finds in the corresponding English tradition, of Will Hay, George Formby, Lucan and McShane, Norman Wisdom and the *Carry On* series. Victor Moore, Jack Oakie and others bring to 30's movies something of the brash, down-to-earth, briskly accurate character vignettes which are as vivid as they are limited, and catch much of the snap-crackle-pop of the American style.

Mae West smilingly acknowledges the applause for her fairground shimmy in *I'm No Angel*, and happily gurgles under her breath: 'Suckers!' The film is directed by Wesley Ruggles, but its credits engagingly proclaim its *politique des auteurs*: 'story, screenplay and all dialogue by Mae West; suggestions by Lowell Bernardo'. The film's plot (pre-Code) is, on paper, ambiguous, but there is so little mistaking its meaning that her films, more than any others, goaded the do-gooders into their successful clean-up campaign.

Yet the film's morality is more complex than opposing the Legions of Decency and the opulent Mae's prime side of high camp. In a climatic courtroom scene, Mae, at bay for her easy virtue, argues that if some men gave her diamonds because of what they thought she was pro-

143

mising, they ought to lose them. The implication that the would-be clients of a supposed prostitute deserved to be bilked is clipjoint morality, and if Mae's male spectators can forgive her for it, it's for a variety of reasons. Certainly her victims are the sort of mean-faced characters who turn up as crooked bankers and sheriffs in B Westerns, and are clearly incapable of matching, even to their nearest and dearest, Mae's conspicuously loyal and generous way with her friends and lovers. Also, however, the film homes in on that challenging old saw which titles a W. C. Fields movie: Never Give a Sucker an Even Break. But as a result of Mae's forensic genius, it is respectability which finds itself in the moral dock. The prostitute's client is not only as immoral as the lady of easy virtue herself, but ten times as ignominious. And when she rounds on her beloved's ex-fiancée and forces her to admit that she wouldn't dream of returning his engagement gifts, she convicts the respectable matriarchy of clipjoint morality in its turn. The comedy's happy end is possible because Cary Grant is generous enough to accept, and to forget, what is, perhaps, most difficult for the proud male: the fact of Mae's close relationship with a man who is clearly a pimp type. Mae clinches her triumph by offering to let any of the jurors 'come up and see her'. But her lover she will ring—any time. . . .

The film manipulates the moral masochism of the mere male as deftly as the more usual blend of puritanism and is, in a sense, a libertarian riposte to it. Mae West is the Statue of Liberties, whose hourglass figure sent Old Father Time into a flat spin, and brought the naughty 90's back to the roaring 20's. Like Westerns, the films are partly exercises in nostalgia, with Edwardian razzamatazz, ragtime pianos trickling notes into the saloon office, music halls with big-voiced tenors and figure-of-8 chorus-girls with high boots and feathered hats. In the streamlined 30's, her sofa contours, her slow-drag way with wisecracks, evoke the epoch of Madams rather than Moms. Indulgent, undulant, monolith, she glides, her hips moving as sweetly as the paddlewheels of a Mississippi pleasure-steamer. Lucky all who sail in her. . . . Her mystery lies in this sumptuosity immingling with a slick, cool, mercenary ruthlessness, a Momist outline with feminine independence, a Nietzschean will to power which has too much humour not to be agreeably self-critical, and a generosity whose tone deliciously blends maternal indulgence and complicity. It's the perpetual possibility of any of these responses which gives tension and wit to lines which, on paper, could hardly seem more mechanical.

Her lover asks her what she's thinking of: 'The same as you, honey.' Was ever the need to court a woman more smoothly put aside? 'I'm crazy about you,' he adds. 'Yes . . . I did my best to make you that way.' The wit in that line lies not so much in any revelation of female scheming as in its almost maternal tolerance of manipulable little boys. Baudelaire likened the superior lucidity of one lover *vis-à-vis* the other to the relationship between surgeon and patient or torturer and victim. Mae's view has a worldlier amiability. Mae's celebrated 'Beulah—peel me a grape!' occurs after a row with Cary Grant and suggests that she is soothing herself after a slight heartbreak by a self-indulgence in luxury and power—slightly provocative, perhaps, in the era of *My Man Godfrey*.

Some lines are almost unanalysable, as when she tells Cary Grant that she's come to a decision about their affair. That was very quick, he remarks, to which she replies, 'Oh, I'm very quick, in a slow way,' a line which might mean almost anything, particularly as accompanied by a broadly sensual resettling of her hips. But, whatever it means, it refers to some blend of impulse and scepticism, of impulsive passion and nonchalant reserve, of stalling and pouncing. The sexual innuendo is a magnificent promise.

I'm No Angel concludes with Mae adorning herself with a white bridal gown, a defiance of society as outrageous as Groucho's teasing of Margaret Dumont, that anti-Mae West of yearning, lonely, inno-cent, respectability. One or two lines work on double-entendres of sexual unorthodoxies much to the taste of the kinky sixties. Thus when Cary Grant over-romantically asserts, 'I would be your slave,' she amiably replies, 'That can be arranged. . . .'

The films themselves have aged and creak in every joint, almost giving a curious double nostalgia. One good turn deserves another, and Old Father Time has gallantly rejuvenated the outrageous Mae, for her whole style has a bland, unruffleable cool only enhanced by her archaic opulence.

Disreputable, disillusioned, dissolute and disgruntled, W. C. Fields was Mae West's comrade-in-arms in bawdy comedy's rearguard action against the galloping pasteurization of the 30's. Like Mae West, he wrote most of his own screenplays, under such pseudonyms as Otis T. Criblecoblis and Mahatma Kane Jeeves (and co-stars with her in *My Little Chickadee*). But his bursts of slow-motion slapstick and ethereal fantasy relate him to Harry Langdon, Laurel and Hardy and the Hal Roach tempo. In the vaudeville tradition of pompous fruity rascality, he may recall Will Hay and Wallace Beery, but his cultivation of a lordly Southern drawl irresistibly recalls the seedier sprigs of decaying gentry, and/or suburban pretensions to such gentility. His sourness at this Hays Code world recalls the Marx Brothers' way with La Dumont, but the butts of his satire are more solidly characterized than theirs. It's no accident that before Sturges, he used Franklin Pangborn and other preferred denizens of the Sturges world. *It's A Gift*, his study of small-town family life, is less hectic, but even more pessimistic, precisely because every humiliation has time to be winced from beforehand, and mused upon afterwards. His world has less warmth, more emptiness; in several films, his nearest approach to human contact is the dour complicity of fellow-topers. In contrast to Mae's all infolding narcissism, he can manage only a mumbling, but obdurate, paranoia.

This grognosed sourpuss is a sort of battered, half-defeated Uncle to the Marx triplets. Where Groucho's frankness is aggressive, Fields mutters to himself in an interminable monologue, compromising between anger and hopelessness. What may have started out with some hope of eventually counterfeiting an elegant Southern drawl has long since decayed, *à la* Tennessee Williams, to an alcohol-grated larynx rasping like a rusty lavatory chain. His extreme suspicion of the world is revealed in his bitter, lopsided lips, narrowed eyes, and the tentative, cagey gestures that give his rolypoly frame the crabbedness of an arthritic teddy-bear. He is a Sir Toby Belch cruelly misplaced in the Prohibition era. Malvolio now is no mere steward, taking orders, but that dread figure, the bank manager, and Olivia's household has become as petty and niggardly as the Bassonets of *It's A Gift* or the Sousés of *The Bank Dick*. Stout, and still as sour as Cassius, he wages a last-bottle-stand against almost everybody, but especially kids, Moms and bluenoses, that is, everything that the American way of life considers sweet and uplifting.

With Mae West, he shared an ultra-slow humour in which part of the joke was what wasn't quite said, but was, as it were, sidled around. He drawls complacently: 'There's been a catastrophe. He's fallen off the parapet. Yes. . . .' Or an enormous blonde waitress tells him: 'There's a something so big about you.' He waits, with misgivings, and in the silence it's as if a shell were whistling over from the enemy lines, where will it land? She says: 'Your nose.' He nurses his ego, and bides his time, while she bends over a table, and then he murmurs, 'There's something so big about you too. . . .' His retort's crudity, its quality of anticlimax, are all part of the defeated mood of the joke. Thus Fields has an odd quality of non-wit, as if wit required a kind of zest that he no longer possesses, because he despairs of mankind. His gags have an eccentric timing, or mistiming, all their own, sometimes loitering on indecisively, sometimes appearing out of nowhere and disappearing almost before one can laugh. Fields himself said that what's really funny is what one doesn't do, and he can almost claim to have developed the shaggy-dog joke to its highest pitch of inanity. (A clerk spends a whole scene wearing a straw hat without a crown, explaining in almost the last line, that he wears it that way because he suffers from hay fever.) His burring-and-slurring of gags combines a hopeless expectation of audience disapproval, with an ever-frustrated aggression which is nevertheless heroically maintained—as when he stands over an exasperating baby with a chopper in his hand, murmuring by way of excuse, 'Even a worm can turn. . . .'

It's A Gift, an unrelenting exposé of small-town life, includes a deliriously cruel episode where Mr. Bassonet (Fields) as the proprietor of a store, has to deal, not only with a baby who releases floods of sticky molasses from a barrel, but, simultaneously, with a customer who knocks over piles of glassware wherever he turns, because he is not only virtually blind but also virtually deaf. (Only Fields could get himself persecuted by creatures so helpless.) All the petty paranoia of the average man is crystallized in a dawn scene where Bassonet, driven out of his bed by his wife's indefatigable nagging, tries to snatch a little sleep on his balcony, only to be disturbed by, successively, the milkman, a coconut bouncing slowly down every tread into the ash-can, a baby in the balcony above bombing him with grapes and screwdrivers, an insurance salesman, his wife, a 'vegetable gentle-man', two females being maliciously polite to each other, and his own couch's collapse. In one film he spent eighteen minutes trying to hit a golf ball. In a nightmare drive to a maternity hospital he gets his car stuck in a fire-engine ladder, and lifted off the road, but not high enough to spare passing traffic from suicidal swerves. This, a classic episode in the Sennett style, is matched by the automobile's racing up and down and around the corridors, staircases and elevators of the *International House*.

His slapstick homeliness brings him quite near Laurel and Hardy, whose taste he shared for absurd parody-realms. But just as in his 'homely' scenes, he exhibits a far more abrasive hostility to the way of the world (where Stan and Ollie just blunder along), so, these 'absurd' realms have, in Fields's films, a function of derisive liberation that anticipates goonery and its indefinable, but pervasive, affinities with satire. In both *Million Dollar Legs*, written by Joseph L. Mankiewicz, and in *Never Give a Sucker an Even Break* (originally released in Britain as *What a Man*), we are introduced to a crazy realm which matches Al Capp's Dogpatch as a parody-opposite of ours.

In the latter film, he falls out of an aeroplane washroom into a strange realm presided over by a Mrs. Haemoglobin (Margaret Dumont), a sort of respectable female Dracula whose ivory tower is equipped with hanging swimming-pools. *Million Dollar Legs* has Fields presiding, like the genially tyrannical Oz, over a Land of Cockayne where all the women are called Angela and all the men are called George (suggesting a happy extreme of democratic equality, and the idyllic community cohesiveness of a South Sea tribe). There's also a vamp called Mata Machri (deliciously played by Lydia Roberti). The million-dollar legs are not, as one might expect, hers, but, of all people's, Andy Clyde's, as an international athlete who, in the old Mack Sennett spirit, keeps in trim by outrunning express trains, and takes his super-superman speed absolutely for granted.[1] There is also a charmingly erotic scene where Jack Oakie and his girlfriend brush each other down with feathers. Such titillation is rare in Fields films, for, in the presence of women, Fields, though hardly lacking in deep dark desires, seemed in his amorous relationships paralysed by a suspicion that all women, however beautiful, were merely harridans in their butterfly stage. *Million Dollar Legs* isn't simply a Dogpatch: or rather it's a European Dogpatch, it's a last zany image of Ruritania, of the lands from which America's immigrants came. It bristles with secret police, yet everyone is content. According to Aristophanes, Cloud Cuckoo Land was the topsy turvy region where you beat your father and got praised for it. Klopstockia is the land where foreign, fuddy-duddy fathers turn out to be champion weight lifters and supersonic sprinters. Andy Clyde's philosophy is the absolute reverse of American earnestness, he's a deferential, almost feudally modest, messenger boy, and he can hardly be bothered to stir his stumps merely for the sake of winning. 'Have you ever studied astronomy?' he ponders, philosophically. 'Have you ever realized how short a hundred yards is?' Backwoodsmanship is in

---

[1] Are these quick motion effects, one wonders, a parody of King Vidor's way of slowing camera speeds to make his heroes run or work faster (in *Hallelujah*, in *Our Daily Bread*) at inspired moments?

there too, and Fields's slow, full-blown style, often nearer the anecdote than the gag, sometimes takes on an almost Mark Twain quality, as in *If I Had a Million*. Fields and wife, having at last hit the jackpot, drive round town, followed by a fleet of spare automobiles; after each smash, they climb out and hail the next in line.

The homely and the exotic weirdly coexist. Fields hears a police-car radio describing a wanted man as having 'apple cheeks, cauliflower ears and mutton-chop whiskers' (shades of Arcimboldo); or he buys shares in a beefsteak mine; or, as a bank dick, he dons a disguise which consists mainly of a length of string running from the bridge of his nose to behind his ear. These improbabilities are presented so as to be quietly mulled over, rather than developed, and have a strange halfheartedness which is itself a joke, and rather a sad one. Fields's humour, instead of falling between two stools, of fantasy and satire, wobbles uneasily, and intriguingly, on the edge of both. He seems to be taking a subdued revenge on the real world by substituting for it a fantasy one. Yet he's also too weary to develop the fantasy. It's as if he introduces, into the familiar atmosphere, little 'air-bubbles' of fantasy, which swell, and slowly subside, and at last burst, leaving a sour nostalgia behind.

The passage of time has perhaps enhanced this effect, since his films abound in parodic reference to genres with which later audiences are less familiar. In *Never Give a Sucker an Even Break*, Fields leads an existence weirdly split between a Hollywood director's and a small-town spouse's; he has simply taken, to a *reductio ad absurdum*, Hollywood's picture of homely Hollywood. In *International House*, the Chinese inventor obsessively trying to get a six-day bicycle race on his 'radioscope' (television) is an idiotically Westernized, passified and cretinized Fu Manchu. Fields's flight in an autogyro, out of which he keeps dropping empty beer-bottles, refers at once to the 30's fascination with long-distance solo flights and an outrageous defiance of still vivid Prohibition. (It's easy to forget just how much any reference to any alcoholic beverage, even the presence of a bottle and glass, meant for Prohibition era audiences.) In one of its musical interludes, *International House* also has Cab Calloway singing about 'that funny reefer man', a line whose subversiveness probably strikes more people now than it did then. But the fact that it got there is one of those happy accidents with which a kindly fate blesses those artists who deserve it. It's ironical that *International House* would today have to lose this scene, or be banned.

The one new innocent of the 30's is Eddie Cantor.[1] His *Roman Scandals* (for Goldwyn) started out in Depression America, from which town bum Eddie dreams his way back into the court of Poppeia, finally returning to save the poor from being evicted by the hard-faced businessman. The mixture of comic topicality and wish-fulfilment opulence is evident enough. Less characterful, less rooted in reality than Keaton, Lloyd and Langdon, Cantor had something of their touching intensity, and, in his personality 'aura' seems to have something of each, as if typifying the way in which the various sections, strata and racial groups of America were coalescing into—not the American ideal, for Eddie, like most comedians, was an anti-hero—but the 'little American'. There's a kind of scuttling nervousness about him which is very much of the period, too, with its hectic pace and its Depression. The stress lies on gags, and bluff-and-cowardice gags, in a way anticipating Bob Hope, a comedian with a slicker, more realistic style. But if *Kid Millions* now seems an awkward anticipation of the Bob Hope style movie, it is saved, like *Roman Scandals*, by the musical numbers of Busby Berkeley, which, in these and other 30's movies, are really little deliriums of the imagination, psychological counterparts of crazy comedy, but, with their lines of milky, healthy, smiling beauties, cosy as well as crazy. As the middle-class tide rises throughout the 30's, Berkeley's Freedonian regiments of lovelies yield, in their turn, the limelight to more intimate and 'cosy' numbers, based on the 'individualistic' couple-of-lovers (Fred Astaire, Ginger Rogers).

[1] He had made *Kid Boots* with Clara Bow in 1926 but the early 30's are his heyday.

13 · Four Against Alienation

Rather less melancholy and vastly more aggressive, the Marx Brothers found highbrow admirers from the moment of screen blast off. It's no accident if Antonin Artaud, prophet of the Theatre of Cruelty, subsequently so fashionable, called *Animal Crackers* that 'extraordinary thing . . . an . . . essential liberation . . . a kind of exercise of intellectual freedom in which the unconscious of each of the characters, repressed by conventions, and habits, avenges itself and us at the same time . . . a kind of boiling anarchy, a kind of disintegration of the essence of the real by poetry . . .'. A few years later, Dali presented Harpo with a harp whose strings were made of baked wire.

On their first appearance in London, at the Coliseum in 1922, the brothers, still billed as 'Herbert, Leonard and Julius', were so unpopular that the audience booed and threw pennies on the stage. Art houses apart, their cinema popularity here was, reputedly, centred on London and Leeds (a distribution presumably related to their often very Jewish humour). In America, of course (mainly through Chico) the Marx Brothers (though themselves German Alsatians) had a special resonance also with the many Italian immigrants struggling along in a strange land, feeling themselves to be 'crazy', by American standards, while contemplating, irreverently, its strange customs and institutions. Prominent among these latter, of course, is Margaret Dumont, the high society hostess with the well-meaning schoolmarm soul. She can never believe that life around her is as chaotic and cynical as it is, with the result that Groucho can insult her with impunity (in *Coconuts*, more by luck than by design, he saves her daughter from marriage to crooks). Through the Marx Brothers, immigrants could take a liberating revenge on that American xenophobia that made them feel third-class citizens until they had brainwashed and transmogrified themselves into conformity. Their successive films rake every aspect of American life; WASP snobbery and high society (in *Animal Crackers*), the campus (*Horse Feathers*), politics (*Duck Soup*), and so on, through the opera, the circus, the Old West, big department stores, and, in *Love Happy*, the conventions of the Raymond Chandler world.

But from the particularly American issue of immigrants versus conformism, their films spread out into a wider application of Bergson's 'mechanism' theory of humour. They also mock the maladjustments brought about by habit, assumption, social convention and hypocrisy. The Marx Brothers are flippantly, scathingly alive, whereas all their victims are half-mummified by a particular position in the social order—whether waiters or foreign ambassadors. The characteristic Marxist posture is opportunism and a bashless nerve. It is scathingly cynical rather than nihilist, for, although it finds nothing sacred (not even the underdog), its view of human nature is as tolerant as it is low. 'Sir, are you offering me a bribe?' thunders Groucho, adding, 'How much?' Well might he parody, in *Animal Crackers*, Eugene O'Neill's *Strange Interlude*, and interrupt a love scene to tell the camera his *real* opinion of the two women he's courting. For his Marxism is, precisely, a long 'monologue', an aggressive saying, and acting, out loud of everything the ordinary, responsible, hypocritical adult finds it easier not to say, and then, in the end, not to think, so becoming alienated from his own heart. Marxism is making instant, not proposals, but propositions, to each pretty woman in turn (or several at a time); it is exploiting and insulting the Margaret Dumonts of this world, as they try to soothe cynicism and reality out of existence; it is flying an airliner no hands, and, only incidentally, dishing the crooks. It may seem odd to describe this 'Marxism' as honesty, since Groucho is a con man, and Harpo is a born liar even though he can't speak. But they never fool themselves. Their hypocrisies aren't even skin deep. The transparency (to us) of their roguery helps blow the gaff and show that, from the point of view of mental freedom, respectability is dishonesty. It wouldn't take much, one feels, for the Brothers to rush into the auditorium of a cinema showing one of their films and insult all their fans for laughing at their jokes without applying the lessons of that laughter to everyday reality. For not to take Marxism seriously is precisely the sin of Margaret Dumont. Because she treats Groucho's truths as jest, she remains the eternal sucker.

The Brothers' least typical film, *Room Service*, throws a fascinating sidelight on their resonance. Here the Brothers are, for once, caught up in the cogs and gears of something resembling a plot (a Broadway comedy which is also the original of *Step Lively*). Impresario Groucho, hardpressed by creditors, shamelessly exploits all the pitiable characters—a pathetic waiter, a decent and hard-pressed hotel manager, the idealistic author of his play, and even the sentimental streak in a hatchet-faced accountant. The final fake funerals are in the hilarious worst of all possible taste. Into the conventionally intricate plot, the Marx Brothers contrive to slip a fair charge of fantasy while Groucho, in particular, sustains a *comic*, as well as *farcical*, characterization. The Marxes aren't so far from the Sturges world of *Mad Wednesday*. (As a footnote, it's strange too how their films found room for three actresses who went on to live hectic, libertarian or tragic lives: Thelma Todd, Lillian Roth and Marilyn Monroe.)

On the strength of their verbal and logical craziness, the Marx Brothers have, justly, and most detailedly by J. P. Coursodon, been called the true heirs of Lewis Carroll. Our surprise at the comparison stresses a difference. Lewis Carroll's common-sensical little Alice justified a childlike simplicity against the arbitrariness of adults, and her simplicity was a decorous, moral innocence. But Margaret Dumont is the matronly Alice of the Marx Brothers' Wonderland. She is the innocent voice of 'square' common sense. She feebly protests to Groucho, 'But I saw you go out of the room with your own eyes.' To which he retorts, scathingly, 'Well, who are you going to believe, me or your own eyes?' All Bishop Berkeley's philosophy doesn't confuse the issue more thoroughly or more instantaneously.

Thus the Brothers correspond to the Mad Hatters, the Humpty Dumpties, the tetchy Duchesses, and all the rude and unreasonable characters who plague Alice in Lewis Carroll. But their unreasonableness goes with their drastic honesty. Hence, they never attain the swollen malevolence of Jarry's *Ubu Roi*. They still have some of his characteristics—Groucho's fake front of respectability, Chico's sullen plots and plans, Harpo's shameless lasciviousness. Instead, they're more benevolent, particularly towards the young lovers, than all the 'straight' citizens, who, weighed down by responsibility, or soured by taking life seriously, have no time or wish to play truant.

In their vulgarity, they are nearest Chaplin (but without his pathos), in their sourness, nearest W. C. Fields (but without his defeatism). Harpo *constantly* does all the things that The Little Man does on running amok in *Modern Times* (only with Harpo it's not twisting off women's buttons, it's cocking his thigh up on to their hands). Chaplin's rollerskating in *The Big Store* is dreamy-idyllic (with hints of tragic danger), whereas the Marxist version in *The Big Store* is chaos come again. (There's also a counterpart of Chaplin's feeding-machine, when an Italian momma and all her brood keep getting trapped in automated beds, which, to add to the confusion, look like safes, automobiles and other absurd status-symbols.)

Between them the Brothers are everything that's disreputable in the city jungle. Groucho is the city slicker with the commercial or professional front. His moustache is painted, while his eyes are as shifty as ballbearings in an earthquake. His scathing cynicism about everything is an inversion of Yiddisher sentimentality. There's a touch, about his cagey leer and rasp, of the Humphrey Bogarts (another hard-bitten, disillusioned city-dweller), while his sneaky, bent-double walk-cum-slide isn't monkeylike, so much as physical metaphor for moral snakeyness. He's the Brothers' front man, and, as the most ambitious, constantly being victimized by Chico and Harpo. They usually descend on him, as a team, in the first reel, to offer their 'help', and, in the end, get him to help the young lovers—generally much against his will, for, of the three, he's the most contaminated by worldliness. He's almost Jack Lemmon before his time. As house manager of the Coconuts hotel, he's eventually ready, in sour, weary irony, to join the two agents of chaos in tearing up his guests' registered mail. He becomes more or less benevolent only after their crazy persistence has worn him down; but they are, in a sense, his fate, i.e. his real nature. He's the most Jewish of the three but he is also all the minority groups rolled into one; thus, in *Coconuts*, he leads the singing of *My Old Kentucky Home* and then adds, 'This programme comes to you from the House of David. . . .'

Chico, the most Italian of the three, has all the humble occupations —peanut-vendor, tootsy-frootsy ice-cream seller, dirty postcard-pusher, even 'the fish-pedlar from Czechoslovakia'. He has most of the practical ideas, and he concocts most of the 'artisan-type' schemes (burglary, theft, etc.). He is the link man between the deliriously articulate Groucho and the deliriously inarticulate Harpo, and he is also the 'ordinary' man, the workman of the trio, dour and solid. With implacable loyalty, he won't be separated from, and he always defends, Harpo, his idiot brother (cousin, pal). In family loyalty he could give points to another Italian immigrant, Rocco. A major scene in Visconti's film has Rocco not retaliating when beaten up by his brother. Similarly, when Chico and Harpo fight, Harpo always fouls, by squaring up with his fists and then kicking, whereupon Groucho says, 'Hey, whassa matter, thas-a-not-fair, you no fight downstairs.' But he never retaliates, just like a responsible but forgiving brother. Harpo's 'angry' looks (puffed out cheeks, gritted teeth, protruding tongue) is based on the mocking glare of a local cobbler at the boys who stared at him as he worked away in his shop window. Just under the surface of the Brothers' fantasy, a documentary is screaming to be let out.

Harpo is the dregs of society, the dumb tramp-cum-ragpicker, a character quite as handicapped as one of Samuel Beckett's, but happy with it, because not impotent. He's the St. Francis of the Rabelaisian hagiography, a moon-calf on roller-skates, the most aggressive of dreamers. Since he's a pickpocket and a sex-maniac, one can't altogether describe him as innocent, but he's the most *spontaneous* of the Marx Brothers. His impulses are the least affected by the world's hostility. He's a satyr in ragpicker's clothes. Pan had his pipes, and Harpo has his motor-horn. His red hair is a traditional symbol for lasciviousness; and he is a special master of such coyly suggestive gesture, such as parking his thigh in a lady's hands, or gently leaning forward to press the bulb of his motor-horn against the stomach of his interlocutor. If he's maniacal in his pursuit of blondes, he's indiscriminate in a kind of innocent-hypocritical sexuality, often smiling at villains and cops like a gurgling baby, while double-crossing, or parking his thigh on, them, too. He steals things like a baby grasps an adult's nose to play with. Like a baby, he tries to eat inedibles, especially telephones, and being a magic baby, invariably succeeds. If anyone frustrates him, his face becomes hideous with wrath, rather like a gargoyle's (by Christian standards, he is, indeed, a little demon). In *Animal Crackers* he does his level best to break a girl's arm, and also shoot several other young ladies, because, when there's more than one blonde in a room at a time, he can never decide which to chase. He also has a kind of nutty tenderness that never quite becomes pathos.

Thus the Brothers constitute a three-pronged attack on society—Groucho's 'front man' outrage of polite conventions, Chico's dour, proletarian scheming, Harpo's clown-and-satire glee. Their verbal humour includes execrable puns, which suggest an immigrant's difficulty with the English language. Harpo naturally combines it with an even more primitive form of communication, gestures, which become a sort of punning sound language. He buzzes like a saw and then makes squirming motions, which means, 'bee' plus 'twist', i.e. 'Beatrice'. Not content with contorted verbal barbarisms the Brothers dwell with cretinizing glee on *faux-naif* bad jokes: 'How much do you charge to fall through an open manhole?'—'Only a cover charge'—'Drop in sometime'—'Sewer'. While reducing words to mere lumps of sound, they also create logical solipsisms: 'I know where the suspects are—they're in the house next door.'—'But there isn't any house next door.'—'Then we build a house next door!' and plan to put the roof in the cellar so as to keep it dry when it rains.

Thus they tear language, and all the conventions and assumptions which language incorporates, apart, in just the same way as logicians caution students against bad logic—by inventing plausible logical and verbal patterns which half-procure one's habit-blinded assent, but which lead straight into utter absurdity. Thus, as detectives in *Animal Crackers*, they reason their way from 'This portrait was painted by a left-handed painter' to 'This picture was eaten by a left-handed moth'.

Not that they're pure logicians—their abuse of polite tags, false modesty, idioms, the very sound of syllables, constitute a verbal barrage whose real aim is to devastate social custom. Every time La Dumont replies with false modesty to Groucho's amorous flatteries, he takes her seriously, and serve her right. 'Welcome to my humble abode,' she coos. He punishes her for this coy nonsense by agreeing: 'Now you mention it, it is pretty frowsy. Come to think of it you're not looking too good yourself,' and tries to sell her life insurance in view of her probably imminent death. He courts her with all the romantic flourishes, and when, playing hard to get, she simpers, 'You'll find some pretty young girl to go off with and leave me,' he retorts, 'I'll send you a postcard. . . .'

Unexpectedly for verbal comedians, Marxist dialogue doesn't read half as funny as it sees. In cold print it's baffling rather than amusing, because it draws its relevance, not only from the Marx Brothers' style of delivery, but from a whole network of references and expectations which appear in the screen setting and action, but not in the mere words. This use of language *reads* negatively, because it is a destruction of language, a demonstration of its falsity, of its conventional functioning, a concealment and alienation. Harpo, who can hardly talk, let alone think, is the least alienated from his *joie de vivre*. They thus anticipate current pessimism about communication, and also go beyond it. Communication is only impossible, implies Harpo (silently, smilingly), if you're fooled by language's habit and lies, and let it trap your heart. For communication is, not explaining yourself to blondes, but wanting them enough to pursue them. Those intellectuals, who, like Godard, affect an anguished feeling that nothing can be communicated except the impossibility of communication, only show that they aren't intellectual enough to challenge the rules of the communications game, to exploit, not serve, its built-in hypocrisies. For the Marx Brothers are intellectuals in that they challenge the habits and the rules. They exploit them, to confuse their opponents, but don't believe them. For them, the rules of language, and of society, are like the railway track in *Go West*. The fun only begins when the train of thought shoots off the rails and starts across the countryside, slicing through houses and bedrooms, while the Marx Brothers chop the coachwork off the carriages to fuel the engine.

Not that language is their only butt. In *A Night in Casablanca* Groucho's date with the vamp is continually disrupted by Chico. This self-appointed bodyguard-cum-spoilsport, in paranoid over-protectiveness (justified, as it turns out), keeps ringing up, or bursting in to ensure that his boss hasn't got a woman in there (like a narrow-minded landlady). To escape his attentions, poor Groucho is reduced to staggering from one room to another under the weight of phonograph, champagne bottle and bucket, roses and all, until he feels less like Don Juan than the Hunchback of Notre Dame. Thus a whole romantic iconography is reduced to its most ludicrous terms, the burden of baggage. Similarly, in *At the Circus*, Harpo cuts the rope mooring a platform to the shore, and an entire symphony orchestra, playing oh, so soulfully, goes drifting away into an audience-less horizon, in a classic image for the pompous, self-enwrapped futility of so much high culture. It's much better, like Harpo, in the intervals of blonde-chasing, to settle down with the clarinet, or the harp, when the whim takes one, with no pretentions at all. He's quite likely to conclude his harp act with a voluminous yawn and drop off to sleep. His music is a refreshment of the spirit, for its own sake, a kind of dreaming, just as during his harp-playing in *The Big Store* his two mirror-images acquire an independent life of their own. This briefly perturbs him until their smiles and nods reassure him that they're friendly.

Similarly the message of the Marx Brothers is not to fear one's inner, unconformist, self, but to let it into one's conscious mind. A film like *The Knack* is, so to speak, applied Marxism–Harpo Marxism.

Because their films have acquired a (well-merited) period charm, it's easy to overlook the virulent callousness of many of their ideas. Thus *Coconuts* (made in full Depression) is set against the background of the Florida real estate boom (the Depression's immediate trigger). Perhaps their most scathing film is *Duck Soup*. The state of Freedonia has been kept from total economic collapse only by huge loans from a gracious American lady, Mrs. Teasdale (Margaret Dumont). She insists that absolute power must be given to a ruthlessly efficient American businessman, Rufus T. Firefly (Groucho), who, on arrival, wastes no time in announcing, in song, the basic principles of Groucho-ism. 'If any form of pleasure is exhibited—it'll straightway be prohibited.' But Groucho's wicked pleasure in wielding absolute power rapidly gives way to his lurking hedonism, for his new marriage laws, it appears, will allow any pretty young wife who's caught in adultery to choose between her mangey old husband and her sprightly young lover (Groucho, of course). Sylvania's attempts to sabotage Freedonia's economy by means of triple agents Pinky and Chikolini almost lead to war, which is not to be averted even by Mrs. Teasdale's peace-making mission. Chikolini's trial for spying is interrupted by the Sylvanian attack, and Freedonia has to radio urgent calls for help. 'Help is on the way!' comes the reply—and we see it on the way —cops on motor-bikes, fire-engines, divers, runners, herds of elephants, baboons scurrying through the treetops, and schools of leaping dolphin.

All this has a kind of permanent relevance to twentieth-century diplomacy. Freedonia's economic difficulties recall the Depression. Mrs. Teasdale's belief in a strong, morally severe, businessman's government recalls the solution offered, in opposition to Roosevelt's New Deal, by the American right-wing (as in La Cava's *Gabriel Over the White House*). The foreign dictatorship theme must also parody Mussolini's régime; and just as *Duck Soup* was being made, Hitler took power in Germany. But even more extraordinary than these contemporary echoes is the film's prophetic quality. The highly irregular trial of Chikolini is like a burlesque preview of the Moscow trials in 1936—while the derisory response to the plea for help forecasts the utter paralysis of the League of Nations. Groucho triggers off the war by his paranoid fear of losing face (he slaps the Sylvanian ambassador's face in case the Sylvanian ambassador means to slap his face, which he doesn't)—and there's a kind of sad truth there about the childish chauvinism and prestige-hunting which, in international politics, can have such disastrous consequences for us all. Even more cutting is the scene where Chikolini's trial is interrupted by a declaration of war, greeted with an enthusiasm which becomes, not only hilariously, but hideously, orgiastic. Everyone in the courtroom, audience, judge, jury, writhe in revivalist-style movements, and chant, of all things, 'All God's chillun got guns.'

The actual war cruelly burlesques all the horrors of 1914–18. For its generals' muddle and incompetence: Firefly is about to award himself the Firefly medal for routing the advancing enemy when his aide tells him, 'But sir, you're firing on our own men,' whereupon Firefly, never at a loss, flings him a couple of coins and says, 'Here, keep it under your hat,' and then, 'On second thoughts, I'll keep it under mine,' which he holds out like a collection plate into which the other automatically places the money. The slaughter of the British volunteer army, and the recourse to conscription, is reflected in Harpo's hopeful attempt to find more recruits by strolling across the battlefield with a sandwich-board proclaiming, 'Join the Army and see the Navy'. When a General radios to say he's resisting a gas attack, Groucho tells him to take a teaspoonful of bicarb (and really it's hardly stranger than the Civil Defence Corps telling us to protect ourselves against fallout with vinegar and brown paper). Looked at from the vantage point of 1965, Groucho's appearing in every scene with a different uniform, from a Davy Crockett hat to a Poilu's tin-helmet, becomes not simply a spoof of history, but a matter of 'The Universal Soldier'.

14 · The New Sarcasm

With the 40's came prosperity, and, ironically, a new bitterness. The paradox isn't uncommon (more recently, English affluence saw kitchen sink and anger). Often those oppressed use movies to dream, while those who feel less need for escapism can relish the release of their discontents.[1]

It is Preston Sturges who, with *The Great McGinty*, first caught, and revealed, this new mood. It's a mood that runs counter to Hollywood theories, which saw the public as intrinsically and externally naïve and sentimental, and anxious to be shown only as conforming to a middle-class ideal. There was, and still is, unfortunately, more truth to this than many of Hollywood's critics have understood, but there has always been less truth to it than the studio heads (as opposed to so many writers and directors) realized. Sturges's success was so disturbing as to be resented rather than emulated, and not only Hollywood, but many intelligent critics, found Sturges almost too much to take. James Agee welcomed the tonic cynicism of *The Miracle of Morgan's Creek*. He implicitly linked Sturges's vision of America to the streak of black derisiveness in Sennett, and wrote 'in fact, to the degree that this film is disliked by those who see it, whether consciously or passively, I see a measure less of its inadequacies than of the progress of that terrible softening, solemnity and idealization which, increasing over several years, has all but put an end to the output and intake of good moving pictures in this

---

[1] This doesn't mean that affluence in itself always leads to entertainment anger; in any case the causes of discontent are subjective and relative rather than objective and absolute.

country'. But even Agee went on to confess that he too found Sturges's films unpleasant as well as salutary.[1]

Sturges's first film, *The Great McGinty*, might be described as Capra with the gloves off. McGinty (Brian Donlevy) begins by beating up pluckily independent shopkeepers on behalf of a party machine boss, becomes a corrupt politician in his turn, and is broken only when he decides to go straight. A scene contrasting his pro-public spending platform with the class-conscious Senator Honeywell—as well as the contrast of names—leaves little doubt that McGinty is a Democrat. No doubt studio chiefs saw this study in Democrat corruption as useful Republican propaganda. But with that artistic cunning which can triple- or quadruple-cross any censorship, the film, in fact, sweeps the snooty Honeywells contemptuously aside, and poses the real alternatives as either utter cynicism or the Democratic ethos. But since the former is a popular, and respected, American attitude, Sturges has McGinty get away—helped by, appropriately, a disillusioned cop—and end his days, not too uncongenially, as a bartender down South America way.

Sturges's tact matches Capra's, point for point, as is evidenced by a very difficult scene where our hero, as Mister Big's strong-arm man, beats a toughly individualistic bartender to make him pay protection. If the scene is morally explosive as it is, it is because Donlevy retains our human sympathy despite his classic villain behaviour. The reasons are: (*a*) we've seen Donlevy on his uppers and like him as an underdog, (*b*) his victim has a bully physiognomy, (*c*) he's so confident in his own toughness that he starts the fight, which (*d*) we don't see, instead it is (*e*) reflected on the face of a comic little man who (*f*) thinks about joining in with a bottle but can't bring himself to. The (*a*) to (*e*) points may be classic examples of entertainment tact, but (*f*) is more challenging.[2] That little man is, and is felt to be, 'the little man', the American conscience which, in historical fact, has so rarely made up its mind to interfere in cases of political bribery and corruption.

[1] Less than a decade has passed before Wilder's black comedies were to be greeted with cries of hatred from critics whose fury would know no bounds if one recalled now what they had said then. No names, no pack drill . . .

[2] To speak of tact is not to accuse Sturges of insincerity, nor to imply that he substitutes mere manipulation for artistry. On the contrary. All concern with communication involves a concern with audience response—and whether this is conscious (as it surely is in Sturges's case) or unconscious is not of the first importance. Far more central is whether this tact is deployed to increase or to decrease the audience's awareness. Shocking is simply a special case of tact.

Cynical, Sturges, explosively, joyously, is, but neither nihilist nor dogmatic. He appeals to no ideology, no perfectionism, no despair, but rather to intuitive decencies and horse-sense (still, Agee's own shock testifies to the extent to which such things rasped against the myths of time). More than almost any other director of the war years, he trusted the audience to possess that mental and moral agility needed to follow his quickfire plots and patterns of sympathy through all their twists and turns. *Christmas in July* begins with the well-tried theme of the young lovers who think they've won a huge prize (in this case, for inventing the winning publicity slogan in a Maxford coffee competition). A 'big scene', where two mean businessmen, Schwindel and Maxford, try to snatch presents back from a crowd of tenement children, is quite as openly anti-Republican as Sturges's quiet puns on the word 'democratic' in *Hail the Conquering Hero*. But Sturges's knack lay in never losing his way through all the subsidiary conflicts which prevented this confrontation scene from being facilely loaded. His likeable characters are full of faults and his dislikeable characters often abound in subtle redeeming qualities. Thus the relationship between the quiet, contented heroine (Ella Raines) and her madly ambitious boyfriend (Dick Powell) is, particularly in the opening scenes, edgy to the point of harshness. The menacing supervisor, who imposes exact timekeeping with the relentlessness that seems to sum up an entire system gives the hero a piece of stern advice about self-respect that liberates him from his overblown anxiety to be a success. He seems to represent an older America, the America of stern, solid, modest inner-direction, as opposed to the more fluid, hectic, anxious, callous values of both the boss and the hero. (*Room Service*, similarly, plays on the Marx Brothers' quick, cunning exploitation of the sentimental side of a stern accountant.) Sturges's picture of success-worship is particularly fair, when, for example, Powell's boss, thinking he's won the prize, enthuses over all his ideas, however bad. But when told that Powell hasn't won the prize after all, he immediately sneers at all his other ideas also. Certainly, he's petty and absurd in that all his enthusiasms are unreal, that he has no mind of his own and is lickspittle to success. But he goes on to admit, frankly, that he's no judge of whether the ideas are good or bad, he's made mistakes before, another man's status is all the guide he has. There's both accuracy and sympathy in this observation, and Sturges prefers this kind of understanding to the too-easy jeer, just as he understands the underlying morality that makes a ruthless businessman keep up an unending stream of pompous, jittery, hypocritical self-justifications. In *Hail The Conquering Hero* he contrives to make one minor character incarnate not only a dogmatic sentimentality about Momism but also a disturbingly callous violence, and, in addition, the hero's bad conscience about pretending to be a tough war hero. By uniting these apparently distinct roles, he spotlights that strange connection, in the American psyche, between apparently contradictory attitudes.

George Seaton remarked that his *Anything Can Happen* was a box-office failure because it referred too openly to the fact that many Americans, being only two or three generations away from immigrants, are bitterly ashamed of any foreign traits, and so cling desperately to the concept of 'Americanism'. Sturges darts that needle in and then withdraws it. It is for no other reason that in *Hail the Conquering Hero* the girl's father suddenly unlooses a German expletive (the krauts being the current enemy), while, in the course of a discussion about families, Franklin Pangborn causes a sudden chill by remarking, 'My grandmother was Lithuanian.' It's just at this period that characterization in American movies generally is most stereotyped, as if audiences were trying to conceal, or, better, obliterate, any tell-tale spontaneities, and renouncing the variety and emotionality arising from their (still faintly foreign) family roots. In fact, the hidden theme of much American comedy is crystallized in Chaplin's title, *The Immigrant*, as carried through to Son of the Immigrant, and, I Was A Teenager Lost In The Conformist Jungle, i.e. *Rebel Without A Cause*, only with Jerry Lewis in the James Dean part. But this is to anticipate.

Sturges's films keep jabbing near the nerves of the American ideal (ambition in *Christmas In July*, puritanism in *The Miracle of Morgan's Creek*, heroism). Their emotional voltage enables them to leap from comedy to pathos, from sentimentality to bitterness, with one line of dialogue, or with one detail—like the disturbingly vivid bruised eye inflicted by the Mom-worshipper on his less reverent buddy. And *The Lady Eve* anticipates Wilder's sadism as on their wedding night, gold-digger Barbara Stanwyck feels obliged to confess to her shy, innocent groom (Henry Fonda) that she has lost her innocence with a man . . . and another man . . . and another man . . . and another man. . . .

Nor is Sturges so afraid of anti-anti-Semitism that he shrinks from stressing the Jewishness of a mean Jewish businessman, Schwindel, in *Christmas in July*. It's only at the last moment, after a nice maintenance of ideological tension, that he has him soundly ticked off by a poor Jewish momma (i.e. 'it's not race, it's class'). But then the salt is rubbed in again immediately, when the pressure on Schwindel enables him to yield to his repressed sentimental side—so he can turn on his WASP rival, Maxford, who is less pennypinching, because he's richer, and also less susceptible to sentimentality. Sturges can even allow himself the box-office luxury of (highly implausible) happy endings without weakening his comic sarcasm. This is partly because, contrary to certain theories, the general audience doesn't remember only endings, its memories stress the big scenes, and Sturges's are edgy rather than reassuring. In fact, the happy ending of *Christmas in July* is so zany that it satirizes itself. The slogan-judging jury is finally persuaded, by one incredibly old-fashioned, idiotic and obstinate member, to give the prize to the worst slogan (the hero's, 'If you can't sleep, it's not the coffee, it's the bunk'). This jury theme hilariously prefigures Lumet's solemn *Twelve Angry Men*, and its moral seems to be that it's the ornery old idiots who, by sabotaging business efficiency, make America a happier place for young couples, i.e. the spectator's screen self. Twenty years later, students at Berkeley rebel, fundamentally, against the logical conclusion of efficiency—a computerized existence.

15 · Pizzicato Pussycats

The causes of this apathy are not only technological. Once, wide-spread poverty gave many lives a common dream. People might compete against each other but they were all competing for one thing. Thus the Hollywood film could postulate simple goals, of a romantic kiss, security and success. But with affluence, and more sophisticated forms of bitterness, the simple, common dream dissolves. With more leisure, and education, people can look further, and think further, and become more aware of the diversity of conflicting social, cultural, moral and spiritual groups. As separate groups become less different, and try harder to get along, the frictions become more surprising, subtler and more painful. There is a disturbing sense that one's every belief, aim and emotion is undermined by the possibilities of some other culture. While tradition-directed societies offer unanalysed, viable, obvious, attitudes and rules, which, being stable compromises between divergent goals, feel firm and secure, our more fluid society offers a variety of inconsistent, or conflicting, positions, from which every individual has painfully to find his own balance. Even the old certainties inspiring the traditionalist lashback tend to find it harder to conceal their cynicism. A sense of common purpose is lost. It's not surprising if meaning is sought more intensely than ever in the only form of personal human meaning and contact which has gained, rather than lost, cultural ground during the twentieth century: that of erotic experience.

It's under the dazzle-camouflage of crazy sophistication that the New Morality achieves, in America, its first unabashed screen manifesto. Clive Donner's *What's New Pussycat?* makes an apt pair with Tony Richardson's *The Loved One*; the one lifting fun morality to the status of a Quest, the other defying the concurrent *bourgeois* tabu-sentimentality about death. Both are American films, directed by British directors (the British, being both less sentimental and less cynical than the Americans, have a head-start in developing Anglo-Saxon morality), both were condemned by American critics for their bad taste (but not by British critics), and both were enthusiastically welcomed by the American public. In both, the crazy comedy enters its post-Christian phase.

What's New Pussycat? is Lubitsch on roller-skates. It's novel not just because it's the Kinsey Report as presented by Mack Sennett, but because it's a festive escape from the current hypochondria about being, or at least appearing to be, normal and well adjusted. Since nuttiness is inevitable we might as well all relax and enjoy it. The hunt for pleasure can be also an ebullition of the soul, at least it can be when it's as devoid of dross as the Don Juanism of Peter O'Toole, who has all but shed the egoisms, malices, competitiveness and pride which encumber and poison *la ronde*. The film says, 'Why should we bother to conceal our whims, obsessions, irresponsibilities, spats, woes and humiliations? Why not display them as brashly as peacocks, and tolerate or relish them in others? Then we can become as good-natured and obliging as we are colourful ourselves.' Accordingly, it shows us a madly maladjusted psychiatrist (Peter Sellers), makes fun of its Don Juan with less affection than it extends a loving fellow-feeling to the perpetually frustrated (Woody Allen).

The film is a *chassée-croisée* between three gentlemen and five ladies. Peter Sellers plays a psychiatrist who pursues his female patients with an invariably frustrated obsessiveness (which they scarcely criticize or resent), and wears, like a cry of longing for eternal youth, a P. J. Proby haircut over suits of red velvet. His performance, in its blend of caricature and intensity, is of the calibre of Groucho's. His amorous misadventures intertwine with the scarcely less un-successful career of Woody Allen (intellectual 'Chico' to his Groucho) and with the very successful career of the (aptly named) O'Toole, who delightedly finds a thousand excuses for not yet marrying his steady (Romy Schneider). If his comedy style isn't a great advance on Zeppo's, at least the Marxist comparison springs to mind. An almost equally predatory team of ladies is headed by Romy Schneider, who spiritedly gives the film what little it possesses in the way of normal domesticity. Capucine displays her gift for haughty-faced knockabout, as if to prove that the aloof and expensive models of *Vogue* are pleasantly equipped with feet of clay ('you, spectator, need never despair'). Paula Prentiss and Ursula Andress exemplify the ready, able and willing goddesses who so pleasantly devastate Peter O'Toole. The former plays a stripper-cum-beat-poetess (a natural combination of alienated occupations) whose voice swings down from amorous wail to gutbucket tenor as wildly as she wavers between, on the one hand, nymphomania laced with frigidity and sapphism and, on the other, suicidal mania (all the sex acts she schemes become suicide attempts). The latter appears as an outdoor Amazon who goes parachuting in a cobra-skin cat-suit and remains an awe-inspiring exotic even in our unromantic times. Each character is built on a paradox (frustrated psychiatrist, exotic outdoor girl, knockabout model) as if to celebrate the dazzling transformation of being in our melting-pot culture. Whatever the film's shortcomings may be (not all the actors have the Grouchian mix of absurd and intense, nor has the script the precise resonances of *The Knack*, so that it periodically and lengthily collapses into facetiousness), its claim to a little aesthetic fame (apart from its nice visual tutti-frutti of *art nouveau*) are, notably, its combination of:

1. Neo-Marxism.

2. Spasmodicism. It is the first American adaptation of the British 'spasmodic school' (*A Hard Day's Night*, *The Knack*, *Help*). Rather charmingly, the American film was directed by an English *émigré*, and all the English films by an American *émigré*.

3. Social Atomicism. The characters' relationships have a fragmentary quality, a contemporary mixture of the cool and the superficial.

4. Molecularism, or, more precisely, 'Introverted disintegrationism'. The characters rush about hithering-and-dithering, helter-skeltering, hardly knowing their own minds for two seconds together, like corpuscles in a rainbow-coloured bloodstream. It all concludes in runaway Go-Karts—Named Desire. Its layabouts are runabouts.

5. Hyperessentialism. Its characters are conceived with what may at first seem an expressionist excess, but in fact they are conceived on the cartoon-and-comic-strip principle of the simple-but-paradoxical bunch of traits (like L'il Abner).

6. Dadaism. In its incessant pursuits it rivals the early films of René Clair (though it hasn't their melancholy and is deliberately non-precise in its gesticulations). It all but calls for two notable Clair titles: *A Nous Le Libertinisme* and *Entr'acte*. Clair's *Entr'acte* was a Dadaist film (and, some allege, actually directed by Picabia).

7. Mack Sennettism. To venture a *Private Eye*-ism, it's about the Keystone Kocks.

8. Fauvism. In the bold strokes with which it depicts fugitive, and essentially volatile, states of mind, in the characters' response to the superficial and decorative aspects of human nature, its sense of soul is fauve.

9. Bouduism. It is an irresponsible, libertarian, Priapic film.

16 · Pleading an Aesthetic Excuse

It is a professional deformity which sees films in order to have an opinion about them. And it is an eccentric minority who judge films by their realism or by their chances of what is optimistically called 'immortality'.

For the masses, the cinema is dreams and nightmares, or it is nothing. It is an alternative life, experience freed from the tyranny of that 'old devil consequences', from the limitation of having only one life to live. One's favourite films are one's unlived lives, one's hopes, fears, libido. They constitute a magic mirror, their shadowy forms are woven from one's shadow selves, one's limbo loves. The cinema is a theatre of cruelty, a land of cockayne, cloud cuckoo land, Parnassus, where passions are always young and in their prime, like the Gods. Wishes are horses and beggars can ride. Cuts and dissolves melt space and time. We live dangerously in safety. *We* are the immortal Gods watching the screen characters live their anguished lifetime-in-90-minutes lives. Our immunity sets us free to participate 'in the round'. Art doesn't really make the artist immortal, but it makes the audience *feel* immortal.

A moth-eaten dogma has it that a director is 'the' creative personality of a film. But even in cases when this is so, the audience participates by identifying with and caring about the characters. We share their feelings, if we like them, or project our repressed desires into them, if they're villains, or hope against hope if, like us, they're made of mingled shades of moral grey.

Awareness of the film as a work of art, and of the director behind it, is already the result of 'alienation', of intellectual abstraction, of *inattention*. Yes, of course, behind Marlene is Sternberg. But it's with Marlene that we feel. To live one's unlived life is to live through and with the screen characters. The rest is culture, and while it might interest us in other contexts, doesn't concern us here and now.

It's often presumed that the star system was a cynical mogul's fabrication foisted on to the public by sheer weight of dollars. Nothing could be further from the truth. It is directly descended from the nineteenth-century theatre and was equally prominent among preachers on the revivalist circuits from the 1880's down to Billy Graham. When film producers, fearing that stardom meant astronomical salaries, refused to name Florence Lawrence, the public countered by writing to 'The Biograph Girl'. As Edgar Morin relates, fan-mail arrived from all over the world addressed to the *characters* of French silent serials—Nick Carter, Fantomas. We have already seen how one brief glimpse of an extra looking longingly at Lillian Gish in *The Birth of a Nation*, or two words by Mae West, elicited a deluge of letters.

Alastair Cooke remarked, the majority of popular stars combine striking good looks (on the screen) with 'certain typical whimsicalities or personal traits of humour, temper, sarcasm—some single quality that is entertaining because it is effective to dramatize. Most movie-goers seem to prefer this compromise (between mere beauty and deep psychology) as a steady diet, probably because it offers superior beauty than anything they are personally familiar with, but is at the same time linked up—by the chosen personality characteristics—with a life they know. Thus Jean Arthur's husky downrightness and loyalty, Claudette Colbert's tongue-in-cheek, Carole Lombard's air of honest-to-goodness exasperation, Ginger Rogers' natural acceptance of hard facts. . . .'

In a sense the star is to the public as the sumptuous women of Tintoretto and Veronese were to the *nouveau-riche* of Renaissance Italy, or as the langorous females favoured by the Pre-Raphaelites: in Edgar Morin's words, 'Movie glamour bears witness to the presence of the ideal at the heart of the real . . . the archetypal beauty of the star acquires the hieratic quality of the mask. . . . The star's ideal beauty reveals an ideal soul.' Movie glamour is part of the artistic urge which tends, not towards the real, but towards the ideal. It is the Platonism of *l'homme moyen sensuel*, for whom 'heaven' is more Garden of Eden than a cloudy realm of sexless angels.

There are stars without superior beauty—Wallace Beery, Marie Dressler—for glamour is, perhaps, just one over-used facet of the life-force which stars assert as the classical Gods asserted (with

Charlton Heston for Mars, Jerry Lewis for Dionysus . . .). Glamour without this streak of life-force can never make a star. Of all Rank's charmschool girls only those who broke the mould made the grade— Diana Dors (by being brash, vulgar and working-class), Jean Simmons (by the glint of intensity, of Celtic feyness, in her well-balanced middle-class *persona*), Belinda Lee (after being liberated by an Italian love affair), and Honor Blackman (after donning black leather, high-boots, and topical fetishists' rig). The physical and the psychological interweave: 'Invariably what made them stars' observes Arthur Mayer, 'was some physical attribute or personal mannerism'—he cites, 'John Bunny's jovial bulk, Mary Pickford's golden curls and sweet smile, Maurice Costello's urbanity, Clara Kimball Young's yearning eyes.' We might add: Alan Ladd's deadpan, Bogart's paralysed upper lip and pebble voice, Veronica Lake's peekaboo wave—far from being just gimmicks, they are more even than icono-graphic emblems: fans take them as metaphors for personality-traits, as lyrical assertions of character. To see such traits as being, by the literary standards asserted by Henry James, psychologically crude, is only half the story. The well-loved characters of Dickens and Conan Doyle, or for that matter of Fielding, Richardson and Racine, are no more complex; Dickens endowed his characters with 'catch phrases' corresponding to a visual medium's visual 'tags'. And what makes an 'unrealistic' star seem, to an audience, realistic, is these feelings of theirs which his personality 'accommodates'. They are his resonance in them. Even when a star does happen to be a good actor, it is none the less in being *an object of the audience's projected feelings* that his stardom consists. The ingredient is some affirmative flashpoint with the audience's experience (the realistic aspect) and ideals (the idealis-tic aspect). If a star who can't act becomes a star, it is because the attitude which he automatically adopts towards his range of emotional material strikes at some emotional nerve-centre, some nexus of half-acknowledged memories, hopes, hesitations, fears. Stars, like poets, are unacknowledged legislators of the world—fans, and others, im-bibe, imitate, their mannerisms, personalities, and implied ethos. More accurately, perhaps, the stars are a reflection in which the public studies and adjusts its own image of itself. The individual adopts those stars, and those aspects of those stars, which he feels suit him. The same is true of poets—which is why neither group are legislators at all, or rather: the artist proposes, the audience disposes.

'What happened to the human face in painting?' inquired Roy Mc-

Mullen recently in *Réalités*, and answered that it has been ousted by a network of 'stylistic' characteristics. The other half of the answer is that it found a home from home in the audio-visual media, which are first and foremost media of personality, like the theatre, from which the cinema is, ontologically, derived. People go to the movies to look not 'at', but 'through' the pictures, at the faces and the events. A few films are primarily visual, in that the spectator, to appreciate its full meaning, must respond to image or sequence as a plastic entity, but in most films the image is merely a transparency, and sometimes is as irrelevant to the basically theatrical idiom as the grooves on a phonograph record are to the music. Who ever went to the movies to count the number of cuts? Most cuts are invisible, just as bar-lines in music are inaudible: the notes of the melody are the faces.

The actor is as central to most movies as the actor to a play when it's on the stage.

The intelligentsia's disdain of the star is motivated by the fact that the public's demands on a star's personality tend to limit the range of his performances. (There are exceptions: T. S. Eliot was a Marie Lloyd fan, and her range was as narrow as Kim Novak's—or as Mr. Micawber's and Sherlock Holmes's.) Second, intellectuals like to identify with creative artists, and current dogma has it that stars are witless things who do only what they're told by the director. This contention is often quite false: Lillian Gish contributed as much as any of her directors, Mae West and Burt Lancaster are famous for directing their directors. In any case, the director works through his actors, just as a painter works through his paintings, and it is the work of art to which we should first respond. An older tradition of film criticism talked about Bette Davis films (rather than Aldrich, Sherman, Rapper films); James Agate and *La Revue du Cinéma* (the grandfather of *Cahiers du Cinéma*) criticized in terms of stars as much as of directors; and it's a pity that such criticism in terms of stars has been left to the ladies of *Films in Review*, or degenerated into half-facetious cults by solemn intellectuals gigglingly off-duty. (Which perhaps explains why *slapstick* is criticized in terms of stars—but not 'serious' films.)

The social history of a nation can be written in terms of its film stars (or indeed of almost anything, but film stars are in some respects better even than newspapers). It's not my intention here to trace the shift from the little-girlishness of Mary Pickford to the Lolita syndrome of Sue Lyon, or from the innocence of Lillian Gish to the bland toughness of Kim Novak; or from eager-beavers like Harold Lloyd and Douglas Fairbanks to nervy young rat-racers like Jack Lemmon; or from the portly young father-figure of the 'teen-years, through the exotic erotic idols of the 20's, the reassuring middle-class figures of the late 30's (Crosby), the bitter deadpan of the late 40's (Ladd, Murphy) to the passionate young rebels of the 50's. Even cartoon figures mirror mores, as we shall see in considering American screen comedy. But our first concern here is with the artistic contribution made by a star to the film *as an aesthetic object*.

For convenience, let us divide stars into the 'plain' and the 'sacred monster'. Plainest of the plain is perhaps William Holden, who said of himself that he was no artist, in the grandiose sense of the word, but he was an efficient and honest 'journalist of the emotions'. This attitude to his acting reflects the very quality that gives it its resonance to the audience's experience. He's not especially good-looking, not especially courageous, not especially cynical, not especially anything; he's the ordinary, self-reliant American, wavering between the meanness and pain of the Billy Wilder world and the reluctant heroics of *The Bridge on the River Kwai*. He's conspicuously devoid of the optimism of the middle-class eager-beaver, but he slides more easily into a middle-class world than say, Burt Lancaster (whose mere presence always implies a proletarian origin). To him there still clings a little of the tough individuality of the Gary Cooper hero; he *can* play in Westerns; yet a tense awareness of his own limitations prefigures the softer, nervier, more anxious 'little men' of Tashlin's heroes. Holden's very plainness is the secret not merely of his popularity, but of his authenticity as a screen personality.

Gary Cooper and Frank Sinatra personify two great currents of American culture. One can hardly imagine a film in which they could co-star; Cooper's Western virtues seem hard to key in with Sinatra's jaunty cynicism. Coop, grave, slow, decisive, rode in from the open spaces; he is a rustic, a small town man; and even when Mr. Deeds Went to Town his straightforward goodness had the city slickers and the intellectuals (a Goldwaterite combination?) driving him almost to a suicidal silence. Coop worries, with dignity; the sudden, bleak, black rage of fear, never dwelt on, but briefly glimpsed, gives much of its strength to his portrayal of Mr. Deeds, as to that of the sheriff in *High Noon* (and its absence is the weakness of Wyler's *The Westerner*).

Coop dreads, and punches; Sinatra shrugs, or drugs, or drinks, or takes a tranquillizer, or another girl, or a plane. Coop is rural, small-town, middle-class, inner-directed. Sinatra's cocky grin has the tough derisiveness of an alley cat, a gritty sensitivity, nerves as taut as his cheekbones. His easy assurance goes with a forlorn vulnerability. His bitchy petulance is that of the cosmopolitan orphan. His best films are all from his 'middle period' of the 50's, notably *Meet Danny Wilson*, *Pal Joey*, *Man with the Golden Arm* which came nearest to the sadness needed to complete his artistic personality. (Similarly, I wish Coop had been directed by Clouzot or Clément, who wouldn't have been afraid of plunging us into the 'black' band of his spectrum.) The same qualities inform Sinatra's singing—his voice is brassy and warm, can open up in a rhapsodic boost, jaunt along cagily, wrench out the sudden dramatic punch, the jab of pathos. However ingenuous the lyrics, he goes along with them, wholeheartedly, in hope. He sings a tourist's panegyric about Granada, and we know that he knows that Granada, like every other town in this over-trotted globe, is just a nightclub with broads, but his warm, even ebullience amounts to a reckless defiance of disenchantment, the raw half-tones easily sidle up to jubilation. But once, just once, he should make a film as uncompromising as *Jeanne Eagels*.

At the other extreme, some stars exist to shock and outrage the audience. The sacred monster's every gesture, every response, challenges the assumed, the expected, the 'right'. He (or she) may be aloofly wrapped in mystery like Garbo, or aggressively tormented, like Brando; either way, the audience is swung between hopeless adoration and noisy contempt, and passionate identification co-exists with something like fascinated hatred. Garbo and Dietrich with their strange accents came from vague foreign lands which are really the 'nowhere' of a late romanticism—indeed, the *femme fatale* is a romantic obsession, burgeoning in Keats' *La Belle Dame Sans Merci*, blossoming in Swinburne and d'Annunzio, whose poems inspire the great Italian divas, who in turn inspire their American adaptations (Theda Bara), and so on through Nazimova, Negri and Baclanova (who import the French interest in Slav *femme fatales*) down to the last romantic vamps of the 30's (Garbo, Dietrich). More often than we realize, Hollywood 'vulgarity' is simply the direct heir of high literary fashion. By the 1950's there are no romantic nowheres that haven't been flown over by the U.S.A.A.F. and Kim Novak, like Dean and Brando, is 'neurotic' so as to be unpredictable, fascinating, exotic. If the silent vamps, male and female, mirror the *dreams* of the kid next door, Novak, Dean and Brando, in an age dominated by psychological realism (not to say self-consciousness taken by popular pseudo-Freudianism to the point of hypochondria) reflects his *conflicts*. Their exoticism is only a pretext, for intensifying, lifting to the level of acting-out, conflicts in which the spectator feels he can recognize his own impulses, inhibitions and sufferings. With Valentino, the 20's audience escaped a brash, bustling world. Brando doesn't don Arab costume, and his name has intimations of immigrant vulgarity rather than of Latin languor. His inarticulacy signals his resistance to the rationalist, optimist, conformist, utilitarian, anti-emotional tendencies of middle-class Anglo-Saxondom. His struggles to speak, his fluttering eyelashes, his evident sensuality, his unreasonableness and male integrity-in-immaturity, subvert the middle-class ideal of the man well and unemotionally adjusted to routine action rather than passionately responsiveness to experience: in short, a ghost in a machine.

Or we may contrast two suffragettes—for the 30's, Katharine Hepburn, who was as hated in many popular halls as she was liked by the carriage trade. To see why, we can safely forget all her 'ladylike' films, like George Stevens' *Quality Street*, and concentrate on Gregory La Cava's *Stage Door*, where an astute storyline deliberately endows her with every trait which audiences (and particularly male audiences) of the time might have found most exasperating. She is (*a*) a topdog—stinking rich with unearned wealth, amidst a boarding-house-full of struggling actresses, (*b*) coolly and positively scornful of their envy, (*c*) bossy, (*d*) a self-righteous suffragette (spoiling a girl's affair with a sugar-daddy by trying to punish him for 'deceiving' her), (*e*) an ambitious and talentless career-girl, (*f*) intellectual, (*g*) arty. She gets another girl's part and indirectly causes her suicide, and feels just enough genuine remorse (no more) to make herself into a successful actress. Throughout the film she proves a verbal match for Ginger Rogers—the tough, bitter, proletarian blonde who is 'our' principal identification figure. One hardly needs the confirmation of La Cava's *Gabriel Over the White House* to detect the rightwing message of *Stage Door*. 'If you're over-privileged, don't apologize—you probably deserve to be: for unto those that hath guts shall be given and from those that hath not it shall be taken away.'

Katharine Hepburn also occupies a particular place in the evolution of the American woman. Amicably battling with Spencer Tracy in one comedy after another, she shows a specifically modern emancipation; but in *The African Queen* she is also the Puritan missionary of pioneer days—in fact if you substitute a covered wagon for a steam-launch, and the desert for the river, and Indians for Germans, the film reveals itself as more original in setting than in human values. In *Suddenly Last Summer* she presents another facet of the forceful woman—Momism gone mad. Perhaps the most moving of her recent performances was in *Summer Madness*, directed by David Lean, a lyricist of life's lost opportunities. She was miscast as a plain, characterless spinster whom no one even notices, but what came through was the story of a woman being lonely because she is too self-assured (strangely enough Miss Hepburn later complained that during the shooting of the film she was lonely because everyone assumed that she was too much the 'great lady' to enjoy their social life). A woman's yearning for her own lost softness and helplessness underlies the later Joan Crawford films, from Michael Curtiz' *Mildred Pierce* (1945) to David Miller's *The Story of Esther Costello* (1957); she was always letting herself be wronged by sleek, soft, effeminate Zachary Scott, or by gigolo womanizer Rossanno Brazzi—Katie's lover in *Summer Madness*. It's amusing to imagine Joan Crawford in Lean's film. Her very vulgarity might have made it as moving, in a different way.

The Hepburn of the 30's prefigures Lauren Bacall, with her rangey physique, husky voice, and dry attack. But Bacall, paradoxically, was less controversial—perhaps because the domineering strength was softened by compensations of sultry sensuality (whereas Hepburn has something distinctly schoolmarmish). But a fan in J. P. Mayer's *British Cinemas and their Audiences* talks of Lauren Bacall's 'slithery virility' and it's possible to see in the 'good-bad girl' of the 40's (perfect specimen: Bacall in *The Big Sleep*) a first step towards what Edmund Bergler establishes as the current fashion of *Counterfeit Sex*, partly confirmed by the quite unusual number of American films in which the manly men are sexually passive and the females have to be the males too, a turnabout reaching a mannerist intensity in Wilder's *Some Like it Hot* (1959) and Minnelli's *Goodbye Charley* (1964).

In a word, many an American woman is Katherine Hepburn posing, for men, as Lauren Bacall. If these generalizations seem outrageous, there's no doubt that they are; nor, of course, can one go into all the rights and wrongs of Momism, 'bringing up father', and other peculiarly American forms of the battle of the sexes. Possibly it's worth suggesting that puritanism (Christian and agnostic), competitive individualism, and the middle-class traits referred to earlier, all serve to stiffen the ego's resistance to erotic feelings, which are intrinsically dangerous to the ego: men, being more volatile, become more inhibited, emotionally, if not physically, or at least feel less assured, than women.

B.B.'s erotic aggressiveness is female, Dionysiac and childish, thus revealing her as post-puritan, post-suffragette and post-*bourgeois*—where the attack of her potential American equivalent, Debbie Reynolds, is slightly more masculine, certainly Apollonic and Momist. (I haven't forgotten Tuesday Weld; but she's ersatz B.B., Hollywood's misconception of B.B., just as Theda Bara is hick America's idea of the Italian diva.) With B.B. the equality of the sexes is assumed, freed from its rationalist-puritan associations, and given a libertarian tinge. The search of the erotically emancipated female is for a male passionate but firm enough, not to subjugate, the spontaneous, and therefore childlike, female (a common misreading of Vadim's first film) but to steady her impulsiveness, and satisfy her need for a paternal love. Instead of 'bringing up father', she's looking for one, and the dramatic mainspring of Vadim's *Et Dieu Créa la Femme* (1956) is that the younger brother (Trintignant) who really loves her is an idealizing 'son' type, the elder brother (Marquand) who has all the male virtues is a moral traditionalist who despises her for being beddable, while the fatherly tycoon (Jurgens) can only offer her money instead of happiness.

Trintignant, disillusioned and hysterical, tries to assert himself by a destructive masculinity (the shooting); Jurgens, though wounded, protects him from the consequences, and, paradoxically, the slap which the young man deals B.B. is a kathartic renunciation of violence, an acceptance of responsibility towards, and rights over, her. The idea that B.B., here or in any other film, is a 'mere' sex-object, a Lolita for Humbert Humberts, is puritans' rubbish. The teenage girls who spontaneously adopted her style, did so for completely different reasons. We all know that today male teenagers find growing up harder than girls (in Victorian days it was the other way round), and 1960's teenage girls adopted the B.B. style to appeal to, and to help, their boy friends to father them. You always see a B.B. girl with a boy of her own age, because this modern paganism, without being 'beat'—it's too straightforward—shrugs its shoulders at money and prefers a hedonism of the heart. B.B. has never played a gold-digger, and Sue Lyon is the very antithesis of the B.B. ethos. It's precisely this that makes Autant-Lara's *En Cas de Malheur* so poignant; it's Gabin, representative of the responsible older generation, who's too cynical to believe that he's anything more than a sugar-daddy to B.B., and so does as much as her weaknesses to precipitate the tragedy.

It's a pity that Sinatra and B.B. never made their projected film together, for leaving aside all the boring in-jokes about 'the clan' Sinatra is not only an American hero. He is twentieth-century cosmopolitanism—first, as the ex-alleycat at the London Hilton, second, as the globetrotting nomad of an endless nightlife. He would be almost as much at home in a French film; it's interesting to speculate what he would have made of the Aznavour part in *Tirez Sur le Pianiste* (1960). Curiously, one finds in a bad film of his for Charles Vidor, *The Joker is Wild* (1958), parallel themes, of the entertainer versus the gangsters, the hero betraying his women. At which point one remembers that Truffaut's film is based on a novel by David Goodis. Sinatra's world interpenetrates Robert Mitchum's—the hardboiled-sensitivity of the one parallels the beefy cynicism of the other. For Richard Winnington, Mitchum in Jacques Tourneur's *Build My Gallows High* (1947) incarnated the joyless masochism of the all-American ratrace. But the Mitchum qualities which Winnington evoked by such phrases as 'the saddest and most laconic dick we have ever known . . . another bout of enervated passion. . . . Jeff is by now too tired to love so he . . . dials the police. Kathie's last act is to release Jeff from the ennui of breathing . . .' have another meaning for Mitchum's fan-following, which is essentially teenage, urban and proletarian. They take these qualities in another sense too, as 'lazy, relaxed, cynical, tough, shrewd, bold enough to be bad but too easy-going to be vicious, solitary, none too happy, undismayed . . .' the eternal outsider. His very shamble has something pre-beatnik about it (though beatniks shucked off the need to be tough). When in the late 40's he served a prison sentence on a narcotics rap, the Press ran photographs of Mitchum in prison gear cleaning up dustbins, and his fanmail soared to an unprecedented level. Publicity which would have annihilated a conformist star only perfected his screen image.

As Mitchum and his public, matured, a new mellowness and humour came to inform the initial blend of barfly cynicism and slumbering violence that made him, in Dmytryk's *Crossfire* a disturbing incarnation of the average man's know-nothing anti-idealism, from which a tough human decency (very) tardily emerged. Most of his films have been bad, content to exploit rather than to explore his screen personality; but such exceptions as Robert Parrish's *The Wonderful Country* and Vincente Minnelli's *Home From the Hill* have delved into its core, of honest nonconformity, where a depressed cynicism is the tragic error of a wry lucidity.

In its day *Sequence* expressed a rather refined admiration for such sappy youngsters as Diana Dors, Audrey Hepburn and Micheline Presle. Otherwise its 'People We Like' were a collection of Aunt and Uncle figures like Claire Trevor, Mary Astor, Catherine Lacey, Barbara Bel Geddes, Ward Bond and George Cole. Since then Bette Davis and Joan Crawford have become the Auntie Fun figures of *Sight and Sound*. All very safe and tepid.

A younger Oxford generation virtually ignores actors and enjoys only the vicarious experience of being a film director—via such easy conformists as Hawks, Preminger, and Leo McCarey.

However, Andrew Sarris once began an interview with a sustained defence in intellectual depth of his *auteur* theory, and concluded by confessing that what really kept him coming to the cinema was its girls. Here is the beginning of wisdom. Here human relationships are re-endowed with the shock of desire which our shallow rationalists, who use Freud only to reinforce their Anglo-Saxon psychological hypochondria, are so anxious to disallow. Here, however shyly, the old Adam peeps out from behind the *pince-nez* of culture, and the bland, shining mask of 'objectivity' cracks to reveal a human expression.

17 · Tales versus Novels

The Biblical story of Samson and Delilah is told so briefly that no publisher would accept it as even the synopsis of a novel. As an inevitable consequence of its brevity, the characterization is sketchy and vague, the 'motivation' nil, the whole lacking in convincing detail, or indeed, any detail at all.

The same synopsis, in the hands of three different novelists, could not but acquire three different themes, three different sets of characters, three different sequences of psychological cause-and-effect; three different 'contents'. Yet it is its sketchy, 'contentless' form that has intrigued generation upon generation of readers.

For the 'tale', bare as it is, intrigues, and communicates, by its structure of paradoxes. An (a) *weak* woman conquers a (a1) *strong* man. He (b) *knows* she is an enemy, but (b1) *acquiesces.* His (a2) *strength* lies in his (a3) *weakest* part (his hair). When at his (a4) *weakest* (blind), he proves (a5) *strongest*, annihilating all his (b2) *enemies*, his (b3) *loved enemy* and (b4) *himself*. The 'eloquence' of the story is in its tension of paradoxes.

The 'tale', a genre distinct from the novel (and far from obsolescent, even though the novel evolved from it) conforms to the comments of Aristotle in his *Poetics*. 'There are therefore necessarily six elements in every tragedy, which give it its quality; and they are the Fable, Character, Language, Thought, *Mise-en-Scène* and Melody.... The chief of these is the plotting of the incidents . . . the fable ought to have been so plotted that if one heard the bare facts, the chain of circumstances would make one shudder and pity. This would happen to anyone who heard the fable of the *Oedipus*' (or of *Samson and Delilah*). Similarly, writes La Charrière, for the reading public of the fourth century A.D., 'whether pagan or Christian, no *Life* of a sage or saint could possess an *edifying* quality unless it had first the quality of *amazement* and conformed to the laws of the aretological genre, laws as strict and binding as the literary conventions which apply today as, for example, in the detective story'.

Myths, fairy tales and folk art generally conform to the same aesthetic. The tales of the Round Table, of Aladdin's Magic Lamp, of the Magic Tinderbox, the tales of Greek myths and Norse Gods are sequences of vivid, powerful situations and paradoxes.

Similarly with characterization. From *Sir Gawayne and the Green Knight* through the tale of Patient Griselda in Chaucer's *The Canterbury Tales*, through Mary Shelley's *Frankenstein* down to, say, Joseph Heller's *Catch 22*, many authors have sought, similarly, the 'striking fable', using either exaggeration or the bold, haunting idea. The 'poetry' is in the paradoxes of the plot.

Jean Cocteau's comment in *Opium* reminds us of the prevalence of this aesthetic in our oral culture, and of its incessant infiltrations into 'high culture'. 'I have come to know Eisenstein. I had seen aright. He invented the murder steps at the last moment. Those steps became part of Russian history. Alexandre Dumas and Eisenstein are the only true historians. . . . Tragic events have the power of those little obscene anecdotes, anonymous anecdotes which are perfected from one mouth to another and finish as the typical stories of a race. Jewish stories or Marseilles stories.' Some other modern 'tales': Dr. Crippen, the Angels of Mons, the Wreck of the Mary Deare, Casey Jones, Frankie and Johnny, Stephen Ward. . . .

In such tales, detailed characterization, where it exists at all, is of secondary interest. But even where authors and spectators are interested in character, such characters, by current academic standards, are 'two-dimensional'. Ulysses, Gawayne, most of Chaucer's pilgrims, Sir Epicure Mammon, Sir Toby Belch, Tom Jones, Mr. Micawber and Sherlock Holmes are, essentially, 'bas-reliefs', rather than 3-dimensional in the modern sense. Sharply realistic details exist in, for example, Defoe's *Robinson Crusoe* and Richardson's *Clarissa Harlowe*, but those exegeses which seek to establish a continuous 'stream' of subtleties smack of special pleading. These early novels are just as limited, just as complex, as L'il Abner or James Bond. 'The popular imagination . . .' writes Louis James of nineteenth-century proletarian tastes, 'is interested in character conceived on a simple, well-defined place, which exists independently of a complex literary form. All popular heroes have been subjects of prolonged story cycles, whether *Odysseus*, King Arthur, Sexton Blake or *The Archers*, the successful English radio serial.'

To the aesthetic of the 'tale' academic culture has, by and large, turned a blind eye. As recently as my grammar school days, English masters instructed us all in the necessity for realistic and deep characterization, logically consistent behaviour, penetrating studies of motive, and that proliferation of vivid detail suggested by Henry James's phrase, 'density of specification'. We were besought to insist upon the 'texture of lived experience', and many of the exegeses we studied had strained to detect such 'density' in such improbable places as folk ballads, or Chaucer's tale of Patient Griselda. Yet it was curious that, rich and complex as was the showpiece of the 'complexity' school, *Hamlet*, each critic struggled to isolate its hero's 'real' motives, to simplify, to synopsize, him into a figure almost as systematic and simple as another famous procrastinator, L'il Abner. For, as Erich Auerbach remarked in his study of the development of European literary realism, 'To write history is so difficult that most historians are forced to make concessions to the technique of legend.'

Nowadays, of course, the 'tale' aesthetic has taken on a new vigour. Science fiction offers a particularly clear example of popular art's inheritance from folk art. A science fiction story may be written in a merely competent style, with scarcely adequate characterization, and yet fascinate and haunt the reader because of the inventiveness with which the author has developed his central 'extrapolation' (or integrated his cluster of them). The ideas have an eloquence apart from the 'density of detail' ('style'). The plays of Ionescou depend, to a great extent, on their qualities of 'tale'. And though the 'texture of lived experience' remains important, the study of motivation through literature has, and it's high time, been overtaken by psychology, sociology, and various other branches of the 'humanities'.

The quality of the tale of Samson and Delilah lies in its paradoxes. Similarly, complexity in 'tale' characterization, where it is present, arises not from meticulously stated detail, but from contradictory traits which build up the tension of paradox. The Frankenstein Monster is *brutal* but *pathetic*; he's a *creature* who masters his *creator*; he's brute *material* capable of a lofty *idealism* that turning *sour* makes him a *devil*—but a *sympathetic* one. Sherlock Holmes is, overtly, far less complex than the Monster. (Mainly: his acumen assorts oddly with such weaknesses as morphine-taking, his non-emotionality with his violin-playing.) But his very *extremism* is, judged by ordinary human preoccupations, if not actually a paradox, a challenge, a shock. It haunts.

Ours is a 'realistic' age, which means, in effect, that we like our fantasies to be readily identifiable as such, and to be realistic in their details (requirements now being challenged by the literature of the absurd). Outside such overt fantasies (e.g. *King Kong*) 'extremism' stops short of the (to us) outrageous implausibilities of, say, Chaucer's Patient Griselda story, which, ontologically, is half-way between a 'realistic tale' and the Byzantine fairy-story on which it is based (and, it may be added, a very awkward half-way indeed).

Similarly, a film story which is, essentially, a 'good tale', may be mistakenly dismissed as a 'bad novel'.

18 · Theme and Variations

Our first glimpse of Johnny (Sterling Hayden) shows us a sad, forlorn fellow, riding slowly, aimlessly, along a dusty trail. He is conspicuously gunless, and unable to intervene in a stagecoach hold-up nearby. He accepts his helplessness with a philosophical detachment—resignation? cynicism? both? He strolls into an opulent gambling-house and humbly asks for a job. Its owner appears—an adventuress named Vienna (Joan Crawford), who is clad in what is virtually a masculine rig-out (black shirt, trousers, boots and guns) and behaves in a hard, bossy way. Her customers include a tough, brawling gang of outlaws— Black Bart (Ernest Borgnine), their boss, the Dancin' Kid (Scott Brady) and a teenager, Turkey (Ben Cooper). Black Bart hates everybody and is always on the look-out for someone whom he can bully. The Dancin' Kid is Vienna's prospective lover, while Turkey boyishly adores her. The hero makes a startling entry into this tough company—with a blue cup of coffee in one hand, a cigarette in another, no guns and a meek, smiling manner. When the others try to pick a quarrel with him, he asks mildly, 'What more can a man want than a cup of coffee and a smoke?' Black Bart sees a likely victim in this thoroughly castrated fellow (jobless, gunless, sexless) and sets about getting him drunk by plying him with whiskies and ordering the hero to consume them—which the latter obediently does.

The theme-song (sung over the credits), the casting (Sterling Hayden usually plays unromantic toughies), the actor's personality and the hero's calm self-possession keep reminding us that Johnny Guitar is the film hero and hinting that he'll come out all right in the end. Still, the audience is mystified and full of curiosity as to what, if anything, the hero's motives can be for his strange mildness and gunlessness. They fear he will take his line of conduct to the point of being thoroughly craven. They wonder whether they despise him, and are mildly mystified to find that they don't. Of course, it isn't long before he and Black Bart swap punches and, in a man-to-man fist-fight, the latter is shown up as a blubbering coward, though still so spiteful and treacherous as to be very dangerous.

Here then we have the thoroughly conventional contrast between the pacifistic but tough hero, and the bellicose but weak villain. All the same, the film has introduced it with a very unsettling 'excess'. One line of dialogue establishes a social-philosophical reason, of sorts, for Johnny's inoffensiveness. Why did he give up carrying a gun? 'Because I'm not the fastest draw west of the Pecos.' In other words, 'if I threaten nobody by disarming myself, I shall provoke no one and live, whereas if I carry guns I shall lose my immunity and meet my match eventually.' The audience thinks of his gunlessness as a deliberate, reasoned-out point of view. Later in the film this position is shown to be just a pretence, or, at most, a subsidiary reason. Still, for the moment, the encounter between Black Bart and Johnny has the quality of a collision of points of view, of ways of life. Throughout the film, Johnny is, vaguely, peace-loving modern man, the man with the grey flannel gunlessness. More specifically, he refuses to be aggressive, or warlike, for sensible, though unidealistic, reasons.

A few minutes later, in another scene, this interpretation is sharply contradicted. Turkey is showing off his marksmanship to Vienna; suddenly Johnny snatches up a gun, outshoots, humiliates and wounds him—indeed, only a sternly shouted warning from Vienna stops him killing the boy. Immediately after his violent impulse, Johnny is suitably contrite, or at least ashamed. This incident paraphrases, and leads into an exposition of, why Johnny and Vienna ended a previous love affair years ago. He is really Johnny Logan, who was not just a crack gun fighter, but actually gun-crazy, an instinctive killer. In a sense, he was, and, under pressure of jealousy, is, blacker than Black Bart: for whereas Black Bart is satisfied with bluster and humiliation, Johnny immediately snatches up a gun, without warning, to kill. Of course, he doesn't forfeit our sympathy: in the first place, he has renounced killing, his current pacifism is an expiation of his previous bloodthirstiness; in the second, he struggles against his psychological taint; in the third, even when unarmed, he is courageous.

Vienna's black, mannish, villain's clothes express one level of her character. Here is your American matriarch, woman as owner and boss, wearing not only the pants but the six-shooters. She and the hero have exchanged roles. She is tough and mannish to a fault, he is passive and inoffensive to a fault. But just as his outburst with Turkey reveals the turbulent virility beneath, so it isn't long before she too reveals that her masculinity represses an 'excessive' playing of the female role. Their debate over their past love-affair, and whose fault it was that they parted, provides a great deal of additional information about their 'present' characters. Although retrospective, their quick, sharp accusations and retorts set up a suspense of moral sympathies and a suspense of 'hope' about their chances of resuming their love affair and finding happiness. The heroine leaves us in no doubt about her past: during the conversation she wears a scarlet dress, and when explaining how she rose to become a woman of property, she cries, 'For each brick, each plank, each beam of this place, I——' He cuts in sadly: 'Don't. . . .'

The general impression we get from the conversation is that for their parting he must take most of the blame. Their past relationship is a 'complement' of their present one. Then he was emotionally hard, she was vulnerable and womanly. Now, emotionally, he is 'subject' to her, having no guns and no job. His 'castration' is really a moral penance. His 'civilized' point of view is really guilt, 'imposed' on him by a woman—or rather, by his harshness towards her in the past, leading up to her present re-rejection of him.

Later in the film, when she and Johnny seem to be coming together again, she changes to a white, full, feminine dress which might be a wedding dress, even a kind of virginity. She is seized by the townsfolk, who truss her up in it to lynch her, but saved by Johnny. She finally reverts to her masculine clothes for the film's climax, a gunfight between herself and the film's principal villain, another matriarch, Emma (Mercedes McCambridge). So there are really three Viennas— Vienna the bad (wo)man in black, Vienna the scarlet (Scarlett) woman, and virginal Vienna, made to be martyred.

Emma, a 'pioneer' type, wears a plain, full-skirted dress and has a raucous, corncrake voice. She is in Vienna's age-bracket, is plump and plain, but very susceptible to the charms of the Dancin' Kid, who, however, resolutely prefers Vienna. Emma is a spinster-cum-harpy, hating the Dancin' Kid and Vienna both, and constantly urging the decent but weak sheriff to arrest them: finally she does persuade him to lynch her rival. Apparently homely, feminine, ascetic and virtuous, she is really more dominating and destructive than Vienna. Vienna is a mannish matriarch and ex-prostitute, but love restores the wedding-dress woman she is at heart. She has pacified a vicious killer (Johnny). On the other hand, Emma's love has turned to hate: the Dancin' Kid 'makes her feel like a woman, and she don't like it, so she wants to hang him'. She doesn't get much sympathy for her frustration, for her personality assures us that her 'love' was never very generous anyway. And whereas Vienna's influence is pacificatory, Emma turns peaceful citizens (sheriff and posse) into vicious killers (lynch law).

When Vienna is seized by the posse, Emma gleefully takes potshots at the gambling-house chandelier (Prohibition-style) and watches the place burn down. It is these flames which, after Vienna has been rescued from the posse, set fire to the train of her white dress. For the lynching, the posse wear ultra-respectable black (having just come from a funeral). And after Vienna has been nearly hanged in her white dress, she is nearly burnt alive in it. Black slacks are certainly more practical in the land of gunfire and fire.

The lynching also retrospectively 'palliates' Johnny's vicious attack on Turkey. Emma's posse find Turkey hiding in Vienna's saloon (very much a son-and-mother situation). They half-promise to pardon him if he frames Vienna. He appeals to her. It's his life or hers, he's only a boy, what should he do. The appeal to Vienna's maternal instinct is of couree thoroughly treacherous. She answers curtly, 'Save yourself.' Emma double-crosses Turkey and persuades the reluctant posse to hang them both. Turkey is hanged, but just as the noose lifts Vienna out of the saddle, Johnny, who has been hiding nearby, cuts her down with a knife, snatches her up on his horse, and rides away. When Vienna asks him why he didn't save Turkey first, he points out that he had to choose between saving him or saving her (he hadn't a gun, only a knife to cut the noose—another 'inversion' of his being unarmed). His calculation is chilly but reasonable. And it's justice: Johnny's choice ('which shall I save?') is an inversion of the choice which Turkey treacherously shifted to Vienna. But, also, Johnny has now done, with every sort of justification, what he nearly did at the beginning, that is, get rid of Turkey and keep Vienna for himself.

The most emphatic antagonisms in the film are between Black Bart and Johnny Guitar, and between Emma Small and Vienna. Black Bart and Emma are both plumper, less attractive and more vicious than their opposite numbers. Emma is a frustrated spinster and a defeated gunslinger, whereas Vienna has lived out her desire to a fault (the scarlet dress, the badman kit). Johnny Guitar and the Dancin' Kid both have 'musical' names, as if to stress their decorative, i.e. sexual, appeal. Both are very dangerous—we have no doubt that the lithe Dancin' Kid would make short work of Black Bart. Both are rivals for Vienna, both are gunslingers. But the obvious dramatic conflict, between Johnny and the Dancin' Kid, is by-passed until near the end, when their gunfight is stopped by Vienna, who sets them both to helping her prepare breakfast instead, a nice housewifely-matriarchal touch. The Dancin' Kid is then accidentally shot by Emma, who appropriately mistakes him for Johnny Guitar. The emotional expectation of a gunfight, set up in the audience as Johnny and the Dancin' Kid bicker, is disappointed, but 'shifted' over into the climactic fight between the two gun-totin' Mommas.

So Johnny Guitar is 'patterned' not only by Black Bart, but also by the Dancin' Kid. And his encounter with Turkey has another undertone. For at this point both are 'subservient' to Vienna—Turkey because he is only a teenager, Johnny because he is a saddle-tramp. Turkey is the 'good' boy, Johnny is the vicious boy who has rejected his mother, made her a prostitute and now seeks reinstatement. In a limited sense, Turkey and Johnny are two 'sons', competing for 'mother'. But, of course, Johnny is older than Turkey, more experienced and formidable, and has had a previous love affair with Vienna. So, in a way, he is a father-figure to Turkey, just as Vienna is a mother-figure. According to Freud, authority-figures, in melodramas as in dreams, tend to be parental figures, so that the Sheriff is another weak father-figure, constantly being egged on by Emma, the 'housewifely mother'.

Vienna even has a father-figure; one of the employees at her gambling house is Old Tom (John Carradine), a lonely old man who dies trying to save Vienna. There is a fourth member of the gang, Cory (Royal Dano), not unlike Old Tom in being self-effacing and unaggressive. At every opportunity he buries himself in a good book —an 'intellectual', thoughtful streak recalling Johnny's 'musical' name. He shows the risks of being thoughtful and quiet by getting himself treacherously shot by Black Bart.

We have presented these patterns in terms of similarities—but only so as to show that these patterns do exist. None the less, the first impression they give is that of strong contrasts. The similarity is there to establish the tension of the dissimilarity. We don't feel Black Bart and Johnny Guitar, or Vienna and Emma, or Emma and Black Bart, as being 'the same, but different'—quite the reverse, it's a case of 'similar poles repel'. Our patterns of similarities are also patterns of differences. . . .

19 · The Emotional Flow

Although *Johnny Guitar* is shaped around a very forceful 'goodies-baddies' polarity, the pattern of emotional shocks and paradoxes is both involved and nuanced. It must be said that the plot is unusually complicated, so much that some of the conflicts are worked through very rapidly, in an almost schematic way, and only half-involve the spectator. This is not a negative criticism, for, being half-serious, they act as a streak of 'comedy-thriller', inculcating a satirical attitude towards the characters. Black Bart, for example, is the butt of a great many laughs, like Cory and, to a lesser extent, the Dancin' Kid.

The dramatis personae fall into three main groups: (1) the gang of outlaws; (2) the townsfolk; (3) the people who live at the gambling house (notably Vienna and Johnny). We might say that the gang groups four 'outlaw' attitudes; the townsfolk are 'respectability', with both its good aspects (the posses are decent at heart, though weak) and its bad one (Emma is frustrated and vindictive); while the denizens of the gambling house are outcasts but not outlaws—individuality with all its faults—and they are the most generous individuals in the film.

Each of the groups is split within itself. Johnny is Vienna's ally in some ways but her antagonist in others. Emma is constantly bullying the posse. The gang, as befitting lawless characters, mostly hate one another, and are constantly bickering. The egghead is less aggressive, but resolutely ignores them, preferring to lose himself in a good book, so perhaps he's just as egoistic. Even so, the discussion is far from schematic—the three groups are unified by 'overlapping' characters, e.g. Turkey (who in some ways is attached to Vienna, in others to the gang) or the Sheriff (who tries to stand up for Vienna and Johnny against Emma).

Each of the principal characters is split within himself. In a sense, each character is a group of characters. There are three Viennas—black Vienna, scarlet Vienna, white Vienna. Each is a different aspect of the same woman, just as Black Bart 'is' a different aspect of Johnny Guitar. Just as each group of characters is a set of variations on a common theme, so each character is a set of variations on a common theme. Very simple melodramas characteristically have the equation, 'one person = one attitude', but a film like *Johnny Guitar*, though, really, a melodrama, has left this primitive level of meaning far behind, it has a lively and stimulating chop and change of emotional permutations.

The emotional pattern is further variegated by the 'infrastructure' of audience response. At first we feel sorry for Turkey, admire his pluck and dislike the hero for humiliating him. We are mildly surprised to find this nice lad is in cahoots with Black Bart and the Dancin' Kid. We hope, we're sure, that he'll reform and save himself. But later the very vulnerability which we pitied betrays the heroine—we may still feel pity for him, but have to admit that his being hanged is poetic justice. The character-trait persists, but, as circumstances 'test' and reveal it, so our attitudes to it change. The audience's feelings towards the characters are like 'invisible' characters in the drama.

All this may seem to be getting us into very deep waters. But in fact scriptwriters swim happily about them every day. When adapting a novel for the screen, one often combines two characters—a 'group of characters'—into one person. Or one abolishes a character, but, feeling one particular aspect of his attitudes is important, transfers the relevant dialogue to another character. Or one may make two hitherto 'unrelated' characters 'accomplices', which one can do only if they have some common interest or attitude, i.e. are 'variations on a theme'. Or one may write in a character so that his 'attitude' will bring to the audience a new range of emotions. Any writer, often quite consciously, whether he is writing a film, a novel or a play, will invent a character whose job is to symbolize a particular response to the problem which comprises the film's theme. Literature abounds in friends, servants, confidantes, etc., whose function is to act as emotional counterpoint to the heroes. Juliet—virginal romantic passion—has an earthily Rabelaisian Nurse, Horatio provides a common-sense 'norm' helping us to orientate ourselves towards the more brilliant but unstable Hamlet, Arthur Seaton has Bert. In talking to them, the hero is revealing himself to the audience. But, simply by being there, they also tend to attract to themselves the role of contradicting or counterpointing the hero, becoming another bundle of feelings appropriate to the film's circumstances. Racine and Corneille, with their exceptionally rigorous approach, tended to keep the 'confidant' very close to the principal character's viewpoint. Even so, the confidant often, unobtrusively, moves into opposition and expresses forebodings, awe, and other forms of 'resistance'. In the Greek drama, the 'satellite' characters often become the voice of common sense, of 'the average conscience'—like the 'chorus'.

Thus one can almost see Hamlet/Horatio as a kind of 'twin' character—as well as being, in other ways, 'opposites', like Juliet and her Nurse. A hero's 'twin' may act as counsellor, or as tempter—suggesting to the hero ideas which are only vaguely and weakly formulated in his mind. In a sense Iago is Othello's 'opposite'—but he is also Othello's tempter, his still small voice; thus, he 'is' the concealed suspicions *in* Othello; indeed, he can influence Othello only because there is something in Othello to which his arguments appeal. Without Iago-in-Othello, there'd be no play, because Othello would be quicker to suspect Iago than to suspect Desdemona. Iago and Othello are opposites *because* they are twins, just as 'close' as Hamlet and Horatio.

However, the fact that the first pair of characters are enemies while the second pair are allies is, of course, an important difference between the pairs. The dramatic relationship (friendship, hostility) represents, in a sense, another 'bundle of feelings', another 'invisible character'. Looking at it from another angle, we can say that a hero who is hesitating between two alternative feelings (shall I trust her or murder her?) is a psychologically more sophisticated version of an argument between two characters each of whom stands for a different attitude. This sounds rather abstruse, but in fact it is a thoroughly practical proposition. An author may create a second character so that the hero can argue with him—when the second character is, up to a point, the hero's alter ego. Or the author may invent a character whose job it is to 'split the difference' between dramatic opposites. For example, given the situation of a good man and a bad man hiding out in the hills together, it is often very convenient to have a third party whose 'vote' carries the day, who can calm down their quarrels, or start them up, or work in different senses at different times. Or one might decide to do without this 'casting vote' and have goodie and baddie argue things out and come to some sort of decision. Or one may have a third person who is open to persuasion and wobbles between the hero and the villain.

Often the hero of the play is a wobbler—like Othello—and the entire play is the saga of his wobbling. Such a character—who splits the difference, has a casting voice, or wobbles—is from one point of view 'transitional' between the other two. But he may also stand for something very positive himself. For example, given our hero and villain hiding out in the hills, the 'transitional' character might be a wise, humorous old prospector, whose canniness both men respect. Or simply by being divided within himself, the 'transitional' character, as a storm centre of a conflict, can stand for the very important and positive *fact* of a conflict. If we distinguish drama from melodrama by the extent to which the former presents conflicts introvertedly while the latter presents them extrovertedly (the 'gearing' of character and circumstances), then it will often be found that in drama the 'transitional' characters are the principal characters, whereas in melodrama they tend to be in the 'middle distance'.

One might produce an inside-out version of *Johnny Guitar*—with one outlaw (instead of the gang) and a group of three women (instead of the three Viennas). The eldest woman wears Vienna's black clothes, another a scarlet dress, the youngest a white dress. Their professions and attitudes, of course, would correspond to these clothes. Or one might have only the black and white Vienna, and the bundle of feelings associated with the scarlet dress might be paraphrased by some dramatic issue or situation. The man they all love might be a combination of Black Bart, the Dancin' Kid and Turkey. He was once as likeable as Turkey, but was hardened when humiliated by the eldest woman's lover; and then betrayed her, becoming as seductive and dangerous as the Dancin' Kid, and humiliating the second woman; but some weakness of character, guilt and drink, say, brings him to the level of vicious, weak bluster reminiscent of Black Bart.

Such a film would no longer 'be' a version of *Johnny Guitar*. In making these changes we have substantially changed the bundles of feelings evoked by the film. None the less, we are working in the same 'key'. Our example is extreme, but the principle is exactly the same as the sort of alteration a scenarist makes to a novel. In a sense, one can't alter anything in a story without turning it into a different story. One can substantially alter the emotional content of a film simply by altering the background music—for example, by replacing a syrupy, consolatory orchestral score by a dry, curt, ironic guitar motif. Again we come to the same formulation: 'style' is just as emotional, just as fundamental, just as much a part of the film's 'content' and 'soul' as the characters, the psychology and the events in the plot. In fact our 'reversal' of *Johnny Guitar* might be nearer the emotional tones of the existing film than many a film is to the emotional tones of the story on whose narrative it is based—where the characters are retained, but their unhappiness softened, the whole thing made more upbeat, etc.

Given a 'striking idea' an experienced craftsman can, very rapidly indeed, develop a complete story, simply by contract-and-repetition —our pattern of similarities and dissimilarities. The 'core' of *The Wicked Lady* is—the wicked lady (Margaret Lockwood). She attracts her natural complements: a meek and good lady (Pat Roc), a victim male (Griffith Jones), an even tougher male (James Mason) and so on. These very symmetrical characters are thrown out of all-too-predictable symmetry by further surprises—it's the toughest male who is killed by the heroine, it's the one she killed for who kills her, etc. It is by throwing the symmetries out of any obvious symmetry that the film creates its 'imbalance', that is, the 'disharmonies' which the 'harmonies' exist to resolve.

One can imagine a version of *Johnny Guitar* in which Vienna is played by Margaret Lockwood, and a version of *The Wicked Lady* in which the wicked lady is played by Joan Crawford. In fact, the changes of personality would necessitate a considerable number of supplementary changes—in dialogue, in the performance of the other actors, in camera-angle, etc. Still, the general resemblance between the wicked lady and Vienna reminds us that the striking idea is itself a complicated balance of feelings, which can be developed in an immense number of different ways. James Mason's highwayman might be replaced by a highwayman with a pathological streak like Sterling Hayden's. Oddly enough, *The Wicked Lady* does give us a young lad, rather like Turkey, the stagecoach guard whom the wicked lady shoots and then, mothers as he dies—it's as if Vienna had had to shoot Turkey to save her own life, which is the opposite of what happens, Turkey sacrificing Vienna to save his.

There is, after all, only a tiny number of dramatic situations (thirty-six is a well-known estimate), although clearly it depends on what one defines as a situation. Most situations are really 'bundles of situations'—i.e., each confrontation between two specific characters can be considered as a sexual situation of some sort, a social situation, a moral situation, etc. If one took these arguments far enough, one could probably demonstrate that every plot is a second-cousin-twice-removed of every other plot. Yet—at the same time—in the sense that a change of music or of actor makes a film substantially different from an otherwise exactly similar film—no two films have more than a general, vague resemblance!

Though *The Wicked Lady* and *Johnny Guitar* work from a similar core—the wicked lady and Vienna—and have some storyline resemblances, we certainly don't think of them as 'variations on a theme'. There are too many differences. In *The Wicked Lady* none of the characters enjoys violence for its own sake; conventional sexual polarities are retained; and so on. A theme is not the 'soul' of a film; its 'soul' is its whole atmosphere, including *audience* response.

People and places are atmospheres—bundles of feelings—too. Often the last scene is set in the same locale as the first (or as the first 'crystallization' of the dramatic issues). Yet the atmosphere of the place has been transformed by all the events that have taken place since. Once, it was a happy house, now the characters are gloomy. There is a sense of 'return' to the place, but there is also a sense of 'no return'. The memory may add a particular tone of desolation, of irony, of melancholy. The place functions like the recapitulation, in a symphony, of a musical phrase, but in a sadder cadence. Feelings snowball round it, just as they snowball round the *human* characters. It creates a pattern, is part of the orchestration of feelings, of the very structure of a film. Its function as a symbol is far less important than its function as a 'motif', recalling the feelings it picks up as it goes on.

Similarly with 'props'—or any object involved in the action. A gives B a ring, swearing eternal love; B tires of him and gives it to C; C . . . and so on, back to B, who is now ninety years old and just hoards it in a box of trinkets. At each appearance, the ring is 'the same, transformed'. There is no pattern of cause-and-effect; the idea is communicated by the simplest and crudest intellectual process, the 'association of ideas'.

Thus settings and objects are used as rolling stones to gather emotional moss. Points of style may function in the same way, like the repeated movement in *Le Diable Au Corps* which we quoted earlier.[1]

---

[1] Possibly academic criticism tends to overemphasize the importance of a specific meaning to a symbol and underemphasize the role of a symbol in creating, resuming and transforming a whole 'atmosphere', a use more complex than a specific 'deep meaning' can ever be.

To say that 'atmosphere is soul' is a way of saying that the story is not there to explain the characters—the characters are there to provide the story, and the story is there to provide the atmosphere. The profundity is in the superficialities—including those meanings which the film exists to stimulate it, and exist only in, the spectator's response. Whether the ideal or the average spectator is another series of problems. . . . Centrally though the audience's feelings 'snowball' with the principal characters. The hero and the heroine are the 'themes', like those of a symphony. But a theme is less than a symphony, nor is a symphony there to express the theme. . . .

20 · Mute Poetry in the Commercial Cinema

So far as the masses are concerned, poetry, in its academically esteemed forms, labours under four main handicaps. Any one of them would alone be sufficient to kill interest, although they generally apply in combination and reinforce one another.

Thus poetry is, alas, first and most insistently (compulsorily) offered at school by missionaries of middle-class middlebrows sweetness and light, whose attitudes and values (*bourgeois* moral uplift and/or romanticism) are frequently ungraftable upon genuine working-class attitudes. It usually concerns 'symbolic' things (rainbows, daffodils) which have little real, intimate meaning for urban or indeed for rural youth. Worse, it eschews 'vulgar', i.e. interesting, subjects, in favour of middle-class feelings about what is 'refined' and 'beautiful'. Fourth, the intellectual complexity and cultural range of reference of genuinely 'modern' poetry handicap communication with untrained audiences. And conversely, academics often ignore or deprecate the popular mythology from which the mass media so often derive their intimacy of resonance with their audience.

'Poetry' is notoriously difficult to define plausibly and clearly. We are not using the word in the common literary sense, to mean verse with a certain intellectual and emotional texture, but in the looser, larger sense, whereby it is possible to speak of certain paintings, Surrealist texts or *objets trouvés* as 'poetic'. The implication is of some lyrical quality which is deep, intense, obscure in origin, and somehow over-and-above or below-and-beneath the obvious, logical 'dramatic' meaning. In fact, this 'overtone' exists out of art, in everyday life, in, for example, the melancholy exhilaration of a sunset, the eerie seductiveness of window dummies, the erotic delicacy of flowers. In art's special, 'meditative', circumstances, these atmospheres are easily and naturally brought to the fore. Poetry, in this sense, consists of the free, intensive, subtle exploitation of these irrationalities.

A famous example is the burglary sequence in *Du Rififi Chez Les Hommes* (Jules Dassin). A burglar alarm is stifled by coils of white sludge exuded from a fire extinguisher. The plaster of a ceiling is pierced from above by the tip of a fabric-muffled drill. An umbrella is poked down through the hole and opened outside-down, to catch falling flakes of plaster. The team of craftsmen work in a dreamlike wordlessness. The scene's realism is documentary and it was in fact used as an instructional manual by gangs of burglars in several countries, one of whom used its techniques to burgle the cinema where it was showing. But, the dramatic tension, the unaccustomed use of objects, the silence, also creates a strange 'Surrealist' atmosphere, over and above the dramatic sense of the scene.

Clearly there can be no hard-and-fast boundary between the 'dramatic' and the 'poetic'. As an example of such 'equivocation' we might glance at the common association of women, horse-riding and sexuality. In John Sturges' *By Love Possessed* Lana Turner rides a horse furioso, and before any plot has developed we know she is sexually frustrated. In *All the Fine Young Cannibals* Susan Kohner goes out horse-riding just before a quarrel with her sexually uninterested husband. In John Huston's *The Unforgiven* John Saxon talks about taming a shy mare and looks at Audrey Hepburn while he says it, which is generally felt to be ample justification for her brother (Burt Lancaster) promising to kill him if he ever talks that way again. In *The Big Sleep* Humphrey Bogart and Lauren Bacall talk about horse racing when everyone concerned, except the Hays Office, means the act of love—with a quite hilarious precision.[1]

An even more recondite symbol is the association of fresh cold water with sexual relief. It's not surprising if, in 'desert' films, water and women go together—in Mario Bava's *The Wonders of Aladdin* the sumptuous Amazons of the Persian desert lure parched Donald O'Connor towards them by pouring water on to the desert sands. In

[1] Obviously horse riding more often than not lacks these overtones. It may stand for social status. In Westerns the cowboy's love for his horse links with power, independence, even loneliness—Howard Hughes' *The Outlaw* would rather have his horse than Jane Russell, the traditional hero rides away from the sad heroine, the hero and his horse (Trigger, Silver) are a kind of joint being. Often the particular helplessness and inarticulacy of animals makes them metaphors for the purest and sincerest human feelings—so that Elizabeth Taylor has *National Velvet* and *Lassie*, Toomai has his elephants, Fay Wray has King Kong, and so on.

Arthur Lubin's *The Thief of Baghdad* Steve Reeves has just braved the magic Ordeal by Fire when he finds himself by a cool clear rivulet, which leads him to a luxurious palace whose attractive mistress tries to poison him. And in Terence Fisher's *The Stranglers of Bombay* Guy Rolfe finds himself pegged out in the Indian sun at noon while a villainous girl with an ostentatious bosom (bosoms would be more accurate) sits by him cruelly showing him the water which he isn't allowed to have.

Similar overtones apply even in temperate zones. In *La Ronde* timid student Daniel Gelin is sweltering with suppressed sexual desire for Simone Simon, and keeps sending her out to the kitchen to bring him a glass of cold, clear, fresh water.

The same association of ideas turns up in the popular myth that cold showers are a cure for sexual longings. Association of 'ideas' is a misleading phrase, really, for the remark isn't 'interpreted'—it's 'understood', or it communicates, because of the sensual shock, the contrast of physical sensation between 'hot' feelings and a cold douche. Here, cold water and warm feelings are antithetical. But in the 'desert' films, cold water and warm feelings are interchangeable —the hero (or the spectator) wants both the water and the women. The pleasantness of cold water makes it 'like' sexuality, instead of its opposite. In neither case is there an 'objective', 'intellectual', connection of ideas or sensations; everything is interpreted in the context of a very subjective thing like the urgency of desire.

These 'dramatic' meanings may be consciously understood by the spectator, or simply felt as 'mood' or 'atmosphere'; but in neither case are they interpreted or decoded in a matter-of-fact way. The general audience doesn't say to itself: 'Horse-riding . . . hmmm. . . . Freud says that in dreams it often stands for sexual intercourse. . . .' Apart perhaps from the educated fad, it hasn't read Freud, it might well think the whole idea ridiculous of it had, nor has it the intellectuals' habit of half-serious, half-satirical play with Freudian interpretations. The 'horse-riding' parallels depend on the lead given by the dramatic contexts (including an off-screen scandal involving Lana Turner), and are felt on the basis of a physical, kinaesthetic similarity. Horse-riding is a physical, exhilarating, rhythmic and legs-astride activity. In any event, the spectator never substitutes the new meaning for the obvious one; Lana Turner *is* riding a horse, the scene isn't just a 'symbol' for how she's feeling. The explanation doesn't explain anything away. The audience *feels* rather than *thinks out* the second meaning, which is not so much a *substitute* meaning as an *additional* one, not so much *deeper* as an *overtone*.

There is a subtler poetry in Marcel Carné's *Le Jour Se Lève* (scripted by the Surrealist poet Jacques Prévert), when Jacqueline Laurent enters a factory workshop, carrying a bunch of flowers, to be confronted by a burly welder (Jean Gabin) clad in a protective asbestos gear. Given this strong contrast, we know without thinking that a girl cradling a bunch of flowers is a bunch of flowers herself. To make the metaphor more conscious—say, by intercutting, as older textbooks recommend—would be too emphatic, indeed, cheapening. For in outline the metaphor, girl=bouquet, is banal. It is given life by the contrast (carrying the sense, industrialization versus the natural), and by nuances of style: the girl's face, her reserved, disturbing expression and presence. She is not *reduced* to a bunch of flowers. Their presence *enriches* hers, but in no way limits her, as, in itself, a 'like' clause might do. She 'is' as fresh as the flowers, but she is herself too, with all her dramatic possibilities. . . .

Thus, a specific metaphor would be an impoverishment. To put it another way, the metaphor, in novels, dramas, or films, is only one way of making us 'feel' girl and flowers on our mental 'screen' at the same time. A metaphor is a 'prop' which couldn't masquerade as part of the plot or scene, and so had to be introduced by the tacit word 'like'.

Because cinema visuals are intellectually clumsy (having no prepositions, conjunctions or grammar to speak of) the commercial cinema's natural tendency, at least in its present stage of development, is to disguise metaphors as props, décor, setting, plot-symbols, locale, and so on. This is so much part of the cinema's dramatic, not just grammar, but spelling, that one's choice of examples is bound to be arbitrary.

In Orson Welles's *The Lady from Shanghai*, Orson Welles and Rita Hayworth have a lovers' meeting in an aquarium in whose tanks silhouetted sharks and octopi are prominent. During an island picnic, shots of the graceful but enigmatic heroine are intercut with shots of high-stepping white birds and a writhing black snake. (The plasticity of the contrasts is important—'high-stepping white' versus 'black writhing'.) In Joseph Losey's *The Sleeping Tiger* the correct, yet chilly relationship between a psychiatrist (Alexander Knox) and his wife (Alexis Smith) is expressed by their smart, yet starkly lit, rooms.

The husband invites a young criminal (Dirk Bogarde) to stay with them. An abrupt cut from bare white walls takes us into a steady, stealthy tracking movement past rubber-plants, whose leaves, in close-up, evoke some steamy, slimy jungle, and, sure enough, our track concludes in a close-up of the trouble maker reading, sure enough, a volume with the sweltering title, *Sexual Behaviour in the Human Female*. The polar clinic is challenged by the tropic jungle.

Henry King's *Snows of Kilimanjaro* offers a rare example of a pretty recondite poetic symbol which is (just about) communicated to a fairly large majority of spectators—though its meaning will cross most people's minds briefly only, if at all. Its hero, a writer (Gregory Peck) looks back on his life as he lies dying and surveys the steady loss of his spiritual integrity. This theme is crystallized by a prologue, a symbolic story about a leopard found frozen in the snows of Mount Kilimanjaro—no one knows how or why he climbed so high. In retrospect, it becomes evident that the leopard is the hero, the snows in which his poetic fire was frozen those of the higher social strata. On several occasions the film compares good writing to hunting big-game; the writer's second mistress (Hildegard Neff) is nicknamed 'Frigid Liz, the semi-iceberg of the sub-tropics' (the same paradox as snow on a tropical volcano); she creates modernistic sculptures with holes (like craters) where their breasts ought to be; and she also has a laugh like the hyena laughing as the hero lies dying. Interestingly, the film begins with the 'parable' of the leopard, challenges the audience with it, offering it as a riddle. Instead of irritating, as obscurity sometimes does, it creates interest, a sense of anticipation—for the imagery is bold and striking, the anecdote has a certain toughness and romance in itself.

The cinema's relatively clumsy syntax and its exploitation of objects gives it an easy affinity of technique with Surrealism. Stanley Kramer's generally mediocre *The Pride and the Passion* has one sumptuous sequence. During the Napoleonic Wars a band of Spanish guerillas haul a gigantic cannon across the mountains. At one point they can avoid capture only by hiding the monstrous thing in a cathedral, and then under a float, which, festooned with pious images, is wheeled through the streets of a city during a religious festival.

This contrast has no precise sense. Are we supposed to reflect that cannons and cathedrals, war and love, however opposite they may seem, are natural bedfellows, since freedom is sacred and this is a clear case of 'Praise the Lord and Pass the Ammunition'? Is it that Christian sanctimony conceals in a hypocritical though necessary way the brute facts of military might: 'right may be right but it must have might too'? Should we concentrate on a psycho-analytical undertone—a cathedral is a cold, stone womb, a cannon is a phallus in a bad mood? At any rate, the contrast of objects with contrary emotional associations has a massive effect. Each of these 'meanings' is created by the spectator, in his own mind. It is, so to speak, his response to the 'problem', the disturbance posed by the film. As we have so often seen, much of a film's 'content' isn't in the film at all, but only in the spectator's mind. Whether the spectator 'solves' the 'problem' in the way the artist foresaw depends on their affinity of culture, experience and temperament. Sometimes, the artist doesn't really mind how the spectator solves it, or wants him not to solve it.

21 · Poetry without Papers

In such poetry there is no intellectual protocol, no received 'tone of voice', no sense of sensitive loftiness. In Hitchcock's *To Catch a Thief* a cigarette is stubbed out in the yolk of fried egg—hinting at the burning out of an eye, but with a tactile sickliness of its own. In his *The Lady Vanishes* a nun reveals that she is not what she seems, her cloven hoof is her high heels, while the patient in her care is really her prisoner, bound and gagged by the bandages. Poetry gears in with melodrama, with narrative, with action, as in the old myths. Its lyricism has not yet become autonomous. Similarly, the pop 'lyric' is still conjoined with music, in the way that 'high culture' has all but lost, or is still rediscovering.

For the most part, poetry is derived from 'obvious' symbols—those of everyday experience, such as window-shopping, or listening to tape-recorders, or looking at the moon, whose poetic spell hasn't been destroyed by its rhyming with 'June' and 'croon'. How could it be, when it has been a literary motif for several thousand years? Just as in literature the 'stock' image can be revivified by sensitive words and ideas, so, in the cinema, the cliché can be brought alive again by sensitive art-direction (as in Murnau's *Sunrise*) or lighting (as in Frank Borzage's *Moonrise*) or photography or by associated imagery (the theme of sun and moon in *Orfeu Negro*, Brahms and whisky in *Les Amants*). Such poetry retains the epic poems' 'narrative' relationship with the world. Its interest is less in intellectual subtlety or complexity than in passionate attitudes and intense experiences. Subtleties arise out of the paradoxical encounter of profound, simple elements (the cathedral and the cannon). On the other hand in much poetry written with a highly 'cultured' frame of reference the simplicities are reached through a 'pointillisme' of subtleties—and so become

203

indecipherable by all but the expert few. Often, as with the Aristotelian emphasis on the fable—the mass media retain older techniques which our academics have not recognized.

In its primitive stage, poetic myth is closely bound up with religion. If the universe is made 'poetic' by means of myths about sun and moon goddesses, it is not to 'prettify' it, but to attempt to explain it. Such poetry, in intention, is documentary and philosophic. In the popular cinema, documentary films, heavily influenced by middle-class middlebrow ideas of poetic 'sweetness and light', try for a lyrical 'poetry' to which mass audiences are healthily insensible. Disney's *Real Life Adventures* restrict themselves to a complacent sentimentality which narrowly fails to banish all wonder and beauty from such films as *Water Birds* and *The Living Desert*. Such 'underwater' films as *Épaves* illustrate the 'superimposition' of documentary and poetry interest. The *Rites of Spring* episode in Disney's *Fantasia* has a certain mythic grandeur. The sun as an inchoate mass whirling and blazing through space; the spectacular convulsions and metamorphoses of the earth's crust before the appearance of any living thing; life's slow crawl from the single cell on the seabed ooze to complicated animals crawling on the shore (a time-lapse 'tracking shot' of poetic compression); the affection of dinosaur mothers for their pups; the earliest mammals scuttling about beneath the legs of the giant reptiles they are destined to supplant; the inexorable and anguished extinction of entire species—here, documentary, spectacle and drama blend into a vision of philosophical grandeur, lowbrow, certainly, but not invalid.

Yet this 'factual' episode is closely related to the least serious of cinematic genres—the monster fantasy (*King Kong, The Beast from 20,000 Fathoms, The Lost World*). The dream meets fact—creating the myth. . . . Science-fiction at its most poignant is the poetry of scientific possibility, i.e. the exaggeration of technology into its 'poetic' meaning . . . hence fantasy and horror films so often have a rich vein of poetry—poetry in narrative form, that is, myth.

The older forms of myth are still valid currency. Superstitions of many kinds afford convenient rendezvous for poetic fantasy and the proto-scientific myth. Ludicrous as it may seem, many people still believe, or half-believe, in ghosts, in poltergeists, in dark forces with which it is as well not to meddle—and, by emotional extension, in their Transylvanian kin. Films about black magic have surprisingly little to surmount in the way of audience scepticism. It's a safe bet that more English people are frightened of cemeteries, or believe that the dead are watching us, than know the meaning of such exotic initials as 'F.A.O.' or 'U.N.E.S.C.O.'

The 'dream sequence' is characteristically the realm of libidinous delirium. In Victor Fleming's *Dr. Jekyll and Mr. Hyde* (1941) women's bodies suddenly turn to sand, and flow away as if scattered by a driving wind.

In all these ways the ordinary commercial cinema maintains something at least of the fullness of the primal myth, blending, in various permutations, fact, drama, the 'Surreal', dream, magic and the supernatural powers at their play. Perhaps we too readily assume the mass media's lack of, and antagonism towards, poetry. . . .

22 · A Great Defect

An over-eagerness to penetrate to the allegorical layer of a film may lead to distortion of that very layer. Jean Cocteau's *Orphée* (1950) affords a striking example.

Orphée (Jean Marais) a celebrated poet, defiantly visits a café patronized by the hostile writers of the *avant-garde*. An old friend gives him two pieces of advice. 'Your greatest defect is that you know just how far to go too far,' and: 'Astonish us.' Orphée catches sight of the Princess (Maria Casarès), a beautiful patroness of the *avant-garde*, trying to prevent a drunken young poet, Cégeste (Edouard Dhermite), from scattering his papers about. A fight develops, and her chauffeur, Heurtebise (François Perier), phones for the police. Cégeste is knocked over by two uniformed motor-cyclists who drive on without stopping.

The Princess orders Orphée to help her carry the injured man into her Rolls-Royce. After Heurtebise has driven them some way into a strangely deserted part of the countryside, Orphée realizes that Cégeste is dead. The Princess is stonily unperturbed, and greets the two motor-cyclists as if they were her agents. She takes Orphée to an eerie and dilapidated chalet; two Chinese servants appear as if from nowhere and serve him with champagne. While he drinks, the Princess resuscitates Cégeste, who recognizes her as 'his death' and enters her service. Orphée catches a glimpse of the Princess leading Cégeste and her aides through a mirror—which ripples like water—but when he tries to follow the mirror is—just a mirror.

He comes to, apparently lost in a sandy landscape, but is hailed by Heurtebise, who, presumably on the Princess's orders, drives Orphée home. There, his wife, Eurydice (Marie Déa) is discussing the sudden disappearance of the two poets, with the Commissioner of Police and with Aglaonice (Juliette Gréco) leader of a League of Women, a friend of the *avant-garde*, and an old enemy of Orphée. Heurtebise parks the Rolls in Orphée's garage and, after pacifying the Commissioner, Orphée begins listening to cryptic lines of poetry coming over the car-radio. He refuses Eurydice any explanation of his disappearance—when she tries to tell him she is pregnant, he refuses to listen. Instead she confides in Heurtebise, who tries to reassure her of Orphée's love.

Night after night the ghostly Princess appears in Orphée's room and watches him sleep . . . as if Orpheus had charmed even his Death. . . .

A journalist friend of Aglaonice publicly accuses Orphée of being implicated in Cégèste's death; but Orphée, utterly indifferent to his wife's pleas and the counsel of Heurtebise, now spends all his time in the car, whose messages have mostly degenerated to meaningless series of numbers. Although Orphée has forbidden her to see Aglaonice, Eurydice resolves to appeal to her. Heurtebise refuses her the use of his car, and, when she ventures out on her bicycle, he vainly tries to drag Orphée away from the radio. Just outside the house, she is run over by the motor-cyclists. Heurtebise carries the injured woman to her bedroom, where he confronts the Princess and her new, still clumsy, aide, Cégèste. Heurtebise is insubordinate, querying her orders, and again tries to warn Orphée, without success. Cégèste broadcasts the messages which keep Orphée in the garage, while the Princess 'strangles' Eurydice and leads her to the underworld. But she forgets one of the rubber gloves which enable her to penetrate mirrors. Heurtebise remains behind and tells Orphée that by following him to the next world there is a chance of reclaiming Eurydice. Orphée follows, not simply because of his love of Eurydice, but also in the hope of finding the Princess.

Heurtebise explains: 'Mirrors are the doors through which death comes and goes . . . watch yourself in a mirror as you age, and you will see death at work, like a swarm of bees in a glass hive.' Beyond the mirror, they traverse a No-Man's-Land, resembling a ruined city. 'Life dies little by little. This is the twilight zone. It is made of the memories of men and the debris of their habits.' The two men appear before an underworld tribunal, not as the accused, but as witnesses. The Princess is on trial for having killed Eurydice, without orders. Her crime is 'Initiative', and her motive, she confesses, love of Orphée. She and Orphée declare their undying love for each other.

Orphée, being a poet, is allowed to reclaim Eurydice, but on condition that he never looks at her again; if he dies, he will lose her. Heurtebise is allowed to return with them to ease them into their new ways during the awkward 'honeymoon' period of living back-to-back. During a tragi-farcical scene of hide-and-seek, Orphée's exasperation mounts. At last Eurydice is convinced that he hates her, and tries to kill herself by creeping into his bedroom and startling him into seeing her: her plan is frustrated by a sudden power-cut.

The next morning, however, Orphée glimpses her in the driving-mirror of the fatal car. Simultaneously, Aglaonice and her friends (the Bacchantes), determined to avenge Cégèste, burst into Orphée's house; Heurtebise throws him a revolver, for self-defence, but Orphée is accidentally shot in a tussle and dies. The Bacchantes scatter, and the police are held at bay by the two motor-cyclists who carry off Orphée's body.

Beyond the Zone, the Princess waits impatiently ('Strange, I almost have a sense of time . . .'), while Orphée and Heurtebise traverse the Zone, this time with the greatest difficulty, for they are going where they have no right to go. The Princess asks Orphée if he will accept any ill-treatment she cares to inflict on him, and then orders Cégèste and Heurtebise to 'kill' him. The death of a dead soul is re-birth. . . .

Orphée awakes beside Eurydice. She remembers having had a bad dream, he feels he has been inspired.

Cégèste watches as the Princess and Heurtebise, guilty of disobeying their totalitarian superiors, are marched off to face a terrible punishment. . . .

Cocteau's remark, via Heurtebise, 'You seek too hard to understand, Sir. That is a great defect,' is of a piece with his many pleas to critics to believe, not to interpret. All the same, he might have saved his breath to cool his porridge, for much critical effort has been devoted to establishing 'deep' meanings. For example—the Princess is Death, Heurtebise and Cégèste are angels of death, the Zone is one of the outer circles of Hell, and so on. (But why is Death a seductive woman, and not, say, an old woman, or an old man? or a skeleton? What does an 'angel of death' symbolize? what does 'Hell' symbolize? The explanation explains nothing.) One might see the Princess as a black angel, a guardian devil, trying to pervert Orphée from a healthy domestic life with Eurydice. Or, if the film is an allegory about the poet and poetry, the Princess is a false muse, a black goddess, a 'negative' of the white variety worshipped by Robert Graves.

In a Jungian interpretation, the Princess might be the 'terrible mother', the witch, menacing the child with an alluring possessiveness, also incestuous. A Freudian interpretation might suggest that the notion of 'Death' symbolizes the punishment for incestuous wishes towards the mother, who is alleged to be responsible; and the land of Death is the land of repressed desire, where nightmares come true. This can point to the overtones of incest and homosexuality which many critics have noticed in Cocteau's work, and which he has hardly bothered to conceal. John Minchinton drew some interesting parallels between the film and the Greek Orphic religion (which, despite its name, had no real links with the Orpheus of myth, but was certainly a death-centred religion, ascetic and puritanical). Jean-Jacques Khim discovered some astonishing parallels between Cocteau's film and the Thibetan Book of the Dead.

Writing from a Roman Catholic viewpoint, Henri Agel complains that the underworld is not really Hellish enough, and accuses the film of a Manichean loathing of the flesh. Certainly one could make a terrifying film about the nuptials of Death in *The Seventh Seal* and the Princess in *Orphée*. But from this angle Cocteau's film lacks the high-voltage tragic protest of Bergman's, and the mutual love of Orphée and the Princess contradicts this interpretation. Death in this film is not particularly physical death—which takes some of the force from Henri Agel's remark. The film contains many personal motifs. 'Astonish us,' was said to Cocteau by Diaghilev in 1913; and Cocteau certainly knows just how far to go too far. One of the lines which Cégeste broadcasts, 'L'oiseau chante avec les doigts,' was sent to Cocteau in a letter by the poet Apollinaire in 1917. The Bacchantes are said to recall the Surrealists, who detest Cocteau and all his works, all the more because outsiders so consistently miscall *Le Sang d'un Poète* a Surrealist film. The champagne offered by Chinese servants in the house of death probably symbolizes opium; in his journal of that name Cocteau describes one of the symptoms of opium-craving as 'champagne in the veins'.

The film bears a general resemblance to Cocteau's relatively clumsy one-act tragi-farce of the same name. There, Orphée is obsessed, not by the radio in a Rolls, but by a horse, which nods its head in response to letters on an ouijah-board. Heurtebise is not a servant of death, but a glazier, constantly appearing to mend Eurydice's windows, which are, so to speak, the anti-mirrors in which, as Cocteau says: 'One sees oneself age and death approach.' (There is a trace to Heurtebise's original profession here: he and Orphée pass a glazier crying his wares in the Zone.) Death, who enters and leaves by mirrors, and uses rubber gloves, is a beautiful woman in a ball gown. Her aides, Azrael and Raphael, are white-masked surgeons. Orphée and Death neither meet nor fall in love. Eurydice, intending to poison her rival, the horse, is herself tricked and poisoned by Aglaonice. Orphée brings her back from the underworld on the same conditions. After he has been stoned, the Commissioner, who is an absurd dunderhead, instead of, as in the film, sympathetic, interrogates Heurtebise. Orphée's head then appears on the top of a bust and answers most of the questions, giving his name as 'Cocteau'. A last scene shows Orphée and Eurydice enjoying lunch together in Paradise.

Heurtebise is a recurrent figure in the Cocteau mythology. In *Le Sang d'un Poète* the character of this name is a muscular Negro with wings. Cocteau's poem 'L'Ange Heurtebise' includes the lines:

> *Angel Heurtebise, with brutality*
> *Incredible, leap on me. Please*
> *Jump not so hard,*
> *Bestial boy, flower of great*
> *Stature.*

And the name means: 'breaking against the kiss'. The same poem features Cégèste as a secondary angel.

In view of this enigmatic personal mythology it is hopeless to attach 'philosophical' meanings to the film. As with *Marienbad* many interpretations *nearly* fit, but none really fits. (Indeed, the idea of an 'interpretation' which 'explains' everything is itself a myth.) Cocteau declares that 'the film sets out to be nothing but the paraphrase of a Classical Greek myth' (though what are Heurtebise, Cégèste doing there?). The film's 'meaning' is, of course, as nebulous as the 'meaning' of the Greek myth (which has never been agreed on). The film is not a message hidden in some obscure code, but simply, a story, a battery of emotional provocations. Enriching as they are, the interpretations mentioned above all have one limitation; they are too simple, they fail to take into account the fact that, far from symbolizing some vague abstraction or other, each character is torn between opposite desires. One can speak of themes, but not of symbols.

Cocteau sees three themes in the film. First, the successive deaths and counter-deaths that a poet must undergo in order to become, in Mallarmé's words, 'Tel qu'en lui-même enfin l'éternité le change' (such that at last eternity transforms him into himself). Second, the theme of inspiration: 'It is when Orphée renounces his own themes, and accepts messages from the outside, that everything is spoiled.' The third theme is that of free-will. 'Heurtebise,' writes Cocteau, 'is not at all an angel as he was in the play and as he is often said to be. He is a young dead soul, in the service of one of the innumerable satellites of death. He is as yet scarcely tainted by death. On several occasions, he tries to forewarn people, for example, Orphée of the worthlessness of the radio messages, and Eurydice of the accident which will happen on the road. But the destiny which he attempts to frustrate by an act of free will is a destiny initiated by the Princess. Hence the Superior Tribunal has no accusation to make against him. . . .

'At their trial . . . the Princess and Heurtebise are forced to avow the shadow of a shadow of the sentiment they feel, for the human kingdom to which they have belonged still has some power over them.' (A power corresponding perhaps to the 'ace of hearts' in *Le Sang d'un Poète*.)

The Princess and Heurtebise are not simply 'Death'; they are further advanced in death than the living. Throughout the film, Heurtebise *opposes* the Princess. There is a continuity between the dead and the living—the glazier in the Zone believes he is still alive, his habits persist. The hotel of *Marienbad* is situated in a posh suburb of the Zone. The state of total death towards which we are all slowly drifting is inconceivable, perhaps it does not exist, perhaps there is always the shadow of a shadow of a shadow, recurring like decimals.

In a general way, death is the opposite of love; maybe it is the ultimate bureaucracy, a concentrationary universe, fate. In so far as the Princess rebels against it, we can call the film *Countess Dracula Versus the Gestapo*.

The characters are divided within themselves. Love and death are inextricably intertwined. Orphée, who is alive, loves his death; his death, because she loves him, kills his wife, and later, when he is killed, undoes his death. Orphée's death keeps him alive, against his own wishes. If Heurtebise tries to thwart her, it is perhaps less for the sake of Orphée, than of Eurydice. In a way, he is the 'negative' of

Orphée—he adores Eurydice hopelessly, as Orphée adores the Princess. Life in each of the worlds is reaching out for the other. Cégèste, too, is a paradoxical figure; the darling of the *avant-garde*, yet shy and clumsy and soon poetically bankrupt. Although the one line is Apollinaire's, he may also recall Cocteau's friend Radiguet, author of *Le Diable Au Corps*, who died young; he may even represent Cocteau himself, as a young poet, accepted by the *avant-garde* but basically uncertain of everything. . . . The Princess cannot be labelled either a true or a false muse; she is a patroness of the arts, yet some of her actions menace Orphée's inspiration, while others renew it. Eurydice, who, if anyone, represents Life and happiness (she is pregnant, loyal, sentimental) at one point tries to commit suicide, and so is on the 'side' of Death as well. The living are morally no superior to the dead—Orphée is killed by the living, the Bacchantes, whom Eurydice trusts. Death is the work of the living, as well as of the dead.

As in all the best dramas, the principal characters are constantly being forced into reversals of their positions, and a cut-and-dried interpretation is likely to miss all the tragic force of these contradictions.

Perhaps the moral of the film is that poetic inspiration comes from the poet's inability to be either alive or dead. In whichever world he finds himself, he feels driven to break through into, or to get himself hounded by, the other. Orphée follows Eurydice to the underworld, for contradictory reasons, one an affirmation of life (to bring back Eurydice), the other a longing to embrace Death. The poet's inspiration is A.C. flashing to and fro between opposite poles. It is an everlasting contradiction, so close and intimate as to leave him perpetually confused. Cégèste's broadcasts are both pearls of poetry—and rubbish. In this 'union of contradictions', which is also an emotional ambivalence, we can perhaps glimpse, obscurely, why Heurtebise in the play and the film of *Orphée* is so different from Heurtebise in the poem and in *Le Sang d'un Poète*. In the poetry he is a sensual, kindly-brutal angel, here, on the contrary, he is lightly, politely and genuinely in love with Eurydice, but always impotent—in the warnings he gives, in his attempted intervention with the revolver, as a lover. However, the final strangling of Orphée on the orders of the Princess recalls the brutal assault which Cocteau's poem seems to crave.

The poet's task is to master—by remaining ever-obedient to—the 'union of contradictions'. He must become 'such that at last eternity transforms him into himself'; but he must also renounce, in the words of *Le Sang d'un Poète*, the fatal boredom of immortality (*l'ennui mortel de l'immortalité*). It is no easy task to distinguish the two; the poet is a lonely wanderer, a man without passports, the Garry Davis of all possible worlds—a fate worse than—yet eerily immune from—and also perhaps a result of—some death of the heart.

But *Orphée* could never be reduced to this meaning. The feelings suggested by the other interpretations are still valid. We can all recognize the Princess as a despot, a vampire, and the idea of women as danger is asserted again in the person of Aglaonice and her 'monstrous regiment of women'. Like Plyne in *Tirez Sur le Pianiste*, Cocteau says: 'La femme est magique . . .'—indeed, the episode of the Bacchantes' intervention might be called *Tirez Sur le Poète*. It is the simultaneous validity of so many emotional strands that gives the film the richness and the mystery of feelings far more real than those we can label with ease.

The film would be much less gripping if it were less convincing on its most superficial level; a spy story, gaining added tension from its supernatural overtones. Although its setting is post-war, it is packed with occupation memories; midnight arrests, power cuts, a Fascist militia who train guns on the ordinary police, spies and counter-spies, collaborationists and Gestapo tortures. Cocteau beat the ton-up boys to the draw in exploiting the Fascist virility of black-clad and be-goggled motor-cyclists, centaurs of a mechanical age.

Orphée is *also* one of the best films about the Occupation, because of its vivid atmosphere of an arbitrary, rapacious despotism.

The people aren't allegorical absolutes, symbols of philosophical principles. They are all what we have called 'wobblers', torn between opposing principles. Only by resisting 'allegory' can we reveal the film's richness, and obviate the short-circuiting effect of premature interpretation. All interpretations are bad in so far as their secret, but real, purpose is to simplify, to explain subordinate themes away, to replace all the uncertainties of dramatic struggle by a definite meaning.

The divergence of 'high culture' criteria from the 'popular' tradition of poetry not only renders many admirable works of art in the former illegible to the masses, but many admirable works of art in the latter illegible to *aficionados* of the former. It induces a naïvely rationalist approach to popular poetry which, if applied to other media, would annihilate poetry as a method of communication altogether. If we use as text J. G. Weightman's remarks on Ingmar Bergman's *The Seventh Seal* (1956) it is precisely because this writer, so careful and thoughtful when he writes about literary culture, often approaches films with expectations pitched so low that no artist could conceivably make himself understood. The reproach is hardly directed at Weightman himself, nor, for that matter, at the other 'visiting firemen' who drop nonchalantly into film criticism from their great cultural heights. As we have seen, those who should have been championing the film medium were contentedly using it to titillate their own complacency.

Bergman's film has a medieval setting. Death, a stern monk-like figure 'comes for' a Knight who, once idealistic, now disillusioned, is returning from the Crusades. The Knight challenges death to a chess game, so earning a brief respite, which he uses to search for someone or something which will checkmate Death. But by the end of the film, all the characters are whisked off in the Dance of Death—except for a family of travelling mountebanks—a young clown, who has visions of the Holy Family; his beautiful but more carthy wife; and their baby. The search for a 'checkmate' is, clearly, not so much a search for immortality, as for a meaning which will 'outlast' Death-as-nihilism—though the 'confusion' between the two senses is itself a meaning: a 'value' with which one can identify is, in a sense, oneself. . . .

Mr. Weightman, identifying Death with evil, comments, 'It is true that, in ordinary living, most people, after failing to cope with evil (which in fact cannot be coped with and merely has to be endured) start on a new phase. The trouble with *The Seventh Seal* is that it is trying to say much more than this, but only offers very confused symbolism. Why should Joseph, Mary and the babe be saved when the knight perishes? What is the connection with the Holy Family? Why should Death appear as a person, who admits that he knows nothing about the mystery of creation? Why should the knight play chess with Death? Psychologically he is not struggling against Death, he is worried about evil, which is rather a different problem . . . why should there be a tremendously impressive return to the knight's castle in a storm, only to be followed by resignation and extinction? Then, having accepted death with dignity, why should the seven victims be made to dance in anguish along the horizon? . . .

To have Death laboriously sawing down a tree to kill a minor character is grotesque. . . .'

But the answers to these questions are, surely, not Bergman's confusions, but his most elementary meanings, which he could hardly make clearer, except by inserting little subtitles which explain, 'I am not confused about this scene, the meaning of it is. . . .'

Very curtly and schematically, then, the answers are:

The clown, his wife and their baby are not Joseph, Mary and the Babe, but a low, earthly, earthy, comic, loving human family. The clown has visions, of Mary and her Babe, i.e. of all he loves, his wife and child, on the plane of ideal immortality. His wife does not have visions, she has womanly wisdom and motherhood instead.

They escape death for a little while because (*a*) he has Visions, which is like immortality-in-a-split-second, and (*b*) one-family-after-another, fertility and love, is as immortal as Death, for a little while, though perhaps one day the human race will die out, and because (*c*) Clown and Woman are the 'lowest common denominator' of humanity (like Picasso's clowns, say). The contrast-identity of clowning and the sacred is used in the anecdote about the Jester who turned somersaults to honour the statue of Our Lady, who kissed him when the monks objected. The durability of 'low' human nature appears in Louis MacNeice's lines:

> . . . *the whore and the buffoon,*
> *Will come off best: no dreamers, they cannot lose*
> *Their dream.* . . .

Only this clown is a dreamer, even if he pretty quickly loses his dignity in reality (when bullied into dancing on the tavern table). The young couple's profession (travelling showmen) has a nomadism like 'one's journey through life, man has no home' and a quality of illusion like, 'All the world's a stage.' Illusions, visions. . . .

Death appears as a person for the same reason that he appears as a person in medieval imagery. Given the human tendency to anthropomorphism, what form could be more easily understood? Analogous examples: Old Father Time, the Four Horsemen of the Apocalypse, Satan. In the language which myth-makers and poets have long permitted themselves, death is not only an inescapable event, it, or rather He, is also the ultimate persecutor. He dresses like a Monk because he does in folklore and because a monk's dress is a way of saying that he has renounced this world, which is what Death is making you do. It is also a mysterious, sinister kind of dress (like Dracula's black cloak). Death is ignorant of everything because he, or it, is the ultimate and total negation. A theological equivalent: the proposition that evil is both a positive force and a non-created Nothing.

The chess-match is a well-known symbol for cerebration and the processes of the intellect. The Knight, Crusader and idealist, represents the human attempt to affirm, or to search for, a 'good meaning'. Like that attempt, he's considerably weary and disillusioned. He is now looking for an answer more sophisticated than that of the sword, for a winning move, some value, which will negate Nothingness. It's not his own skin he wants to save, particularly; as a fighting man he has faced death without complaint before. It's absolute death, the death to man's values posed by The Absolute, that he's facing now, and this isn't quite the same thing as evil, although, of course, it's associated with it, traditionally, as in 'The Wages of sin is death.' The Bible often equates evil with Death, good with immortality. It's not a 'confusion' of Bergman's, but a venerable cultural association, and presumably has its origins in the inability of the unconscious mind to come to grips with reality and its nuances. The only punishments it knows are violent ones (castration, abandonment, approximity to 'death'), while on the other hand, the feeling of virtue catapults into omnipotent fantasies ('I'm going to live forever'). It would seem to be all but ineradicable from human thought.

The Knight's return to his castle is his reunion with his faithful Lady, the feminine equivalent of himself. His idealism has drained her life of happiness, but he hoped to find in her patience, faith and approval a value, a communion, so impervious to the chances and hazards of this world that she would, so to speak, 'check-mate' Death. He was attacking Death with his Queen, the most powerful fighting piece on the board, and his Queen is taken, by her unhappiness. The 'return home' is a dramatic symbol for the 'self-confrontation', the 'moment of truth', the 'summing-up', the 'home-stretch', the 'driving things home', the climactic point of the knight's return from the disastrous Crusade. I'm quite unable to understand why an impressive storm scene shouldn't be followed by resignation and extinction. It's common enough, surely, for storms, in literary convention, to precede disastrous events.

We may think we accept death with dignity, we may put a brave and philosophical face on it, but nature screams out against it and tugs away but gets tugged on, and that's the dance, which isn't a dance at all. We are all conscripts, members of a chain-gang, hold hands in a compulsory 'solidarity' which we may hate; we like it or we lump it, but we all go off into the dark.

The character in a tree is an actor-seducer, and the slick scintillating illusions of his profession and his hobby contrasts with the gross and cogent materialism of Death as a slow but sure old manual labourer. The scene's 'laboriousness' is presumably Swedish humour. It also relates to a general tradition, like the antiquated old car driven by Death in Dreyer's *They Met at the Ferry* (1948).

If modern rationalism can no longer follow the poetic language of a film so clearly in the folklore idiom, so much the worse for modern rationalism; one doubts whether it's even rational, except in trivial mannerisms.

It's not as if a film had to be particularly sophisticated to blend dramatic, poetic and philosophic meanings as Bergman's does, and our last chapter will, provocatively, concern itself with their confluence in the screen equivalent of 'pulp' idioms.

23 · The Wedding of Poetry and Pulp— Can They Live Happily Ever After and Have Many Beautiful Children?

Much science fiction is in the tradition of *Paradise Lost*, in that it relates the human condition to the basic physical and mental structures of the cosmos. Its explorations of 'other worlds' are akin to metaphysics. Usually, it 'decapitates' metaphysics, for, instead of leading up to the crowning-and-unifying notion of God (or a hierarchy of Gods) it often hints that all our acting, and even thinking, assumptions will be further undermined from outside our present 'unity'. From this point of view, science-fiction whose intention is to satirize our society is less science-fiction than satire; or at least is, poetically speaking, best read in reverse, ignoring the author's satirical purpose and dwelling on his other world. In either event, of course, no *s.f.* story entirely escapes the gravitational pull of society today—if only because its readers are formed by that society, and must refer everything to its terms.

Yet little of this aspect of *s.f.* has penetrated to the screen. For in the cinema, with its mass public, prevalent professional theories, whereby the public seeks above all familiar reality either ameliorated, melodramatized or 'comicalized', are compounded by the prevalence of critical theories determined to prove that the cinema medium is essentially realistic, sociological and psychological. As precious as rare therefore are those films which, developing within the tradition of childhood like Flash Gordon, not only lead us on an odyssey through space-time, but into the terms of interplanetary ethics. One thinks avidly of what might have been done with the ideas behind a few turnips, notably Sid Pink's *Journey to the Seventh Planet* (1961), where an extrastellar creature, defending its terrain, weaves destructive mirages out of the spacemen's own minds. . . .

Yet, whether a film whisks us to the twenty-first century, or to

218

Atlantis in its prime (*circa* 10,000 B.C., according to Umberto Scarpelli) the spectators remain, alas, in the pedestrian here and now. As bizarre as the robes, the décor, the technological contraptions, may be, they must refer back to the structures of our *musée imaginaire*, our lives, our unconscious, our society. It would be oddly hard for most of us to adjust to the sight of a space-hero dressed according to a time when narrow, drooping shoulders were considered smart (though they were, less than a hundred years ago). It's hard enough to understand certain assumptions of the Samoans, the Balinese or the Americans, and all but impossible to empathize into the perceptions and drives of, say, a boa constrictor. How much more difficult then to identify with the notions of, say, the immortal twelve-sensed telepathic polymorphoids whose natural habitat is the ammonia clouds of Galaxy X7?

As with sensations, so with ethics, philosophies, emotions. Flash *v.* Ming is the cowboy against the Yellow Peril (from Ming to Mao . . .), is James Bond against the intergalactic No.

If here we endeavour to focus on the pedestrian 'resonance' of five 'assonant' fantasies, it is in no way to deny to the fantastic cinema that beauty which is all the more disturbing for being so radically anti-anthropomorphic, the beauty of its super-romanticism. On the contrary; we imply a plea for a greater audacity in extrapolation, as well as to pose a challenge to the alleged 'seriousness' of 'realism'. For the dream language of fantasy reflects reality, too; often, more clearly, for camouflaged undercurrents are allowed nearer the surface. Ming is Mao, before Mao.

These reflections were stimulated by Umberto Scarpelli's *The Giant of Metropolis* (1962) an Italian film which, involuntarily perhaps, is the reactionary retort to all that is democratic and happily pagan in Vittorio Cottafavi's *Hercules Conquers Atlantis* (1961). With Fred M. Wilcox's *Forbidden Planet* (U.S.A., 1956), Kurt Maetzig's *First Spaceship on Venus* (East Germany-Poland, 1959), and Joseph M. Newman's *This Island Earth* (U.S.A., 1955), the films of Scarpelli and Cottafavi form a quintet on the theme of: a 'modern' man discovering a dying, or only posthumously active, civilization. In Scarpelli's film—related to Lang's futuristic *Metropolis* only by cashing in on its name—Metropolis has become the city of Atlantis ten thousand years before Christ (it might as well exist in the twenty-first century). The name indeed suggests the futuristic, super-capitalist tyranny in Lang's vision, that of Marxism stood on its head (a universal change of heart solves all class tensions; its scriptwriter, Thea Von Harbou, became a passionate Nazi). In Scarpelli's film, the 'concentrationary' future is that of a scientific totalitarianism, even though it is in the past (Atlantis). For the scientific hubris which destroyed one civilization may destroy another. . . .

The two Italian epics have much in common. Both assent to the startling recent mythological *volte-face*, whereby the social basis of Atlantis is not, as the novelist Pierre Benoit, in his *L'Atlantide* and his screen adaptors, Jacques Feyder (1921) and G. W. Pabst (1932) presumed, the erotic despotism of a Queen, but a system much nearer *s.f.*—the transmogrification of man into Superman.[1]

Both films locate Atlantis on a mist-shrouded, rocky island, which is sunk by a cataclysmic atomic explosion. But if the new generation of historians have certain points in common, so far as the general geo-political picture is concerned, their interpretations of the decline and fall of Atlantis are more diverse than ever. For Cottafavi, Atlantis was, morally, doomed because the do-or-die experiments perpetrated on an expropriated peasantry in order to make of them fanatical warriors were part of a totalitarian system inimical to democracy and the dignity of the individual. But for Scarpelli, the corresponding scientific experiments are seen as sins against Nature, whom man was not meant to master. Again, whereas Hercules (Reg Park) smilingly tolerates the effeminate dancers temptingly paraded before him by the high priest of Antinea, Scarpelli is indignant that a young dancing lady should be sandwiched in a *pas de trois* between two muscly youths, one of whom, moreover, is black. It's true that the trio's intensely lascivious motions suggest a yet more closely integrated activity, and it's also true that the girl in the middle has been hypnotized into it, that is to say, that her liberty has been infringed. But the affiliation of these factors characterizes puritan classifications; libertarianism is associated with all possible vices, all the

[1] The nineteenth-century realms of the 'eternal feminine' *à la She* seem, like the vamps of the time, to have been the day dream of a paternalist and puritan ethos. In our hedonistic and feminist ethos, the realms of fantasy and fear are macabre, or harbour our male ideal. For the same reason, the Western, hitherto a hick's or kid's genre, flourishes among more sophisticated audiences than ever before in its history. Conversely, Robert Day's recent version of *She* (1964) stresses less the female's enormity than political upheavals (the slave tribe seeking freedom) and desert adventure. The originator of the 'transmogrificatory' Atlantis is George Pal, in his *Atlantis the Lost Continent* (U.S.A., 1961); Edgar Ulmer's *The Lost Kingdom* (1961) is a none-too-convincing throwback in which Antinea plays second-fiddle to her Frenchman.

virtues being reserved for the other side, a division justifying the intolerance and vituperation specifically repudiated by the smile of Hercules. Nor is it accidental that Scarpelli's film speaks less of 'liberty' than of 'freedom of the will and of the intelligence'. The Thomism of this last juxtaposition is quite evident. In this context, there is a special pointedness about the anti-scientific Jeremiads placed in the mouth of a very old, kind, good Sage, who, slain by the wicked Regent, returns as his own ghost—thus incarnating *both* 'tradition' and 'immortality'. All this has an odour of incense. Whether or not the film's producer is Roman Catholic I don't know; his film is.

In any event, the moral pattern of every film fantasy is as studied as that of any other type of film. The critical Round Table of *Motion No. 6* raised, in connection with Cottafavi's film, the question of whether Hercules and his friend the King of Thrace, in refusing to inform his ship's crew of their true destination, had, in effect 'conscripted' them, trampled on their rights. It was only on seeing the film a second time that I realized that Cottafavi had given the reply. The crew consists of convicted assassins and criminals; the trip is part of their jail sentence. And when they mutiny and attempt to assassinate Hercules, he makes no attempt to punish them further, simply marooning them, prophylactically, on an island. For they were now seeking to avoid the journey to Atlantis, and Hercules, having saved his life, respects their right to attempt to regain their liberty. The argument relates, of course, to those arguments of Hobbes which most clearly reveal that under his totalitarianism is a fierce anarchist undertow.

Easy to decode morally, too easy, even, are the events of *First Spaceship on Venus*, that semi-Ulbrichtian endeavour to renew the fantasy traditions of U.F.A. The only hypothesis I can advance to explain the general platitudinousness of post-war German films (and post-war is two decades, a very long time) is that those German filmmakers who might have become leading artists hesitate between the 'respectable' dramatic emphases—modern, liberal, 'American' sentiments—and the retrospective guilts which they too readily arouse, if allowed to deviate from prim little dotted lines. There are also, perhaps, the sullen but powerful tendencies established by Siegfried Kracauer, that is to say, towards authority, hierarchy, submission, boundless desire, all neatly tucked away under a bland insensitivity towards, and unawareness of, the moral and emotional complexities of which German film production is almost uniquely devoid. One could hardly expect much better from an Ulbrichtian entertainment.

In any event, the dramatic interplay of Maetzig's film is of an astonishing incompetence. Apart from the agreeable Yoko Tani (whose presence is, of course, not only anti-racist and anti-patriarchalist but, then, pro-Mao), even the faces of the supposedly 'sympathetic' astronauts are set, brutal and cold. The first rocket to Venus finds the débris of a very advanced civilization which was preparing to destroy the earth by projecting on to it extremely powerful radiations. The radiations ran amok on the home planet. One thinks of *Forbidden Planet*, whose 'Robbie the Robot' (a benevolent pre-Dalek) si echoed in this little armoured tank which, uncharmingly, resembles nothing more than the teleguided mines developed by the Nazis towards the end of the war. Subtle laughter about the lack of gravity and the ineluctable meteor bombardment (scratches on film), decorate the film's morality: 'Let us have nuclear disarmament before we blow ourselves and our planet up,' a morality near in spirit to that of the American film. It would be fair to see it, not just as a parallel, but as a not unfriendly riposte to its American predecessor, shifting the latter's Freudian, non-political terms into the Kruschevite party-line.

The M.G.M. film's moral patterns are richer and more complex. The Forbidden Planet of the title is Altair–4, on which a U.S. Army spaceship lands, only to find, to its chagrin, that Professor Morbius (Walter Pidgeon) has got there first, by some sort of blend of scientific wizardry and private enterprise. As is well known by now, *Forbidden Planet* is, quite deliberately, a transposition of Shakespeare's *The Tempest*. Altair–4=Prospero's island, Morbius=Prospero, his daughter (Ann Francis)=Miranda (she has never seen a young man before), the spaceship commander=Ferdinand, Robbie the Robot= Ariel. But who is Caliban? Well, Morbius's scientific researches ('magic books') have led him to explore the city of the long-dead Krells, and he is hot in pursuit of their incredible power of converting mental energy into colossal physical forces.

Despite warnings, this scientific Prometheus refuses to draw back, and involuntarily unleashes, not only his own mental energy, but his own destructiveness—a King-Kong-shaped outline described as The Monster from the Id. When he calls on the daintily omnipotent Robbie the Robot to suppress it, Robbie, suddenly neurotic, refuses —for this hatred is Morbius himself, his 'Mr. Hyde'.

More complex still are the moral patterns of *This Island Earth*, one of whose merits is its resonance with certain psychopathological traits in American political thought.

The story develops very, indeed excessively, slowly (probably as a result of a rather pedantic thoroughness in establishing resonance with familiar reality). The producers have apparently convinced themselves that they must aim primarily to please the tastes of older male children, for the hero, Cal (Rex Reason) lives their day-dreams through. We discover this handsome young cadet-cum-tycoon, already President of his own electronics corporation, at the controls of his private executive jet. But a mysterious green light suddenly fills his cabin—green, once the colour of fairies, having retained its associations with the supernatural in popular art—accompanied by a mysterious force which takes control of his craft, forcing it down to an uncannily perfect three-point-landing. Clearly, this was only a demonstration—or a warning. . . .

As Cal returns to his office, he finds that a company, hitherto unknown to him, has sent him, as sample, an electronic item of an unprecedented, but clearly very advanced type. Cal writes off for their catalogue, receiving, by return of post, instructions to construct an enigmatic object described as an 'interociter'. (Thus the fantasy develops by 'resonance' with (a) mail order catalogues and (b) do-it-yourself constructors. I suspect that the original novel began here, but that the film opened on the premonitory green light to reassure a public less familiar with *s.f.* than its addicts that eerie marvels are to come.)

The interociter turns out to be nothing more than two-way TV, whose triangular screen is bathed in changing coloured lights (another of the film's more childish ideas). On the screen appears Mr. Exeter (Jeff Morrow), whose kindly expression does not suffice to reassure us, in view of the forces at his disposition, and who explains that the construction of this apparatus was only an 'entrance examination', which Cal has passed. He invites Cal to join an international team of idealistic scientists who are working together, in secret, to perfect a method of rendering war impossible. And then, from long-distance, he reduces the interociter to a heap of smoking junk.

Despite the misgivings of his buddy, Cal goes to the meeting, drawn more by scientific-intellectual curiosity than by idealist naïvety. At midnight he enters a Dakota whose interior and windows are completely white and in whose empty cabin the controls move as if of their own volition—a visually very beautiful mutation of the theme of the 'phantom carriage'.

Cal begins work on the project. Among his colleagues are Ruth Adams (Faith Domergue) and her fiancé (Russell Johnson). Around this trio the possibilities of an eternal triangle float without actually settling (a rather weak solution to another problem—reconciling children's impatience with romance with adults' liking of it). The likeable Exeter has a more disturbing associate, Brack (Lance Fuller), younger, stronger, fiercer. Both have very high, bulbous foreheads, and the stiffness of their hair faintly suggests the wig of English judges. Thus we know they come from another planet long before the script officially informs us of the fact. And from the conversations between Exeter, Brack, and, on the screen of their own interociter, The Monitor (Douglas Spencer), an elderly man with a noble but sharp face, we gather that their world, Metaluna, is at war with Zahgon, beneath whose attack the hitherto impregnable 'ionization barrier' is at last giving way. Exeter and Brack have been 'kidnapping' the researches of the world's scientists, to find a substitute for the failing barrier. Brack wishes to hurry progress by brainwashing their guests, a procedure forbidden by Exeter as utterly repugnant to the decent Metalunar ethos.

Meanwhile Cal, Ruth and Steve have come to the conclusion that they must escape. But before they can do so, the Monitor orders Exeter to destroy the terrestrial plant and return at once, so that the spaceship's energy can reinforce the pulverized barrier. Guiltily conscious that his scruples have brought Metaluna to this plight, Exeter equally guiltily gives the order to assassinate the scientists. Steve sacrifices himself for Cal and Ruth, whose escape attempt in a propeller-driven light plane, fails when what they thought was a green hill 'erupts', and from beneath its grass crust arises a gigantic flying saucer. Its green rays draw the light aircraft steadily upwards, and into, its ventral hatch.

Against all 'waking' logic, but following a sort of dream-reasoning, the appearance of the flying saucer helps to guarantee the story, to add to its plausibility. For we have all considered the possibility of such machines; the U.S. air force has reported sighting them; they are mentally familiar to us all; and here, at a crucial moment, we see something we *know*. . . .

To survive the various pressures of the voyage, the humans and their humanoid hosts alike are obliged to stay in a transparent tube and to undergo what Michel Laclos has called 'the integral striptease' —their clothes, skins, muscles, veins and bones successively dissolve as their molecular structure is dissolved and held in 'protective suspension' in the tube.

Thus the 'indefinite duration' of interstellar travel (and all the problems it poses for the scenarist) is 'paraphrazed', in an intimate and unexpected manner. Outer Space becomes Inner Space. Two disturbing notions are fused into a vivid, yet exceptionally economical, image. This kind of reinforcement-by-contradiction, as audacious poetically as it is opaque to Cartesian analysis, is a transposition of mental sensation immediately comprehensible in terms of the 'dreamwork'. And its 'anatomical' key sets the key for some dream overtones of subsequent passages.

Approaching Metaluna, the ship must volatilize the incandescent meteors which Zahgonian bombers hurl, like guided missiles, against it. Finally the ship lands, and not just on the surface of the planet, but *into* its crust, which, ravaged by the Zahgonian bombardment, is by now little more than a spider's web of stone holding together a network of craters (this 'insubstantiality' is not unfitting for a meta-moon). After gliding across an impressive panorama of the riddled planet, the ship slips itself into a crater to glide further underneath its surface and finally rests in the wreckage of the once proud civilization of Metaluna.

The Monitor, barbarically stern and desperate, orders Exeter to transform his captives into mere automata. And they see another, less benevolent, aspect of Metalunar science, a guard-slave, human in form, except for an insect-like hand, with huge eyes and a mass of exposed brains bubbling up out of sutures like gaping fontanelles. This grotesque achievement of Metalunar science permits us to watch, without unbearably sharp regrets, a high civilization crumble beneath the hammerblows of the barbarians.

The moment the Monitor is killed and the too-loyal Exeter is freed from his pledge, he helps his human friends fight off the guard, and restores them to their native planet. Then, despite their invitation to stay with them, he maintains that he must set off in search of other worlds on which Metalunar knowledge can be a power for good. But Cal and Ruth suspect that his ship has no more energy, and it is with a heavy heart that they watch his craft rise, and then plunge, like a shooting-star, into the ocean.

The construction of the story is extremely disciplined, in a characteristic Hollywood manner, metamorphosing a few basic themes in a quasi-musical manner.

Theme A; Brains. 1. Emphasis on know-how. 2. Brainwashing. 3. Exeter's and Brack's noble brows. 4. The Guard-slave's ignoble brow, whose extruding brains are an 'excess' of Exeter's bulbousness. (Excess becomes contradiction—a characteristic of the folk aesthetic.) Exeter is Metaluna's Jekyll, the slave, his Mr. Hyde.

Theme B; Remote Control. 1. Of Cal's jet. 2. Of (by destruction) the Interociter. 3. Of the Dakota. 4. Of (by surveillance) scientists in the laboratories. 5. Of the light aircraft. 6. Control of the meteors by Zahgonian bombers.

Theme C; Penetration. 1. Gruyerization of Metaluna by meteors. 2. Transmolecularization of the human body, with 3–4. Associated theme of being sheltered and passive: the ionization barrier complements the glass tubes. 5. Transparence of the insect skull. 6. See theme E.

Theme D; Crescendo of voyages. 1. Personal jet. 2. Funerary Dakota. 3. Escape attempt by automobile and then light plane, climaxing in their converse. 4. Flying Saucer. (Measured against the private plane, the saucer is about the size of an ocean liner. In turn, it appears tiny against the sloping flank of Metaluna—illogically, since the fact that it's visible at all against the planet's globularity should prove that Metaluna's very small. But, by onirist logic, the curve tells us that Metaluna is 'an entire planet', a boundless immensity, a whole world.)

Theme E; Unusual landings. 1. Cal's, under remote control. 2. The Dakota's. 3. The private plane 'lands' in the saucer, *upwards*, and *into* it. 4. The saucer lands into Metaluna, flies along under the muddy, sulphurous, desert-like surface of the planet. 6. The saucer lands *into* the ocean (giving the contrasting series: green valley—desert—ocean). 7. Impact of meteors.

Theme F; Crescendo of altruistic suicides. 1. Cal risks himself for his scientific curiosity. 2. Steve risks himself for Cal and Ruth, and is killed. 3. Exeter sacrifices himself to die with his race (death-wish?).

Theme G; Tension of malevolence. 1. Exeter (sinister but reassuring). 2. Brack (more sinister). 3. Monitor (ascetic, dictatorial). 4. The guard-slave, like a giant insect.

Theme H; The film's basic opposition is between (1) Metaluna, which kidnaps (*a*) research, (*b*) scientists and (*c*) brains, that is, mental things; whereas (2) Zahgon kidnaps matter—meteors. These resemble little suns; incandescent, they are the most terrible of deserts. Finally, under their blows, the desert of Metaluna explodes 'like a sun', says Exeter. There is a crescendo from the green hills of earth to the desert craters of Metaluna to—a sun. Parallel: from the intellectual curiosity of Cal through Exeter's brow-and-wig to the insect's 'exploding' grey matter. *Metaluna, planet of scientists, is also a gigantic brain,* visually; we have returned to Theme A.[1]

But these threads interweave with a much tougher and stronger thread, of *moral* suspense. Is Metaluna, an advanced, largely humane civilization with its back to the wall against a more barbaric foe, justified in kidnapping a handful of Earth scientists? Exeter is pretty sympathetic, which helps us to see things from the Metalunar viewpoint, so we want to reply, Yes. But we have a still closer identification with our co-terrestrials, so we also want to reply, No. Instead of looking for a compromise between our two attitudes, the film maintains both simultaneously, creating a moral suspense which is completely unstated but none the less intense. We can't decide without pain. An associated paradox: it's Exeter's moral scruples which lead him to fail Metaluna, just as his lofty loyalty leads him to menace our heroes. Clearly, overall, in all interplanetary clashes, the earth is our

---

[1] Although of course the film has a pleasing variety of event and mood, it is, as this analysis suggests, very 'ordered' in construction, and also respects a relatively tight thematic unity.

Apologists sometimes try to defend the cinema by saying that Shakespeare, were he living in the twentieth century, would have been a Hollywood scriptwriter. This is true enough in so far as both Hollywood and the Elizabethan theatre are popular media (though modern audiences don't have the same tastes as groundlings), but it is also interesting to query whether his genius would have flourished in view of the screen's special requirements, and whether, in fact, he would have been a very good scriptwriter, so important in films are such qualities as terseness, crispness, and precision in the construction and inflection of situations and reactions. Screen dialogue is telegrammatic. Indeed if Shakespeare weren't a great poet he would be one of the worst scenarists in literary history. His situations are fuzzy, messy and uncertain, the narrative movement of his plays fitful, his characters speak at great length because their creator isn't too sure what his own themes are, nor which of their sentiments are relevant to the story, which indeed appears to change in his mind as he goes along.

On the other hand, Racine would have been an excellent scriptwriter (and said that a play was virtually finished once he had constructed the 'scenario' in prose). From the point of view of a film script, many a novel is full of 'false starts', gropings, repetitions, etc., and is virtually its own rough draft, or rather, all its own rough drafts jumbled up. A really good scriptwriter can establish with one short line of dialogue what many a novelist chooses to spin out into a chapter of rumination, trivia, noodling notation, and so on.

In other words, the film has its own skills, its own qualities of genius, just as novels have—though many novels would benefit from scriptwriters' economy.

motherland, and we're all patriots. But we're distinctly worried patriots. Finally, as between Zahgon and Metaluna, the film's attitude is a tragic acceptance of amorality, that is, of force.

But this Mother Earth of ours is also 'the free world'. Let us put ourselves in the place of the average American spectator. Which country is always kidnapping and/or deluding scientists and eggheads? Russia. Which country organizes so-called 'peace' congresses? Russia. Which country specializes in brainwashing? Russia. At the laboratories the screens reveal to Brack (Big Brother) and Exeter (Little Father) all the scientists are doing—this is the Stalinist 1984. Exeter's disobedience to dictatorial orders that pain him is all that is best in Russia, no doubt.

But the film's political moral isn't at all an equation of Russia and Metaluna. The conversations between Metalunans lead us to accept their thesis that Metaluna has so far been too scrupulous, too peace-loving, too cultured, too passive, too complacent behind its 'Maginot Line', too slow to mobilize. Though, at the beginning of the film, we fear that Exeter is a Communist undercover agent, towards the end Metaluna is not at all Communism. It is: 'What will happen to us if we're sluggish and passive towards an unscrupulous enemy.' And from this point on it is Zahgon which is Russia—Communism battering at the gentle, defensive Free World.

One can follow this symbolism in another direction. The wigs, the very English name, 'Exeter', his expression, his scruples, suggest a certain gentlemanliness. His situation of a weak Father, too obedient to hierarchic loyalties is England's (historically, as Gorer points out, the 'weak father' of America, and ever since, her alter ego—a surprisingly strong and courageous land, considering how effete it seems, and with a perfidious streak, but none the less, too weak to 'hold' America). The implication is that *because* Exeter and Metaluna were weak before, now they must kidnap and brainwash. It repeats the switch from Jekyll to Hyde, but in a more realistic way. Exeter represents 'England and our other pretty-soft-on-communism' allies. But above all, he incarnates the last stage of the temptation against which the U.S.A. must be on guard—confidence-in-advanced-technology, and isolationalism, without an aggressive counter-initiative, a warlike readiness.

The ionization barrier recalls, perhaps, the 'early warning' systems. They are only a Maginot Line. The Zahgonians' technique is relatively crude, but, given their obsessional persistence, effective. Instead of hithering and dithering about scientists' work and brains, they scoop up huge lumps of incandescent matter and hurl it with neither scruple nor subtlety. It's Russia's technological 'crudity', the mass attacks of the Chinese in Korea. And it can succeed.

If we go so far as to see in the 'International Congress of Scientists for Peace' a reference to the United Nations we can see that in the course of the film Metaluna becomes, successively, the U.N., Russia, Britain and a too-liberal U.S.A. The symbolism depends on associations, not on a consistent code. This 'sliding symbolism' isn't at all unique in movies. We can find an analogy in *Henry V*, where the English are the English but Agincourt is D-Day, where the French are the Germans, until Henry courts Katherine, whereupon the French are probably the French. Such 'contradictions' are typical, also, of Freudian dreamwork, where symbolism is dominated less by the 'objective' correlative of each mental entity than by polarities in an emotional situation.

The McArthur-like morality of the American film is fundamentally mitigated by our sympathy for Exeter, a sympathy due to his 'liberal' scruples, and it is this ambivalence which creates a great part of the film's emotional excitation. In a sense, it is only 'accidentally' a committed film. It exploits the current international situations to insert a 'plausibility', an 'everyday correlative', to its own story. Left-wing critics can enjoy it with a clear conscience. Many, perhaps most, American spectators will see in it only a philosophical meditation, a reflection of violence and idealism, in the 'abstract' of Outer Space, so to speak. If they have hitherto taken aggressiveness as axiomatic, they may be surprised to find themselves feeling so concerned for the alien Exeter—and in this case the film's 'meaning' ('effect') would be anti-racist, anti-xenophobe, pro-liberal. The effect and meaning of a film is rarely provable by however meticulous a textual analysis; one must also know what assumptions, in the mind of its spectators, it is coming up against.

But *This Island Earth* probes more deeply still into American attitudes. Exeter with his 'binary' Brack, the Monitor with his 'binary' the Insect, are paternal symbols (Exeter and the Monitor via their age, their superiority and their control over the hero's destiny). The Metalunar civilization is, in short, a weak father. (But let us beware of a cruelty hidden in this benevolence. . . .) Yet, Metaluna, the moon, round, like a dry breast, devastated—is the dead mother. The association is underlined: Metaluna and the saucer are both globes, the light plane enters the saucer's belly (birth in reverse), as the saucer enters Metaluna's pores (birth in reverse), before plunging into the sea (birth in reverse). The Metalunans are not exactly feminoid men, but passive—and feminoid in the sense that, for Americans, passivity, pacifism, moral scrupulosity, gentleness, altruism, and preoccupation with education and culture are associated with the 'schoolmarm ethos' (cf. Hofstadter), with the 'cissy'. The Zahgonian bombers are dart-shaped (as opposed to globes) and throw little suns (phallic-sadistic) against the moon which at last becomes the sun—the female, tormented, ravaged, by the sadism of the nightmare father (opposed to the reasonable, weak father) becomes male, explosive. Femininity disappears. In fantasy, even the women are masculine. 'Vienna', that feminine name, all waltzes and romance, has 'caught fire' and become a black-booted gunslinger. Indeed, Faith Domergue wears black slacks and boots throughout. Fathers are passive, women no more so. . . .

Thus Metaluna is simultaneously breast and brain. Both are attacked simultaneously. We knew that Americans fear that to be intellectual is to be cissy, and we may suspect that their obsession with mammary hypertrophy conceals a certain fear of the castrating female—just as their anti-intellectuality goes with an obsession with dangerous Masterminds (mad scientists, Mr. Bigs, and so on).

If we indicate these Freudian categories, it is only to underline that the film is founded on the *confusion* of sexual qualities, a confusion arising from the presence of an uncontrolled, scarcely sublimated sadism. The meteors (which we have characterized as 'phallic-sadistic') are also globes (feminine); Metaluna (the body of the dead mother) is inhabited by a hierarchy of Fathers (with Brack as 'elder sibling'—i.e. both brother as competitor and threat, and 'Father as pal'). The Insect signals the undertow of Zahgonianism in Metalunar culture. Between Zahgon and Metaluna the 'sympathetic self-preservation' of Cal, Steve and Ruth is the best compromise (and a heterosexual *camaraderie*).

The Metalunans are more sympathetic than the Zahgonians, but they lost. Thus a 'puritan' morality of liberal scruple is contrasted with the cynical 'morality' of success. . . .

If we assume that the film responds to authentic currents of American thought, we could have deduced from it how deeply rooted in the American psyche were attitudes which would naturally try to emerge, on the political plane, as McCarthyism, McArthurism, or

Goldwaterism. The old 'isolationism' turns into bellicosity. There is a haunting fear that a 'liberal' policy towards Communism is the policy of men who are, not exactly feminized, but neutered, castrated, by their scruples. Similarly, Margaret Mead and Geoffrey Gorer tell us that in America the woman rather than the man tends to possess the moral ascendancy within the family; and it may be that this ascendancy is subtly reinforced by the masculinization of woman imposed by an individualistic, and therefore competitive, society. Thus, femininity disappears on Metaluna, and Faith Domergue, the woman dressed like a man, has undergone a transmogrification analagous to the insect-slave's.

Exeter, the gentle father, is vowed to autodestruction by observing the 'severely obeyed gentleness'. The paradox of the American soul is that a strongly competitive, puritan ethic, whose principles, for all the mitigating effects of a subsequent 'fun morality' are, in their stern, simple imperatives, 'masculine'. Yet they are imposed by women, who thus become not so much the indulgent member of the family, as the taskmaster. Within the family, 'Pop' is Exeter. But, outside the family, in the jungle of 'rugged individualism' (the ratrace), father's ideals are (or are supposed to be) more Zahgonian. Simultaneously, in the very bosom of the family, Oedipal rivalry creates 'monsters'— the insect-warrior-slave, malicious and ugly, being the symbol of the jealousy faintly suggested by, but never crystallized, between, Cal, Ruth and Steve. And so the middle-class 'quiet American', with his picture of himself as gentle, reasonable, liberal, conscientiously re- presses his Zahgonian undertow until he finds an enemy on whom he can project it—which justifies a Zahgonian brutality in his own reac- tion. How often have we not seen, in American war films, the American forces napalm and pulverize the enemy with a Zahgonian mindlessness?[1]

---

[1] There is a similar opposition in Byron Haskin's *From the Earth to the Moon* (1958), adapted from Jules Verne's novel. On the one hand, Stuyvesant (George Sanders), a scientist with Confederate loyalties (gentlemanly, 'olde-worlde', doomed to defeat) invents an impregnable armour (passive defence) which he idealistically hopes will render war impossible. On the other, Barbicane (Joseph Cotton), an ambitious Yankee capitalist, invents an atomic shell which volatilizes that armour. Stuyvesant ⌐ Metaluna, Barbicane ⌐ Zahgon. The President of the U.S. appeals to Barbicane to turn aside from warlike applications of his hideous power; Barbicane consents, but, rebelliously, refuses to destroy it, turn- ing it, by way of compromise between his egoistic will to power and the President's will to peace, to peaceful purposes: a moon rocket. Stuyvesant pretends to generously forgive him, and they pool atomic power and armour. But once in Outer Space, Stuyvesant reveals that he has sabotaged the rocket, to doom them

The general polarity can be seen in other American films. Thus in Kazan's *On the Waterfront* the hero's apparently friendly elder brother (Rod Steiger) and 'meta-father', Johnny Friendly (Lee J. Cobb), have 'sold him down the river'. Thus 'Metaluna' is rapidly revealed as 'Zahgon'. There is a basic conflict between Brando's 'Zahgonian' ideas of revenge (guns, fists) and the softening influence of the fatherly priest (Karl Malden)—a 'Metalunar castrate'—and a schoolmarm (Eva-Marie Saint). This 'Metalunar' approach to racket-busting, however, accommodates his virility: first, the schoolmarm enjoys being raped by him, and second, he asserts himself *vis-à-vis*, the dockers as one of them by a fist-fight with Friendly's men (which he loses). Again, in Zinnemann's *High Noon* there is a clash between Gary Cooper's aggressive ideas of self-defence and his Quaker wife's 'treacherous' passivity. Clearest of all is the overt propaganda of Tay Garnett's Korean war film *One Minute to Zero*, which contrasts Robert Mitchum as a tough U.S. Army Colonel and Ann Blyth as a 'schoolmarm' U.N. worker who isn't at all sure that North Korea is really the aggressor. After he's slapped her and saved her she finally sees his point, and even acquieses in his final 'Zahgonian' ruthlessness; he orders his artillery to blast a column of South Korean refugees which include women, children and Commie infiltrators. In King Vidor's *Duel in the Sun*, the kind, reasonable, liberal son Jess (Joseph Cotton), with his woman's name, is his mother's favourite and is pacifistic about gunslinging, preferring the (intellectual-moral) law, is the 'Metalunan' son. He loses the passionate girl to his brother Lewt (Gregory Peck), the egoist-assassin,

all, himself included. His pretext is outraged idealism (rockets are sinful), although it's plain enough to Barbicane and ourselves, whose viewpoint we have by now adopted, that his motive is repressed hatred of Barbicane. Thus, again, the apparent, and no doubt, sincere 'weak idealist' reveals a hidden brutality; again he is associated with altruistic suicide; and he has a female association; where Barbicane has a son, the only thing Stuyvesant loves more than his principles is his daughter (Debra Paget). Again the two young people re-establish the heterosexual ideal in a film that might be called *From the Earth to the Meta-Moon*.

It's arguable that Haskin's film is a deliberate copy of Newman's (rather than an independent confirmation of it, except in so far as imitation can be a valid index of relevance), which is one reason why I relegate it to a footnote; and certainly it *advocates* a turning-away from the arms-race, a channelling of energies into peaceful competition, which itself is felt to be sufficiently aggressive, rebellious and not devoid of risk. It maintains the aggressiveness of 'rugged individualism' as, on the whole, better and more decent than Stuyvesant's love of 'peace'.

There is a scarcely different permutation of the same conflicts in Delbert Mann's *Our Man Flint*, 1966.

the father's son, who dies, in the desert, under the sun, together with a shotgun-carrying (masculinoid) girl. . . .

Universal as is the resonance of these films, can we not recognize in them a preoccupation, an atmosphere, a tonus which are specifically American? After all, the Wild West, with its deserts, its killings, its men-without-women, is—Metaluna. It would be easy to translate Newman's film into a Western—*Duel Under the Moon*—although its tragic breakdown of a social order might well be resented, as a criticism of the American way of life. . . .

Revealing as it is, the film is not a masterpiece; its style is rather plodding, it respects too many American sentimentalities. Notably, Cal and Ruth are 'pure', they are implicated, a very little, but too little, in the emotional paradoxes. Despite the title (which is ironical: No Planet is an Island) the film doesn't complete the spiritual voyage whereby Zahgon is also in the hero's heart. It's still, perhaps, interesting to see how many moral complexities an 'ordinary' film can bear. What lifts this out of the ordinary is that, to a sufficient complexity of moral sympathy, is added a certain fantastic poetry.

Morally, one may prefer it to *Forbidden Planet*. Not that this doesn't maintain some of the main points. For Morbius is Metaluna and his Mr. Hyde is Zahgon. Once again, the intellectual with the daughter reveals a hidden destructiveness, remains passive under the attack of active evil, and commits suicide, though retaining, like Exeter, our respect and love; while the 'honest militancy' of the U.S. Army is the really peaceful force. But the film goes further than either Newman's or Haskin's in imputing Morbius's hidden aggression to all of us. The phrase, The Monster from the Id, imputes such a creature to every man jack of us.

The visuals of all these films play the same 'parodic' game with reality. Even Scarpelli's film whirls up its potpourri of clichés in such a way as to attain a certain charm—thus we find characters in pharaoh-shaped blue helmets peering through tele-periscopes, brain-transplanting operations determined by astrological conjunctions, an operating-table whose form recalls an anvil, circular arches over triangular doors (the triangle is quite a 'supernatural' shape, what with interocitors too), hairpin-shaped doors cheek by jowl with octagonal windows and Gothic ogives, and pagodesque structures hobnobbing with aerodynamic edifices in the style of William Cameron Menzies' *Things to Come* (1936).

Far more Corneillian is the décor of Cottafavi's film. As Jean-

Louis Barrault remarked, the true colour of classicism is not ivory-white but blood-red; and Cottafavi has given us such a classicism, the only genre possible in an epoque as profoundly marked as ours by psychoanalysis. The film's soul is not only in the physique of the amiable Hercules (Reg Park), whose muscles stand out like bunches of grapes, purple in Technicolor, but in the contrast between this benign strength of flesh and the temples of Atlantis—with their scarlet columns and heavily barbaric decorations; with its chariot, drawn by flowing-maned white horses, bounding through flames between the massive pillars of hillocky-floored catacombs whose roof slopes steadily, oppressively down; with the buildings jumbled among yellow rocks, like Monkey Hill; with the simple but striking off-key harmonies between the black, gold and electric-blue colours of Queen Antinea (Fay Spain) and the yellow and coral green of her apartments. Hercules himself is a kindly soul who smiles and sleeps until the very last moment, not only preferring *la Dolce far niente* to *la Dolce Vita*, but as far removed as possible from 'Zahgonism'.

The merits of *Forbidden Planet* are more literary and moral than architectural, and the furnishing of Prospero's planet isn't without a certain flowers-and-leopard sentimentality. By contrast, *First Spaceship on Venus* more than compensates for its moral poverty by the work of art designers, Anatol Radzinowicz and Alfred Kirschmeier, and its team of special effects designers, who, very cleverly indeed, transpose pictorial motifs from, among others, Dali and Tanguy, and find in the junk forms of a derelict planet, an opportunity not only to match, but to go beyond, the old expressionist delirium Ever since 1945, Polish films have been notable for the tragic virulence of their sense of devestation. . . . What atrocious beauty invests these ruined and incomprehensible installations! Bunches of steel plates are warped into arcs recalling the wind-bellied sails of tea-clippers; huge, half-molten domes evoke white skulls from whose eye-sockets drip dissolute forms like white worms; from a bird's-eye-view a reactivated 'energy complex' suggests Broadway Boogie-Woogie as it might have been rendered into a grotesque contraption by Jean Tinguely. And the inconstant winds of Venus are evoked by white and oxblood washes drifting across the images.

Less rich in ideas, perhaps, but convulsive, too, are the Metalunar desertscapes, whose craters recall the pores in the giantesses' breasts to which Gulliver clung in Brobdingnag. . . .

234

Appendix · Depth Psychology and Popular Cinema

In discussing *This Island Earth*, and the uneasy link which it establishes between an unconscious conflict, certain cultural stereotypes,
a philosophy of violence, and Cold War attitudes, we are in no sense
offering any summary of American thinking on any of these levels.
We are discussing one 'myth' (or configuration of archetypal images)
among many myths. This is not at all to suggest that this myth is 'the
key' to American attitudes. A myth, like a dream, is only a partial
picture of the unconscious processes; and even within its field it is
distorted and disguised. And of course the primitive quality of the
attitudes is refined, restrained by and overladen with the more obvious considerations of rational political thought. It's just because they
are held in check that they appear more clearly on the level of film
entertainment than anywhere else.

Hence entertainment, like dreams makes its own contribution to
our general self-awareness. To say there is a joker in the pack is not
to reduce the pack to its joker. Insofar as this exegesis of *This Island
Earth* refers to actual political attitudes, it is no more than a study in
one particular aspect of the 'hidden persuasion' to which respectable
political rhetoric never dares make open appeal but which, if
'Dichterism' has any validity at all, must influence political feeling,
to, no doubt, a limited extent. All the same, our intention is not to
throw light on American politics, simply to underline the fact that
the emotional and moral 'catchment-area' of an apparently 'escapist'
film may be far more extensive, and realistic, than its overt content.
The political link-up (which the film itself suggests) is a way of stressing that these emotions can't be dismissed as 'mere triviality'. Thus
poetry is indissolubly blended with philosophy. To indicate a paranoid streak in American political thinking is not to indulge in that

favourite pastime of European intellectuals—scoring off American 'vulgarity'. That that is in no way the burden of these remarks, the tone of earlier chapters should make clear. Indeed, of all the movies examined in this chapter, it is the two American movies which show the most sophisticated and self-critical awareness of inner tensions.

This Island Earth has everything against it. It's fantasy, it's science-fiction, it's slanted at adolescents, it's a routine product from a studio with no intellectual pretentions, it has no *auteurs*, its artistic 'texture' is largely mediocre—and for all that, it has a genuine charge of poetry and of significant social feeling. It's not cliché; with its sense of inner tensions, of moral tragedy, it's myth.

Our suggestion is that academic criticism is condemned to misunderstand the film, to dismiss it as routine trash, because its psychology is straightforward, its terms melodramatic, and so on. 'High culture' is preoccupied with what Henry James called 'density of specification' and what F. R. Leavis calls 'texture', with the question: 'Does it work on my level?' But such criteria are irrelevant to this as to most movies. The question must be, rather, 'Does it work on its level?' (for people who freely respond to simpler textures).

The temptation then is to swing to the other extreme, and fall into the studiedly uncritical acceptance of any and every form of popular art as 'myth' and 'folklore of the twentieth century'; or, at a slightly more aware level, to abandon oneself to the ironic relish of 'camp'. Too often this is both a studied falsity and a (completely unnecessary) surrender to the (supposed) naïvety of popular thought. Our implication is that some pulp-movies are very much more considerable than others, that the mythic can be distinguished from the cliché, that, through the myth, movies communicate with people's *real* doubt and feelings, that such movies are in a very real sense 'good' art as opposed to others which are in a very real sense 'bad' art. This isn't to elevate the subversive possibilities of entertainment above its reinforcing of social attitudes; *This Island Earth* isn't subversive, for most of its spectators. But its tragic sense of moral tensions is very different from the comic-strip images which many 'pop-artists' prefer to plunder.

If stated baldly, the moral of *This Island Earth* would make it an expression of American right-wing extremism (obviously, it is not suggested that right-wing extremism is confined to American thought; it's obviously virulent in European politics too). It would mean: 'Look out for aliens! rearm!' And 'aliens' would be definable as 'intellectuals' (high foreheads), 'idealists' and 'internationalists' (UNO, pseudo-allies). By the vast majority of spectators, its moral won't be stated baldly, or even seen clearly, because of its mythic quality and its ambivalence. But, as Richard Hofstadter remarks, 'It is the use of paranoiad modes of expression by more or less normal people that makes the phenomenon significant.' It's probably no coincidence that the themes emerging from *This Island Earth* exactly fit the titles of Richard Hofstadter's books: his (Pulitzer Prize-winning) *Anti-Intellectualism In American Life* and his *The Paranoid Style In American Politics*.

Certainly, Hofstadter relates these themes to socio-cultural 'images', and doesn't go on to make, as we have done, a further link with themes culled from depth-psychology. The (necessarily summary) sketch of family tensions which, though not unique, seem in America to be a conspicuous or prevalent variety of universal conflicts, is congruent with that offered by Nathan Leites and Martha Wolfenstein (in, particularly, Chapter Two of *Movies: A Psychological Study*) and by Geoffrey Gorer in *The Americans* (especially his opening chapters). This is not to imply that the family situation is the simple cause of which socio-political thinking is the simple effect. The total social situation also influences the family situation. In no way are we hinting at a 'simplistic' reduction of politics and art alike to infantile conflicts.

Nor is our exegesis meant to suggest that 'the' American character is fixed, once and for all, in the conflicts we have described. Obviously the film's relevance to individual Americans is as 'artificial' as all cultural myths about character—(though a myth is not a cliché, and may be as false, yet as significant, as the statistic that the average adult has 1.1 children). For these characteristic myths evolve as fast as the culture evolves. Wolfenstein and Leites point to the fact that in American movies of the late '40's two situations predominate. In films which are overtly about family relationships, fathers and sons are usually presented as being on idyllic terms, whereas melodramas abound in situations in which apparently benevolent father-figures turn out to be treacherous and ruthless. The emphasis was significantly different, or, indeed, reversed, in French and English films (which also differed from each other). *This Island Earth* is an example of this genre.

Nonetheless, during the '50's, father-son conflicts, which had hitherto been idealized away (and only paraphrased in melodrama) now began to appear overtly; notable examples included Nicholas Ray's *Rebel Without a Cause*, and John Frankenheimer's *The Young Stranger*. One reason for the immense prestige of Arthur Miller's plays *All My Sons* and *Death of a Salesman* is that they were among the first plays to combine overt father-son conflicts with other central, and rarely acknowledged, conflicts in the American conscience. During the '50's, too, many films which weren't overtly about father-son conflicts made references suggesting an awareness, at least by the makers, and certainly by many spectators, of the underlying 'Freudian' pattern. Thus Marlon Brando in *The Wild One*, while being beaten up by the head of the lynch-mob, mumbles, 'My old man could whup me harder'n that', and Brando, again, in *One Eyed Jacks*, is pitted against the apparently benevolent, actually evil 'Dad' Longworth. Westerns abound in stories about ambivalent love-hate relationships between young men and older men who father them (*Tribute To a Bad Man, The Tin Star*). It's fair to say that American movies of the '50's are preoccupied with parent-child and sibling relationships, while adult sexual conflicts are treated with vastly less sophistication and intensity. By the '60's the situation seems to have been stabilised, or, at least, little further development is suggested from American movies.

It's clearly an advance in self-consciousness if covert conflicts can be made overt (and a regression of overt conflicts become covert).

In a parallel way, the paranoid undertow in *This Island Earth* becomes the subject of Stanley Kubrick's *Dr. Strangelove or How I Learned to Stop Worrying and Love the Bomb*. The connections between Kubrick's film and Hofstadter's remarks on 'the paranoid style' are very clear; General Jack D. Ripper, with his fear of fluoridation is a pantechnicon of political paranoias, and, for that matter, of related sexual ones.

But the philosophical and psychoanalytical catchment-areas of *This Island Earth* are not its whole story. It is, also, a story about these people, these worlds, in outer space.